'In its usual context, "purchasing power" is an adman's banality but the idea itself packs a real punch once you ally it to a conscious effort to use your discretionary income wisely – and well.

The Global Consumer is just the kind of book we badly need to point the way to wisdom.'

Anita Roddick

New Consumer

New Consumer is a charitable, membership-supported research organisation which aims to mobilise consumer power for positive economic, social and environmental change. We produce publications that inform consumers about the policies and practices of the UK's biggest companies; our research is used by the press, campaigning groups and by the companies themselves. In April 1991 New Consumer released *Changing Corporate Values* (Kogan Page, £48), a widely acclaimed detailed reference book on business and social responsibility.

September 1991 saw the launch of *Shopping for a Better World* (Kogan Page, £4.99), a paperback consumer guide based on the same research. This guide enables consumers to choose brands from the companies most responsive to the issues facing society today. In February 1992 comes the *Good Employers Guide* (Kogan Page, £9.99), a book specially for those thinking of taking their first job in industry, the professions or public service but wondering how their personal values will fit in with the ethos of the organisation they are hoping to join.

The Authors

Phil Wells and **Mandy Jetter** are staff members of New Consumer. Both have a particular interest in trade with the third world, having worked for several years for Traidcraft (the UK's leading independent alternative trading organisation), where Phil Wells set up the educational work while Mandy Jetter was responsible for the company's relationships with its third world partners.

THE
GLOBAL
CONSUMER

Best Buys to Help the Third World

Phil Wells & Mandy Jetter

LONDON
VICTOR GOLLANCZ LTD
1991

First published in Great Britain 1991
by Victor Gollancz Ltd
14 Henrietta Street, London WC2E 8QJ

Copyright © New Consumer Ltd 1991

The right of Phil Wells and Mandy Jetter to be identified
as authors of this work has been asserted by them in
accordance with the Copyright, Designs and Patents Act 1988.

A Gollancz Paperback Original

A CIP catalogue record for this book is available
from the British Library

ISBN 0 575 05000 4

Typeset by John Button using Ventura Publisher
Printed in Great Britain by
Cox & Wyman Ltd, Reading

CONTENTS

ACKNOWLEDGEMENTS

As with any book, this one owes a debt to a large number of people. We have drawn on the research and campaign material of agencies around the world for the general analyses in each chapter, though we have placed on it our own interpretation on many occasions.

However, there are those to whom we owe more personal thanks: Astrid van Rij and Annette de With, whose work experience at New Consumer enabled our research budget to stretch a little further, Charlie Fisher for helping with the research, and the other staff at New Consumer for the many discussions we had. Thanks also to the editorial staff at Victor Gollancz, who have endeavoured to keep us to the point in each chapter.

We're also grateful to Belinda Coote, Ed Mayo, Catharine Howe, Peter Madden, Sheila Page, Stanley Please and Alison Stancliffe – whose criticism and advice on draft material often gave us pause for thought and (we hope) made the analysis a little more useful. Thanks also to Ed Mayo and David Boyer of WDM for the first draft of the chapter on money. Mistakes and faulty analysis are our responsibility.

We would also like to thank Christian Aid, the Twenty-First Century Trust, The European Commission, and CAFOD, for helping to fund the research and writing.

Finally, staff of several companies have been particularly forthcoming in responding to our questions, many of which were not easy to answer. While such cooperation is, of course, no guarantee of enlightened policies with respect to the third world, or a favourable review in this book, our thanks are due to them.

Without whom . . .

Consumers are powerful; of that there is no doubt. But, when it comes to influencing the behaviour of the world's largest corporations, there are many other groups of people and institutions that have been at work for far longer.

In the third world, unions have been defending their members, often at great cost, against malpractice, and sometimes direct oppression, of their employers. International solidarity from unions in other countries has also been a force for standardisation in labour codes. Individual workers and informal groupings, where unions are illegal or legislatively shackled, have similarly risked their lives to secure the rights of their fellow workers.

Outside the formally employed sector, too, groups of peasant farmers, fishworkers, homeworkers and others have taken action to ensure the accountability of large companies. As they have seen their livelihoods and communities threatened by decisions taken many thousands of miles away, they have not sat back, expecting consumers to defend their cause. They have organised from their small villages in ways that belie their isolation and lack of formal education.

Concerned citizens' groups have been active, particularly in environmental issues such as deforestation or industrial pollution. These groups have often risked, and sometimes suffered, repression from governments more concerned with courting the economic power of the transnationals than in securing justice or sustainability.

We should not forget individual executives within the big companies, aware of the potential for positive and negative development impact of their own companies, whose moves towards policy change can be strengthened by an active and critical consumer movement. We tend to see TNCs and other large companies as monolithic and rational; in fact their policies are the outcome of debate and a mix of values.

It would be presumptuous to dedicate this book to any of these groups; suffice it to say that, without their work, we would not be in a position to mobilise the power that we as consumers have.

AUTHORS' NOTE

We have drawn on the research and campaign material of agencies around the world for the general analyses in each chapter, though we have placed on it our own interpretation on many occasions.

To the best of our knowledge, the information in this book was correct at the time of first publication. The omission of any particular brand, company or any other organisation implies neither censure nor recommendation.

ABBREVIATIONS

ACP	Sixty African, Caribbean and Pacific countries, ex-colonies entitled to preferential access to the EC market under the Lomé Convention
EC	The European Community
FTZ	Free Trade Zone, offering incentives for foreign investment
GATT	The General Agreement on Tariffs and Trade, a rolling negotiation intended to liberalise international trade
GNP	Gross National Product, a measure of a country's income; figures in this book refer to GNP *per head*
HDI	Human Development Index, a ranking which reflects the quality of life in a country
HDI v GNP	A rating comparing a country's HDI ranking with its GNP ranking; a measure of relative social provision
MFA	Multi Fibre Arrangement, which controls the export of textiles and clothing from the third world to the EC
NIC	Newly Industrialised Country, one showing significant recent growth through export-led manufacturing
TNC	Transnational Corporation, a company operating across national boundaries.

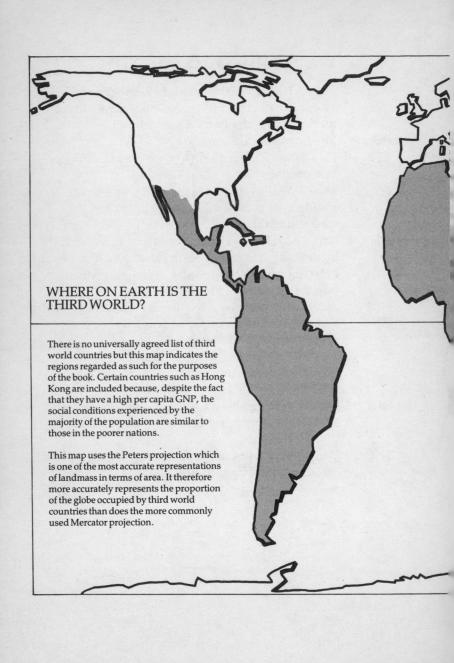

WHERE ON EARTH IS THE THIRD WORLD?

There is no universally agreed list of third world countries but this map indicates the regions regarded as such for the purposes of the book. Certain countries such as Hong Kong are included because, despite the fact that they have a high per capita GNP, the social conditions experienced by the majority of the population are similar to those in the poorer nations.

This map uses the Peters projection which is one of the most accurate representations of landmass in terms of area. It therefore more accurately represents the proportion of the globe occupied by third world countries than does the more commonly used Mercator projection.

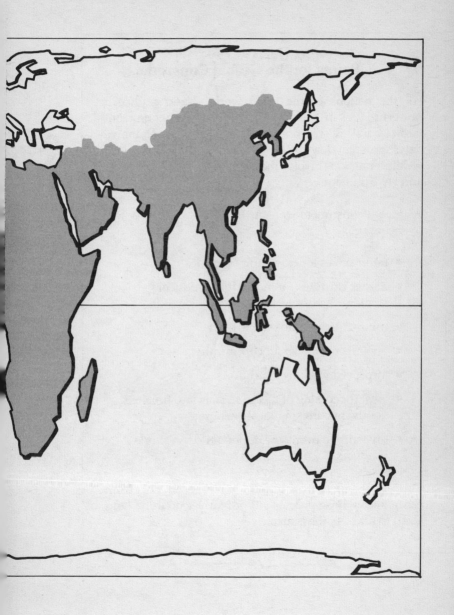

Key Points for the Global Consumer

For the nations of the third world, trade can be a powerful tool in overcoming poverty, combating environmental destruction and achieving sustainable development. Too often, however, relations with wealthier nations involve the exploitation of both people and environment.

As global consumers we can use our spending power to encourage:

- fairer prices for exporting countries
- higher earnings for individual producers – farmers, factory workers, etc
- minimal environmental impact
- benefits for the wider community
- improved working conditions
- local processing of raw materials into finished goods, maximising local earnings
- diversity to overcome dependence on single products

This book identifies brand name products from companies whose policies and initiatives do most (and least) to address the issues.

Introduction

The Global Crisis touches each one of us. Only a few years ago, people warning of impending ecological breakdown were labelled as cranks. The new slimmer ozone layer and global warming have made even the most blinkered politicians realise that the time has come to look beyond our own back yard.

We cannot escape the fact that what other people do – even people on the other side of the world – affects us and affects our children. Just as importantly, what we do affects others. We are having to become experts at calculating not just the price of our shopping list, but also its *real* cost; what are the implications behind our everyday decisions? We have learned that retailers and manufacturers *will* respond to our demand for greener, healthier products – if we can persuade them that we care.

But how far has Green Consumerism brought us? It has certainly helped us to feel that we can each do something to save the world; that it's not up to the politicians and the powerful alone. But while we are rightly concerned about aerosol cans and excess packaging, environmental destruction hits hardest in the poorer countries and is continuing apace. People without land to grow food, people unsure where their next meal is coming from, people working for hours in unbearable conditions for just a few pence, are hardly in a position to care about global crisis. In many cases the environmental damage that threatens them is due to factors quite beyond their control.

All too often it is our demand for more goods, cheaper goods, and (ironically) environmental safety that causes problems in the third world. We frequently end up exporting the global crisis to those countries least able to deal with it. If our world is to become a safer place, we are going to have to take seriously the need to make it a fairer place.

When we go shopping, we become involved in a trading system through which we benefit from the poverty of the third world. As poor countries compete for business, they end up exploiting their people and their environment. Not only is this unjust; it also winds up the global crisis a few more notches. Our concern for the kind of world we want to leave to our children is not just a matter of ozone layers and clean seas; it's a matter of people too. Our world is riven by conflict and marred by poverty, damaging both the people and the environment. We need to move on now, from an environmentally-conscious consumerism to a world-centred approach.

You have the power to make real changes. Read this book, and become a New Consumer, with the world at heart.

The Third World and the Consumer

'The act of buying is a vote for an economic and social system, for a particular way of producing goods. We are concerned with the quality of goods and the satisfaction we derive from them. But we cannot ignore the conditions under which products are made – the environmental impact and working conditions. We are linked to them and we have a responsibility for them.'

Anwar Fazal,
International Organisation of Consumer Unions, Malaysia

The UK is a trading nation; the goods in our shops come from all over the world. Though most of our trade is now with the other EC countries, we still import a great deal from the countries often grouped together as the 'third world' and many of our EC imports originate in the third world too. Each year, we spend well over £14 billion there; over £700 for each household in the UK. To a large extent, these imports are in an unprocessed state, so the amount consumers spend on such products once processed and packaged is far more. And many imports are of components used in UK manufactures. Just looking at the products featured in this book, we spend some £60 billion a year on purchases containing significant third world elements.

As consumers, we are heavily involved with the third world. But in order to decide what our response should be, we need to know more about the impact of our trade on the countries we buy from; on the people and on the environment we share with them. At its simplest, the question is, do we buy from the third world or not?

There are many reasons why this is not a naive question, after all, third world trade is commonly reported in the context of the depletion of tropical forest resources, the poor pollution standards of the factories and the lax environmental safeguards of governments. The low wages and poor working conditions of the people engaged in producing anything from coffee and clothes to tin and televisions are topics for documentaries. This book, by contrast, takes the view that trade is potentially a Good Thing. Examples abound of the way involvement in international trade has benefited poor countries; the four 'Asian Tigers' – Singapore, Hong Kong, Taiwan and South Korea – are the classic cases in point.

Trade may be environmentally damaging – as can any area of human endeavour – but the alternative may be more so. We need to look, not just at the problems, but at the realistic solutions to them. For example, a farmer growing bananas in the West Indies may well be farming in an unsustainable manner, with few resources to improve the soil, but to stop buying his crop will exacerbate the situation, not solve the problem. Still dependent on his bananas, but lacking a market, he will have to accept a lower price, and grow more bananas on the fragile soils further up the hillside to compensate.

We cannot just shrug our shoulders and do nothing, however. The answer is to find ways to assist such farmers to farm sustainably. And our role as consumers is to support those initiatives with our custom. Let us not forget that the environmental damage caused by big banana plantations is far greater, and the pay and conditions of their workers is poor; our farmer's smallholding is part of the answer, not part of the problem.

This example illustrates a fundamental principle outlined by Ben Jackson of World Development Movement in his excellent book, *Poverty and the Planet*: 'The seedbed of ecological destruction is the global division between rich and poor.' Time and again in *The Global Consumer*, we will find that it is poverty and the impact of the powerful upon the lives of the poor that is at the heart of environmental degradation. This is where trade can hold part of the answer.

Rather than concentrating on poverty, this book sets out to explore the contribution that trade can make to **development**. Trade and investment can certainly benefit a country in terms of money. But development is not just an economic process; it is most importantly a people process. Development must in the end empower people, enabling them to take more control over their lives as well as feed their children. Trade is a powerful engine of development, for better or for worse, and it is here that the Global Consumer comes in.

A further quote from Ben Jackson is worth noting: 'People in the North need to wield their consumer power in order to pressure companies to purchase or produce goods grown or manufactured in an environmentally sustainable way *and to pursue fair employment and marketing practices in poor countries.*' As consumers, we are important actors on the scene, though it is the people in the third world themselves who are doing the work, and the policies of their governments are crucial in determining whether 'development' is really progress at all. But we can do more than just watch; we can help to remove some of the barriers; we can help to make sure that our companies are on the right side, that their activities push in the right direction.

Encouraging the best and avoiding the worst is at the heart of this book. The same applies to coffee and computers as to clothes; but we need the information, and we need to look at the successes and the failures and decide what has made the difference. We can use our 'economic vote' to reward companies that are having a more positive impact on the people and environment of the third world. This book looks at the products we buy from the third world, finds out where the benefits go, and shows what consumers can do to encourage changes that ensure that ordinary people get the best from the trade.

There is one further specific issue that needs addressing concerning trade. Transporting goods half way round the world clearly has environmental implications, in terms of energy consumption and pollution. These are factors to consider, though the implications of not trading may be even more serious. Trade is the major motivation behind all contacts between countries; without trade, cultural isolation would inevitably result, with the likelihood of more friction and wars than we have already. It would also consign most third world countries (and indeed many wealthy countries) to an existence based solely on what they can produce internally. Like someone trying to be completely self-sufficient, food might be available, but manufactured goods? clothes? medical equipment? Unless a country has a good resource base and a large population, many industries would simply not be possible, and economic development similarly so.

We also need to put transport costs into context. The cost of transporting goods from India may account for a few pence in the pound, and the fuel costs are but a small part of this. Driving to the supermarket can easily use proportionately just as much fuel – and with a greater environmental impact.

Where is the third world?

The 'third world' is such a familiar term that we have almost stopped considering what it means. Common images that affect the way we think are poverty, destructive climatic conditions, famine, corruption, overpopulation, little industry. In fact the third world cannot be so simply summed up; it is a complex and varied grouping of more than 100 countries on four continents and home to two thirds of the planet's people. The term refers to the countries of sub-Saharan Africa, with their extreme poverty and recurring drought, and to the comparatively wealthy countries of Latin America, newly democratic after years of military rule. Also included are the economic hot-houses of Taiwan and South Korea and the centralised bureaucracy of China.

There is no simple definition of the third world; even international agencies such as the World Bank and the UN do not agree. It is in the history of their relationship with the countries of Europe and North America that we find the reason these diverse nations have been classified together.

How the third world became – and other stories

As civilisations have risen and fallen, some have become colonial powers. Over the past few hundred years, European civilisation has been the dominant force – due initially to the sea power of countries like Spain, Portugal and Holland. As the UK became the first industrial power, its colonies were ready to hand to provide what was needed. Without them, it is likely that the industrial revolution would have taken a very different course.

Colonies began as a source of raw materials: sugar for consumers' increasingly sweet teeth; slaves for the sugar plantations; cotton for our growing textile industry; gold for our banks. But, as industrialisation took off, the colonies provided something else: a captive market for products made by the UK's growing industries. In order to expand and improve profit, factories needed to find customers beyond our shores. The new textile and clothing industry, which began by importing cloth from India, then used India as a market. The colonial government even levied taxes against Indian made cloth sold within India, to ensure the success of imported British products! Gandhi's insistence on wearing Indian cloth was not merely a rejection of British culture; it had an economic purpose.

This kind of relationship continues to this day. Raw materials such as cotton, coffee or copper from the third world find their way into the goods in our shops. Manufactured products are sold to the third world in exchange. But the price of primary commodities doesn't keep pace with the rising cost of manufactured products; though we may feel our jar of coffee gets ever more expensive, the amount which the producer country needs to sell in order to pay for its imports increases year by year; the *terms of trade* are declining year by year. So third world countries find themselves running in order to stand still – growing and exporting more and more agricultural products, for instance, for the same small benefit. The human and environmental cost of this is huge, as more land is turned over to agricultural production.

This unsatisfactory situation has arisen because agricultural commodities are sold in a 'buyer's market', unlike oil, for example. Back in the mid-70s, the major oil-exporting states (OPEC) agreed to increase their prices. We are still feeling the repercussions from that; the debt crisis of today stems from the 'energy crisis' of 1974. The OPEC countries, of course, came into comparative riches. And, with an eye to the future, when the oil will eventually run out, they invested their petro-dollars. The Western banks that accepted all this wealth then had to lend it out in order to earn enough to pay the interest due on the OPEC deposits.

Countries in the third world, in need of loans to industrialise – and, ironically, to pay for the hugely increased cost of oil – were ideal customers. The interest rates were low, because there was so much money in the system, and, crucially, no one asked the right questions. Not just, 'Can you afford it?', but 'Will the loan increase your earnings?' Paying the interest was never going to be easy, so for a poor country it was important that the loan would yield enough income to meet the repayments.

From the late 1970s, the biggest debtor of them all, the US, began to borrow huge sums of money to finance its dreams (and its budget deficit). This put up the interest rates – they quadrupled during the 80s – and the debt crisis was born. Some countries are now spending half their income just paying the interest on their loans. And, when countries have to tighten their belts, it tends to be around the necks of the poor.

Many of the banks that lent money with so little apparent thought have now had to write off some of the debts, though many more are still due for payment. There are calls for further remission of debts as the banks shoulder part of the responsibility. And the poorest countries still need loans (on more favourable terms), but now no one will lend to the third world except on the safest possible terms (and only to the richer countries at that!) The loans available from the international institutions require the countries to apply austerity measures that penalise the poor. The banks have to find other borrowers instead (how many offers of loans have you received in the past year?). The problem has come full circle.

In 1974, the same year that oil prices went up, several Latin American countries tried collectively to increase the price they got for their bananas. But political pressure from the US made them back down – and, besides, the threat that the big banana companies controlling the trade would buy from elsewhere was very real; bananas rot within days if not sold. Oil just stays in the ground and its price goes up. Though in fact oil prices are now lower in real terms than before the 1974 watershed; even OPEC has its internal difficulties.

Another problem is dependence; many countries still rely on a few crops established in colonial times and cannot afford to spend time haggling when the crop is ripe. Uganda, for example, earns 97% of its foreign exchange from just one crop: coffee. Third world countries also depend on the goodwill of the rich countries, who are often quite open about the linking of aid money or preferential trade deals to 'good behaviour', such as voting the right way in the UN. The recent US embargo on Nicaraguan exports as punishment for not toeing the US line is a case in point. Or compare the massive US aid for Egypt with that of Ethiopia; one might be forgiven for thinking that Egypt was much the poorer. But if the producing nations were paid a price that covered the true cost of production, they wouldn't need charity.

While the terms of trade in commodities have declined over time, from month to month prices fluctuate wildly; unforeseeable events, such as late frosts affecting the flowering of coffee bushes in Brazil, can wreak havoc upon the economic planning of third world countries. Many commodities are traded on the 'futures market', in which traders contract to buy crops before the harvest – a single crop may be bought and sold several times while it is still growing.

This at least offers the growers security against such eventualities, though many companies speculate on the futures market, risking all on a big win should prices increase suddenly; the speculation itself fuels the price fluctuations in the same way as speculation on the stock market.

In the long term, it is better for everyone to have stable prices, otherwise no one can continue to produce the commodity. Sustainability isn't just an ecological buzz word; it is also an economic term. Can I afford to keep producing coffee? Can I feed my children *and* produce coffee? Changing over to new crops may take time – coffee bushes take four years to begin producing beans for example – but eventually, producers will move on to other crops, or lose their land and their livelihood altogether.

Several international commodity agreements were drawn up to set quotas to limit production and to stabilise prices. However, such agreements are fraught with problems, since the countries that control the agreements are the big consumer nations and the big producers, who rarely depend for their lives on the commodity concerned. The International Coffee Agreement, virtually inoperative since 1989, is dominated by Brazil and the USA; Brazil earns a mere 10% of its income from coffee, though producing nearly a third of world exports, and coffee amounts to only 0.2% of total US imports. The big producers can afford to overproduce and accept a lower price just to get an advantage in the longer term. The past few years have seen virtually all the agreements on important commodities such as coffee and sugar come crashing down.

Cash crops (growing money or food?)

This rather begs the question, why do countries grow crops for export at all? Countries, like farmers, have to sell something to pay for necessary imports: oil, machinery or medicines. So it seems like a mutually beneficial arrangement; we buy their crops and sell them our machines. But in the real world, nothing's that simple. A particular issue at present is the driving need to pay off debts, which is forcing countries to grow for export at the expense of food security. Governments may encourage the production of cash crops to increase exports, even at the expense of the poor, by giving free advice, fertilisers or credit only to farmers who grow a cash crop. This will inevitably mean that food crops are less favoured.

This may be because the country has become dependent on the crop, since it was developed as a 'plantation' during colonial times. In many cases, farmers began to grow crops for cash only when colonial governments levied taxes that had to be paid in cash. Uganda's dependence on coffee is extreme, but many countries earn more than a quarter of their income from just one crop. As was pointed out earlier, the value of a crop grown for many years may well have declined so far that it is no longer economic to grow, yet the country is locked into its production. The processing factories, transport facilities, marketing arrangements and the knowledge and skills of the farmers may take many years to change to a new crop.

Whether the production of cash crops for export is a Good Thing or not is very much a question of who benefits; the money earned from the crop may go principally to a rich landowner, while the local poor go hungry; it may enable smallholder families to earn enough to buy food and still have something left for the things they cannot grow themselves. The social impact depends on the growing system.

The extent to which the growing and processing of cash crops links in to the local economy is an important consideration when evaluating their social and economic value. Many cash crops can be processed locally before being sold; the tea leaf is withered, crushed, fermented and dried before being sold as black tea, sugar may be sold on as refined white sugar, or even as sweets. In that case, many other people besides the farming community may gain employment and the benefits are multiplied. This kind of linkage is a vital factor in development, but can often be hampered by importing countries putting tariffs and other barriers in the way of processed goods.

One criticism often levelled against cash crops is their

environmental impact; many are more damaging to the environment (and to the people who grow them) than traditional food crops. They are usually monocropped, need more chemical inputs such as pesticides and fertilisers to produce a good crop and consumers 'demand' a higher 'quality' in terms of size and appearance than would be the case for foods consumed locally. Cotton is a particularly heavy user of pesticides, as are bananas; Central America is the heaviest user of pesticides for that reason, and 75% of those used are banned in the US or the EC.

It is also a question of priorities; if cash crops are given resources that food crops need, such as land, labour or other inputs, there may be a problem of food availability. However, this is not always the case; for example, coffee is often grown on small farms, and the farmer can grow food crops between the coffee bushes so they do not directly compete for land. The cash crops may need labour at a different time of year, and may even help to fertilise the soil for the food crops if grown in rotation. Pineapples grow well on soil too salty for other crops – though they are often grown on prime land instead. Tobacco can be intercropped with food crops, too.

So an ideal cash crop is one that can be eaten if times are hard, does not compete for land or labour with food production, can be processed locally to create jobs, is environmentally benign and fetches a good price! Few crops are ideal in this way, but it is important to consider these factors when looking at individual products. Cotton is one crop that comes out pretty badly measured against these criteria, while peanuts compare favourably.

Land (for people or profit?)

Cash crops may make sense to a country, but why do people who don't have enough food choose to grow coffee instead of grains or vegetables? That is a question that has crossed the mind of many a concerned coffee drinker. The answer is, basically, they don't.

The majority of people in the UK don't own a lot of land;

certainly not enough to grow food; we earn our living in other ways. But in a country where most people still rely on the land for a living, the issue of land ownership can create many problems. In most countries, the land is divided up into many small plots and a few very large ones. Smallholdings of a reasonable size can enable the peasant farmers to make a living growing food or crops to sell as they choose. But this is not always the case.

While land is very unequally distributed in most countries, there are some extremes; in Brazil for example, just 2% of the landowners own 69% of the land. This leaves far too little for the majority to scrape a living. The people without enough land – often the majority – must work for someone else. All too often, such work is very insecure, perhaps only available at harvest time. It is often very poorly paid and the conditions on the plantations may be insanitary, unsafe and lacking in schools or medical care. Increasingly, plantations are employing people on a casual basis – hired only when work is needed. The workers may have no alternative places to find work, if the plantation is far from the city.

Many of the commodities the UK imports from the third world are grown on plantations, which can prevent the benefits of the trade reaching the poor. In particular, cash crops may be grown because they need little labour for planting or harvesting – so unemployment takes its toll. And smallholders, who have some degree of choice over what to grow, may be limited by the organisations which buy their crops.

The situation turns full circle when, in order to grow cash crops, large corporations or wealthy families acquire land from peasant farmers to extend their plantations. Peasants may leave because poor earnings and large debts force them to sell up; they may sell up in search of better security on the plantation as paid workers; in some cases, they are forced from the land by private armies. But all too often, they move on to marginal land, such as the edge of the desert or forest to try and scratch out a new living there.

Whichever way land falls to the large landowners, the decision about what to grow is based, not on what food is needed, but on what gives the best return. Historically, it has been more profitable to grow crops for export, such as coffee or cotton (or even cocaine). Whether or not this is a Good Thing again depends on how the benefits are shared. If the return does not yield benefits to the community, economic laws must be tempered by the needs of social justice.

The conflict between what makes sense economically and what is socially desirable is not unique to the third world, but in this situation can only be resolved by ensuring that the benefits flow equitably to the whole community. Land reform is one common approach to the problem. This may mean buying up or even requisitioning unused land for distribution to the poor. It may mean setting a limit on how much land can be owned by one person or company. Some countries take such land into government control. In essence, it means giving power (back?) to the powerless.

A common fear is that breaking up large holdings creates less efficient agriculture. But many studies show that the productivity of small farms is actually higher than large ones, due to the fact that a poor farmer is dependent for his/her livelihood on the size of the crop. Susan George, in her now classic book, *How the Other Half Dies*, quotes a World Bank study as showing that smallholdings in Latin America are far more productive than large farms; in some countries 14 times as productive. In some cases, a rich landowner owns so much land that very little is farmed at all. Yet when peasants scratching a meagre living on the hillsides of Latin America occasionally try to occupy and farm unused land owned by the wealthy, they are repelled by armed guards.

In particular, when land can be bought very cheaply, it is snapped up by wealthy families or corporations as an investment rather than as a productive farm. Much of the ex-forest land used to raise beef in Brazil is essentially a hedge against inflation. The whole issue revolves around the policies of governments – our own and those in the third world.

So, the short answer to the question, 'Should I buy this or that pineapple or tea bag from the third world?' is a resounding 'maybe', without much more specific information. The answer depends on the crop, the country and the way it is grown and traded; and that is what *The Global Consumer* sets out to find answers to.

Overpopulation

Of all the causes of poverty, overpopulation is widely seen as the most significant. With more and more mouths to feed and jobs to create, the problems of countries like Bangladesh are all too easy to understand. Whatever technological advances are made, and however fair the system, the earth cannot support a growing population for ever. But we cannot lay the blame for the poverty and hunger we see on our TV screens on the baby boom without another look.

Through the 1950s, life in the UK for most people became relatively good; pre-war recession and post-war rationing came to an end. For the first time, the majority actually had some choice about what to spend their money on, and the consumer society was born. As rationing went out and luxuries came in, economic life moved into another gear. While our standard of living doubled in the hundred years to 1961, it has doubled again in the next 30. Consumers have never looked back in terms of possessions and expectations. Today we use vastly more of the world's resources than we did then. In fact, the increasing demands of the West have put more pressure on resources than the increasing populations of the third world.

Energy use in the UK has more than doubled in the last 20 years, despite energy saving initiatives and a static population. The number of households with colour televisions has doubled in 10 years; those with a car has doubled in 20 and with a VCR in just four. The amount we spend abroad trebled in real terms between 1976 and 1988. Increasing consumption in the rich countries is a luxury that the world cannot afford, when the rather more legitimate need of people in the third world to improve their standard of living is largely going unmet.

Looking at it another way, to maintain his/her lifestyle,

the average Briton uses up something like 50 times more energy than the average Indian. In this situation, we can hardly lay the blame for resource depletion at the door of the third world. Birth control is vital; without it, deepening global crisis is just a matter of time. But it is also a matter of resource control, and that is very much an issue for the rich consumer.

A measure of this is the extent to which the UK depends upon the third world for its food; it comes as a surprise to many that the countries of the third world export more food than they import. The UK imports about £8 billion worth of food (at import values) – twice as much as it exports. Nearly £1 billion of the UK's food comes from the third world. The EC as a whole imports £34 billion and exports £19 billion worth. Half of these imports come from the third world.

It is nonetheless true that families in the third world have more children than families in the rich countries, and that this can cause great problems locally. The idea of regarding our children as a 'cost' is quite new; until recently, they were regarded as a source of labour. In the third world, this is still very much the case. For poor families with little security and no government provision for old age or unemployment, children are an asset as soon as they can work (or even walk). When many children die before reaching an age to support their parents, family planning is an impossible task.

Population growth is undeniably a cause of poverty – wealthier countries have slower-growing populations – but Tanzania's GNP (income) per head is little more than half Kenya's and only a quarter of Côte d'Ivoire's, yet its population growth rate is actually a little lower. A major reason for this is that Tanzania has invested far more in measures to improve its services such as education and health care; people now need fewer children for their security. Or compare Sri Lanka with Nigeria; their GNPs are the same, but Sri Lanka's social provision is far better. And Sri Lanka's population growth rate is a third of Nigeria's. Population growth is as much a result of poverty as it is a cause. The population time bomb cannot be defused just with a condom.

Food (and famine)

Any popular image of the third world revolves around food – or the lack of it. Since that horrifying TV report on the Ethiopian famine of 1984 first opened the eyes of the people of the UK, many have supported Band Aid, Live Aid and Comic Relief, yet the problem is still with us. Drought destroys crops one year, and flood the next.

War adds to the problems, too. Supplies could reach the disaster area were it not for the war; opposing factions threaten to destroy convoys going to enemy territory. War drives farmers off their land, through fear or directly through conscription into an army. It destroys crops – most infamously in Vietnam and Cambodia, where US bombers deliberately destroyed vegetation over a huge area.

Some people are beginning to wonder if all this aid is just delaying the inevitable; that perhaps we simply have to accept that many will die until the situation stabilises. But war also distorts development even before the shooting starts. In 1985, the world spent well over $900 billion preparing for war. Less than two weeks' military spending would have financed the Tropical Forest Action Plan, the UN Action Plan for Desertification, the UN Water and Sanitation Decade and the provision of contraception to all those who want it.

For many of us, the most horrifying thing about the African famines of the 1980s was the knowledge that there were huge stocks of unwanted food sitting in warehouses all over Europe. We could put men on the moon and fire rockets at Mars (and at each other). We could even fly reporters and camera crews in and out of the stricken area; could it really be true that the entire resources of the Western world could not get food to starving people?

In fact, food shortage is rarely the key problem; even in the Ethiopian famine of 1984, there was food available in neighbouring countries. Famines don't happen overnight, they are the culmination of inadequacies in social and economic structures, and quite predictable. In countries like India, with its own food stocks to guard against lean years, many people are still malnourished. As Indian economist Amartya Sen observed, 'Starvation is the characteristic of some people not *having* enough to eat. It is not the characteristic of there not *being* enough to eat.' The people who starve in famines are those without money, poor farmers whose crops have failed, not, by and large, the people in the cities. The key problem is poverty itself; all the food in the world is not enough if you have no means to pay for it.

Poverty also affects food production directly. In many countries of the third world, most farmers cannot afford to buy inputs like fertilisers, or even adequate irrigation, to improve their yields. Farmers cannot afford to buy fertilisers if the local people cannot afford to pay them good prices for their crop.

However, food production is itself a key issue for the countries of Africa bordering on the Sahara desert. Drought need not lead to disaster, but, complicated by poverty and lack of resources for agriculture, it certainly will. At one time, North Africa was the bread basket of the Roman empire; not too long ago, the desert was fertile. Now it encroaches year by year on to the land needed to grow food. Each year another 6 million hectares of productive dryland turns into desert; an area equivalent to the UK every three or four years.

There are many factors at work here, but poor farmers, scratching out a living on the edge of the desert, turn their own land into a wasteland. Without the resources to develop the land – and with too little land anyway – they cannot avoid destroying it. As is also commonly reported in the context of the Amazonian rainforest, poor farmers, pushed to the very edge of existence by more powerful people, often appear to be the culprits in environmental damage.

To put the crisis in Africa into perspective, there are two quotes that are hard to beat, put side by side. The first is from the World Commission on Environment and Development ('the Brundtland Commission'):

'Triggered by drought, its real causes lie deeper. They are to be found in part in national policies that give too little attention, too late, to the needs of smallholder agriculture and to the threats posed by rapidly rising populations. Their roots extend also to a global economic system that takes more out of a poor continent than it puts in. Debts they cannot pay force African nations relying on commodity sales to overuse their fragile soils, thus turning good land to desert. Trade barriers in the wealthy nations – and in many developing ones – make it hard for Africans to sell their goods for reasonable returns, putting yet more pressure on ecological systems. Aid from donor nations has not only been inadequate in scale, but too often has reflected the priorities of the nations giving the aid, rather than the needs of the recipients.'

And from Lloyd Timberlake, of Earthscan, talking about a meeting with the US congress:

'The politicians wanted to focus on Africa's difficult climate and poor soils, on its rapidly growing population, on its political ideologies – all things over which they had no control. They most decidedly did not want to talk about debt relief, trade barriers, or more effective and increased aid – things over which they do have some control, issues in which they have direct responsibilities.'

When thinking about food shortages, it is important to bear in mind that in the UK we rely on the poor countries for much of the food we eat. That doesn't mean we shouldn't buy it – many poor countries depend on the trade – but it does mean that we should be cautious about saying the third world doesn't have enough food.

Transnational corporations

Along with the globalisation of trade has grown the globalisation of companies. This century has seen the formation of a new breed of corporation that spans the globe, crossing national boundaries and able to make the most efficient use of resources in any part of the world. As they have grown, some have developed their own trading system, with their own plantations, processing plants, shipping lines, factories and even retail outlets and insurance cover.

The major cash crops imported from the third world are

mainly bought and sold by big transnational corporations (TNCs). For example, 80% of world tea exports are by TNCs; and just four big corporations control 94% of sales in Europe. TNCs control 85% of the world's trade in coffee and four firms sell 85% of Europe's coffee. TNCs export 95% of the world's pineapples, 85% of the world's wheat . . . the list goes on. Unilever (one of the biggest food corporations in the world) even accounts for 75% of India's domestic tea sales, and an astounding 98% of its packet tea market!

In financial terms, the largest TNCs are bigger than most of the third world countries they operate in. **Nestlé** and **Unilever**, for example, have turnovers of around £20 billion a year; bigger than the value of the exports of all but five third world countries. Thus they have tremendous resources, and tremendous power over the way decisions are made. If a big company wants to invest in a poor country, they can to a large extent dictate terms. Despite their size, however, their influence on trade is out of proportion to their importance as employers; while they employ 10% of the workforce in the richer countries, only 1% of the workers in the third world are employed by TNCs. We shouldn't get their role out of proportion.

Because they are transnational they can play one country off against another. They can invest in the country that offers the 'best' terms: the cheapest labour, the best tax holidays, the weakest unions. Examples of this can be found near to home if you look at the car giants; we have become so accustomed to them playing off the UK against Germany for the site of the next car plant, for instance, that most of us don't even think about it. Yet they are holding even rich countries to ransom for the most profitable deal.

Their power was summed up by the Brundtland Commission: 'But mutual suspicions still exist, usually because of an asymmetry in bargaining power between large corporations and small, poor developing countries. Negotiations are often made one-sided by a developing country's lack of information, technical unpreparedness and political and institutional weaknesses.'

Of popular concern at the moment is the issue of safety

and environmental impact. As legislation makes life more difficult or expensive in the richer countries – with firms having to pay compensation or clean up bills – TNCs have more opportunity than national firms to avoid their responsibilities by transferring dirty operations to countries with less rigorous policies. Accidents such as that in Bhopal in India have raised consciousness worldwide, but countries in need of investment are in no position to haggle – and many lack the technology to enforce standards anyway. Interestingly the Organisation for Economic Cooperation and Development (OECD) does not recognise a general responsibility of parent companies for damage caused by their subsidiaries. That is a position we as consumers must challenge.

In the past, many transnationals owned large plantations growing crops for export, as well as owning shipping companies, processors and even retail stores to sell the products back home. This 'vertical integration' gives the company a great deal of control over prices, and, when only three or four corporations dominate the trade, there have been accusations of price fixing that are difficult to refute. But the tendency nowadays is for the TNCs to let locals do the growing, which is a risky business, while still controlling all other aspects of the trade – even down to providing the seeds and fertilisers.

The ability of TNCs to trade within themselves gives plenty of opportunity for 'creative' accounting. By using artificial pricing between subsidiaries and the parent company ('transfer pricing', as it is known), TNCs can ensure that profits are made in countries with the most favourable tax regime. Estimates of the amount of international trade that is intra-firm vary, but 30–40% would be a fair guess.

But, of course, we don't buy only agricultural products from the countries of the third world; increasingly, they are manufacturing products for export. Figures for the UK are hard to come by, but according to the UN, US based TNCs account for half of that country's imports. The most important of the products imported from the third world are textiles and clothing, shoes, toys and, more recently, electrical and electronics goods.

The resources that TNCs have at their disposal, however, also give them tremendous power for the benefit of developing countries. Much of the investment, most of the research and development work and almost all the delivery of goods and services are carried out by private enterprise. As the debt crisis has taken hold, direct investment by TNCs has become more important as a way of financing economic development as third world countries have had to become more willing to accept TNC involvement.

The extent to which a country really benefits from TNC investment is a function both of TNC policy and the government's ability to encourage firms that will bring technology suited to the economic and technological development of the country. Third world countries cannot be passive recipients if the investment is to bring genuine development. Joint ventures between TNCs and governments or local companies are a means of facilitating this development. These allow more easily for the transfer of technology in its broadest sense, but not all TNCs favour such a loss of sovereignty. Another factor is whether or not the investment is in genuinely new projects or merely the takeover of existing enterprises; the latter may well mean a net reduction in employment. TNCs vary in the extent to which they involve local firms in providing inputs or services; such linkages can be a valuable boost to local economies.

Problems arise when commercial goals and social goals do not match. As the United Nations Centre on Transnational Corporations says in the epilogue to its report on TNCs and world development: 'National firms accept wide responsibilities to employees and society, and undertake social goals beyond that of narrow profit seekers. But when firms engage in transnational activities their sense of social responsibility often falls short of their global reach.' It must be said, however, that in many cases, the standards set in more developed countries (in health and safety, for example) often influence TNC operations in the third world, gradually transferring improvements to local firms, too.

TNCs dominate the trading system that delivers our goods from the third world: how well do these corporations respond to social and environmental goals? In the following chapters we look, product by product, at the response of big companies to the issues we are facing together at the end of the 20th century.

Free Trade Zones

Many third world countries set up Free Trade Zones (FTZs) or Export Processing Zones to encourage investment by TNCs. These zones offer good facilities, lower taxes, non-unionised workforces and other benefits; the country earns foreign exchange from the exported goods and gains increased employment. Many countries from the Philippines to Mexico now have one or more of these areas, and, while it is a small proportion of the total workforce, well over a million people work in them. Many of the clothes and electrical goods we see in our shops are made in FTZs.

But are FTZs a Good Thing? For the people who work in them, they at least provide a job, though unions or strikes are normally banned and so working conditions can be bad. The companies operating in FTZs employ mainly young unmarried women, on the grounds that child raising disrupts the work, and governments sell them as a cheap, compliant and industrious workforce. The jobs that are gained are also often short lived; older workers also become more demanding.

The financial benefits to the host country are not as good as might at first appear: foreign firms send profits back home, taxes are not paid for a good while, and TNCs may move on to another country once taxes become due. Technology, much needed to develop the local economy, does not 'rub off' onto local businesses in the way it would if FTZs were not isolated from the rest of the country. Investment in infrastructure, such as electricity, water supplies or roads, is frequently diverted from other areas in order to create the FTZ.

The policies of individual companies and governments

determine the extent to which FTZs or any other kind of foreign investments really operate to the benefit of the people. The Zones themselves are merely a microcosm of the way government and industry interact; many of the same factors are at work in the wider economy, some countries effectively operating as giant FTZs.

Industrialisation (stepladder or tread mill?)

Countries dependent on agriculture need to diversify in order to survive and compete: making manufactured exports, processing their commodities, so adding value to them. But all too often, their products are kept out of rich countries by barriers such as tariffs (taxes) or quotas (limits on the quantities allowed in). Voluntary export restraints (VERs) are another barrier, where exporters are asked to cut back in order to avoid retribution from importing countries. No problem selling cocoa beans, but if you try and sell cocoa powder, it attracts a higher tariff; and the tariff is still higher on the chocolate you make from it.

The first big step for many – as it was for the UK 200 years ago – is the textile and clothing industry. It is a trade that requires little expensive technology and can employ a lot of people, yet the added value is high. It is on the income from clothing that countries like Hong Kong, Singapore and Taiwan have developed into industrial powers, and on which Bangladesh is attempting to grow. But, in developing their own industries, such countries begin to compete with the rich countries; development becomes a threat and the response is often aggressive.

In 1974 another international 'agreement' was signed: the Multifibre Arrangement (MFA). This was to restrict the exports of textiles and clothing from third world countries to the rich countries, in order to allow industry to restructure and cope with the new reality. It was a way to protect jobs until new ones could be found – and was supposed to last for four years. In 1991, the MFA was still in force, and negotiations about whether and how it should be phased out were taking place as we went to print. The signs are that it will continue in some form until at least the end of 1992.

The arguments about the effectiveness of the MFA in protecting employment in the UK rage on; jobs continue to decline due to imports from other rich countries and changes in technology, and the cost to consumers is far higher than the wages protected, at around £30,000 per job, according to National Consumer Council estimates. But its effectiveness in hampering the development of a clothing industry in poor countries is clear. The irony is that, as third world countries find a way of becoming less dependent on export crops, the rich countries find another hurdle to put in their way. We see the same sort of barriers placed in front of imports of electrical items, footwear and many other manufactured goods. All too often, trade between 'strong' and 'weak' countries is a one sided affair. And the consumer foots the bill as prices are held artificially high.

This situation leads many people to question whether it is worth the countries of the third world trying to play the international trade game at all when the dice are so loaded against them. Perhaps it would be better to turn their backs on the rich 'north' and plough their own furrow. Trade agreements between relatively equal partners are more likely to carry equal benefits, so is 'south–south' trade where the future lies? That is certainly part of the answer, but if it were *the* solution, this book would be very thin indeed.

Unfortunately, withdrawal from trade with the powerful nations carries costs; countries need imports, such as oil, if they are to run machinery, cars and tractors. They need imports of medicines and other chemicals until they can develop their own industry. They need access to technology and investment in order to carry forward their development plans. Some countries have pursued a policy of 'import substitution', protecting home industries and keeping imports out, not without some success, but the costs of access to technology and inefficiency are high. This is not to argue that 'development' is always good, that imports are never earmarked for the Western lifestyles of rich elites, or that appropriate health care needs the expensive (or even unsafe) drugs that are sometimes marketed by Western companies.

But it is undeniable that as countries have developed economically, the relative shortage of skilled labour, the changing structure of production and the involvement in international trade has tended to improve wages and working conditions. However, low wages, poor working conditions and the repression of unions are certainly not a thing of the past. And, crucially, poor working conditions are not justifiable as necessary for the kind of development that ultimately will benefit the working people.

Working conditions

The most significant social factors people commonly consider when thinking about products imported from the third world are the wages and working conditions of the people who make the goods. They are often invoked with a mix of motives by unions in the UK campaigning for controls on the importing of products made by cheap labour, threatening jobs here. The clothing industry is a classic example.

We've heard of child labour, of people working (and living) in such cramped sweatshops that they are physically damaged. There are factories in which unions are banned, workers being harassed or even beaten up when they try to form one. Some workers are locked in all night to finish urgent orders, some are not paid for the overtime they are forced to do. And the clothes from factories like these do find their way into high street clothes shops in the UK.

But the answer is not to avoid third world goods. For one thing, there is exploitation in the UK industry too (homeworkers are a vulnerable and very badly paid group). More importantly, the export trade in the third world is often a much better sector to work in than the local market; foreign owned companies often have the resources to lead the way in improving working conditions. Refusing to buy from third world countries will only force people back into even poorer conditions.

Since many third world countries look upon manufacturing industry as the best way to finance the development that can lead to improvements in wages and working conditions, a blanket boycott of third world products would be very damaging. The 'economic miracles' of South Korea, Singapore and Taiwan may not be social and economic utopias, but it is undeniable that wages have increased for workers in manufacturing as a direct result of their success in exporting.

Though work in export-oriented factories offers better conditions and wages than either factories in the local market or agricultural work, for most people in the third world, it is not an option. The majority live in villages and job opportunities in manufacturing are few and far between; third world countries and communities will depend on agriculture for the foreseeable future, and the need for other labour intensive work will increase rather than decline as more people look for jobs.

Clearly poor wages and working conditions are an inevitable feature of industries in any poor country and we need to encourage the kind of developments in trade that will lead to improvements. To refuse to buy from a country because of its poverty is certainly not going to achieve that. So we have to be discriminating consumers, buying from the sources that offer the best deal all round – for ourselves, certainly, but also for the producer.

Living in one world

A few centuries ago, countries were self contained, the environment big enough to cope with all we could throw at it. But that time has long passed. Everything that happens in the third world, be it deforestation, debt crisis or democratic change, has repercussions here.

The demands, initiatives and policies of the richer countries equally have enormous impact on the third world – for good or ill. It has become a cliché to refer to One World, but it has to affect our thinking more and more if we are to sort out the mess that threatens us in the rich nations, and already engulfs the poor in the third world.

As consumers we do have enormous power, were it focused in the right direction; a typical school leaver of today will bring around a million pounds to bear on the world's trading system during the course of his or her working life. Companies work within an economic system that militates against many concerns that consumers have; a company that invests too much in social goals will lose out to harder-nosed competitors. What is socially or environmentally desirable and what is economically feasible are sometimes poles apart.

As consumers we can bring them closer together by placing our economic vote in the tills of companies that develop initiatives addressing the issues outlined here. We can make it worthwhile for companies to respond. Already, there are enormous differences between companies who take a broad view – plan for and invest in the future – and those whose search for the immediate return draws them to bite the hand that feeds them. We are all consumers. Let's not apologise for it, let's make it work.

Consumer Power
in Action

The principle behind consumer power is clear: if we place our vote in the tills of the companies doing most to address the causes of the global crisis, we can begin to make a real difference. The biggest companies are very powerful, and what they do is fundamentally important. None of them is perfect; most far from it, and, to be fair, some would even admit it. But a small change will start the process, and rewarding the best, even if it isn't very good, will encourage the rest.

The decision about which product to buy – which represents the best value for people and the environment – relies on information. We need to know what issues the companies have to address on our behalf, and which companies are responding. This section of the book sets out to give you the tools with which to make your choice.

Selecting the products and companies

Most products we buy are not made in the third world, but many use third world components or ingredients. The first job in our survey was to assess the major areas of consumer expenditure that were significantly third world sourced.

Products were excluded for a variety of reasons. Some markets are very diversified with a large number of small companies involved – for example handicrafts – which would make the assessment of company policy far too big a task. Some items may be sourced to a considerable extent from the third world, but do not represent a significant level of consumer expenditure – false beards and wigs for instance, a large proportion of which apparently come from South Korea!

Other increasingly important product groups were not included, but may well feature in subsequent editions of *The Global Consumer*. Essential oils from the rainforest, and the tiny but growing proportion of cars from the third world are just two examples.

Some products have less coverage than others. This does not reflect their importance; it is simply because there was little information available that would help consumers make informed choices. Some goods have been given longer chapters, since they introduce general concerns relevant to other chapters – clothing and textiles, for example, raise similar issues, as do DIY products and furniture.

Selecting the companies to focus on was the next stage. In most markets, the top few companies account for most of the sales, giving them great power and responsibility. We also analysed each market to decide whether the power lay with the retailers or with the manufacturers. There seems little point in trying to focus consumer power on clothing manufacturers when clothing retailers set the standards and put their labels on the products. On the other hand, when we choose electronics goods it is the manufacturers' names we know.

Finding the information

We have gathered information from many sources; from international trade unions, from campaigning groups here and in the third world, from international institutions such as the International Labour Organisation and UN Conference on Trade and Development, from academic sources and from newspapers and periodicals. This information was used to highlight the most important issues arising from the trade in each product; issues which the companies must respond to.

Much of the information contained in this book results

from a high level of communication with the companies themselves. This not only ensures that we can more fairly judge their policies, but it also increases company awareness of consumer concerns.

Companies were sent questionnaires tailored to their areas of manufacturing and/or retailing. They covered all the issues related to the products concerned and asked specifically what policies each firm had developed to address them, and what practical outcome there had been. They also sought to find out companies' level of involvement – whether they own manufacturing facilities in third world countries or rely on suppliers, for example.

Combining information from the questionnaires with information from other sources, we drafted a profile of each company, which was then commented upon by the company (most of those that had not responded to the questionnaires did send information at this stage!). Those that refused, or neglected to respond in any way, are indicated in the product chapters.

Some firms were particularly helpful, and this is reflected in the amount written about them in the product chapters. While cooperation is no guarantee of good policies, a lack of cooperation does suggest that companies do not take these issues seriously, or are unaware of the problems that arise in trade with the third world. It is no coincidence that the most helpful firms are often those that have operations in the third world. In general these have proved to be far better informed and to have developed relevant policies. This is only to be expected, as the bigger they are and the greater their involvement in the third world, the more responsibility they have to take the issues seriously.

By contrast, retailers and manufacturers merely sourcing in the third world have not by and large developed appropriate responses. Even an acknowledgement that they have a responsibility for the social and environmental impact of their sourcing is beyond some. 'We buy only from reputable suppliers' is a common refrain, but it is simply not good enough. It is important that companies first and foremost recognise that they have responsibilities; some retailers have woken up to this and it represents a significant step in the right direction.

It has to be said that even the best responses fell far short of addressing all the concerns we raised. However, the intention of this book is to highlight the best of what is available; to compare like with like and enable consumers to vote for the best. That way lies progress.

It is clear that companies must increasingly become accustomed to collecting and monitoring information centrally on social and environmental issues. A company that did not collect information on sales or output from its subsidiaries would soon be in trouble. We need to see some of the effort that is applied to financial management at work on social issues.

We should also make clear that our research, which relies on material submitted voluntarily and information already in the public domain, gives us no right to claim special knowledge. There may be corporate policies we have no knowledge of, and indeed, such policies may be rapidly developed or modified.

Our survey included only the top firms in each product area, and consequently some brands on the market are not mentioned. This does not mean that the companies not included are any better or worse than those that are; merely that most of us buy from the biggest, and that they have special responsibilities.

What you can do

In the following chapters we explore the issues from the perspective of the consumer. We look at the way the various products are made or grown; at the impact the process has on the people and their environment. We look at the main countries that export to the UK; at what particular factors we can consider in relation to each. In particular, we look at the wealth of the country – its Gross National Product (GNP) per capita, which measures total earnings divided by the population. In general terms, the lower the GNP, the poorer the country and the fewer resources available for social developments. The figures given are for 1987 (the latest available for the range of countries included) and refer to GNP per capita.

We also look at how the wealth is divided up in each country, and at its Human Development Index (HDI), which measures the quality of life in terms of life expectancy, adult literacy and purchasing power to satisfy basic needs. This produces a ranking that can be compared to the GNP per capita ranking. A country is 'expected' to have an HDI v GNP ranking of 0; a positive ranking implies a higher than expected quality of life.

Some countries show huge variations between HDI and GNP; Sri Lanka has a low GNP per capita but a high HDI ranking, indicating that in spite of comparatively low level of economic activity and wealth, a reasonable level of human development can be achieved. Saudi Arabia, a comparatively wealthy country, has a low level of human development. Together, these measures can be used to indicate countries offering good 'value' in development terms; those in which any income from trade is likely to reach those people who need it most.

At the end of each chapter are suggested Consumer Choices; these include a 'Best Buy', when there is one. This represents the best value in world terms. Which widely available product, pound for pound, is likely to yield the best return for the third world? The best buy may work out more expensive than alternatives; in that case, your response will depend on what you can afford.

Sometimes analysing the issues points to a clear consumer response; sometimes not. Occasionally consumer power is limited. But there are other ways of responding, and working with public interest organisations is an important way to do so. There is no doubt that consumer power can sharpen up thinking in places where it matters – in the boardrooms of the most powerful companies – and we make no apology for encouraging you to take action in such circumstances, where it has clear benefits for the third world, however small.

It must never be forgotten that in many cases the decision

to consume less is more desirable than informed choice between brands. This releases resources for use by others – as Gandhi pointed out, the world has enough for everyone's need, not for everyone's greed. But it also releases money, which we may be able to use more creatively.

After all, buying as cheap as possible has brought us to the point of crisis; cheap products mean cutting corners – or wages. Someone has to pay the bill, and it should be the consumer, not the person who makes the product.

Consumer action is more than just choosing the right product. Sometimes other forms of action are even more effective. Consumer Choices gives some ideas. More are to be found in **Going Further** at the end of the book.

Money

A third world export? While we commonly think of our relationship with the third world as one in which we give money to *them*, the reality is far from that. The debt crisis has resulted in more money flowing back to the rich countries than is invested in the third world. The World Development Movement, the UK's leading pressure group on development issues, has launched a consumer campaign focusing on the links between third world debt and the banks; this chapter is based on material supplied by WDM and gives an interesting light on what consumers can do beyond the everyday shopping trip.

To the people of a country such as the Philippines, the consequence of the country's debts are enormous. While it is the government that pays the debt, it is the ordinary people who foot the bill – late in 1989 the government signed an agreement with the IMF in which it undertook to put up electricity and water prices, a measure which particularly affects those who depend on these services to make a living. The government said it was compelled to put up charges in return for international loans. But many of these loans were simply designed to pay off interest on debts inherited from the time of the now-deposed dictator, President Marcos. Such loans were rarely used to benefit the ordinary people. One, attracting huge interest payments of $335,000 a day, was for a nuclear power station at Bataan which was sited on an earthquake fault and has never functioned. Five British banks, including **Barclays** and **National Westminster**, lent $11.7 million for the project.

The Philippines currently uses 40% of the money it receives from export sales to service its $27 billion debt.

The rise of third world debt

Back in 1973 and 1974 the oil-producing countries of the Middle East organised amongst themselves to demand higher prices for their oil. Excess funds were put on deposit in Western banks and financed a lending spree to developing nations. Banks need to earn interest from loans in order to pay the interest on deposits, and loans, at the low interest rates of the time, were made to virtually every third world country. Most, however, went to nations seen as having the most promising economic potential, mainly the large Latin American states – Argentina, Brazil, Mexico, Peru and Colombia. Poorer countries in Africa relied more on government loans.

When the world economy went into recession, repayments due on the debt increased with rising interest rates and commodity prices declined in real terms. Interest payments could no longer be met and the banks woke up to the fact that many loans had not been invested productively. While the banks are still making profits, the countries of the third world are saddled with a debt now worth $1.3 trillion ($1,300,000,000,000). The most indebted countries owe something approaching $1,000 for each adult and child.

With a debt this size, developing countries descend into a spiral of increasing indebtedness. Banks are unwilling to lend new money, except to pay interest on the old money, which simply builds up the amount owed. And in order to repay the remainder, poor countries have to cut back on basic development programmes such as education and health. This simply undermines their efforts to develop. They also have to ensure that they sell more of what they grow to consumers in the North, to earn foreign currency to pay the debt. The debt crisis is one reason we have so many cheap third world products, like tea, coffee and even exotic fruits, in our shops.

This debt spiral can be illustrated by the figures relating

to nineteen of the worst-hit countries. At the end of 1982 they owed $328 billion to commercial banks. Over the next seven years the nineteen countries paid out more than the capital they owed in interest payments to service the debt. But amazingly, by 1989 the amount they were left owing had risen to $356 billion – not as a result of any new loans, but as a result of rescheduling interest payments or converting them into capital amounts owed. In addition, the amounts they owed to official creditors (governments and international financial institutions) rose by $107 billion – incurred to help pay interest on the debt owed to commercial creditors.

The debt crisis is also the reason that over the last few years the third world has paid us far more money than we have given it. In 1988 the 69 developing countries hit by the debt crisis transferred to their creditors $30 billion more than they received in new loans. Banks received $28 billion of this excess. Such statistics make a mockery of the idea that the rich world is the charitable benefactor of the poor world.

For Latin America the result has been a 'lost decade', with a decline in per capita income of 10% (compared to a 40% rise in the previous decade), a one-third fall in gross investment, and true hyperinflation for the first time anywhere since World War II. The losers in this crisis are the millions of people across the southern hemisphere who have seen their standard of living fall to inhuman levels. Each one of them nominally owes us around $290. Rather than being used to lift them out of poverty, the money they earn is going to banks and our governments in the North.

The banks

Anyone who has borrowed money from a bank knows that they are used to weighing up the risks and benefits of overdrafts or loans. Banks are sheltered in two ways from the risk of their loans to developing nations. Firstly, they have strength in numbers. Because of the huge amounts involved, the banks issued loans in syndicates, sometimes involving scores of individual banks from a large number of countries. Secondly, they used 'floating' interest rates: when the loans were made levels were comparatively low. But the terms of most of the loans stipulated that the rates should vary according to international interest rates. These are set, of course, by Northern countries and had tripled by the early 1980s.

Having limited the risk, banks anticipated substantial gains. There was a short-term killing to be made from huge commission fees and a longer-term income to draw from the gradual repayment with interest.

Even so, normal bank prudence was still cast aside. By 1982 the nine biggest US banks had loaned nearly three times their total capital to the third world. Many years on, even bankers now go some way to acknowledging the folly of this. Sir Kit McMahon, as Chairman of **Midland Bank**, stated in 1990 that he 'had no hesitation in admitting that the banks do bear some responsibility for the debt crisis, simply through having lent too much.' The former Managing Director of the IMF (International Monetary Fund), H. Johannes Witteveen, is harsher, condemning the banks as having 'engaged in an irresponsible competitive race in sovereign lending. Many of these banks short-sightedly felt that sovereign risk did not exist.' They just couldn't believe that countries could default on borrowing.

Money for nothing?

Before the crisis broke, the conventional wisdom was that large loans to finance new industry were the easiest way to allow developing countries to catch up economically with the West. Many governments in the third world accepted the loans freely offered to them from the best of motives.

Many others, however, did not. Much of the money borrowed was never intended for industrial development or the provision of social services. For a large cluster of corrupt and military regimes supporting a powerful minority within their country, these loans were 'money for nothing'. In fact, on many occasions corrupt politicians actually re-deposited large amounts of the money in their own names with the same banks that had loaned the money in the first place.

In the Philippines, in the era of Ferdinand Marcos, British banks lent money to companies headed by his cronies, such as the sugar mills of Roberto Benedicto. A number of Marcos associates channelled the loans into their own secret bank accounts or used them to support their luxurious lifestyle. When their companies went bankrupt, the Marcos government took them over, together with the liability for their loans.

For many countries, particularly in Latin America which was largely under military rule at the time, around a third of the debt was incurred to buy arms. Millions of dollars were also spirited straight out of countries such as Venezuela, by rich individuals (so-called 'capital flight'). More was borrowed for ill-conceived and environmentally damaging projects that never worked.

A crisis in the making

In themselves loans are not a Bad Thing. If they are invested in a project that yields more than what is needed for repayment, they make sound business sense. However, other factors conspired to ensure that there was a debt crisis in the making almost from the word go.

From the end of the 1970s three events formed a lethal cocktail for the third world. In 1979 there was a second, unprepared for, rise in oil prices. Following this, interest rates began their steep rise. At about the same time the world price of many primary foodstuffs and minerals exported by third world countries took a nose-dive.

The capacity of countries to develop vibrant industrial sectors, and to protect existing ones, was hit badly by high oil prices. Repayments turned into economic nightmares with the jump in interest rates. Revenue from exports to cover these repayments fell drastically with the drop in commodity prices.

As development moved into reverse, banks lost all interest in providing fresh credit and hardened their resolve to retrieve the money already lent. It was from this time, the early 1980s, that the debt crisis began to bite.

The debt burden

The priority for the creditors was to ensure that no developing country refused to pay off the debt. That, they feared, might have created a 'domino' effect of default right across the third world. Developing countries, still needing new loans for investment, have been pressured by their creditors to 'adjust' to the new burden of repayments. Such economic adjustment programmes have been promoted particularly by two international financial agencies, the IMF and World Bank.

The programmes are effectively a massive exercise in debt collecting. Sir Jeremy Morse, Chairman of **Lloyds** (the British bank with the largest third world loans), says that the purpose of the IMF should be to ensure that economic policy in the third world is addressed to 'containing inflation and earning a sufficiently large trade surplus to enable them to service their debt'.

The main creditor banks cooperate through 'advisory committees' they have set up for each of the main debtor countries. 'With new loans,' explains **National Westminster's** John Hilbourne, 'we work increasingly with agencies such as the World Bank and International Monetary Fund.' In order to ensure that debtor countries continue to pay off the debt, most have been cajoled and pressurised into reaching a belt-tightening agreement with the IMF.

The central idea in this strategy has been that, even with the burden of repayments, developing countries can grow their way out of the crisis. Back in 1986 Sir Jeremy Morse explained this idea to British MPs: 'the generality of developing countries, that have either been caught up in the debt crisis or on the edge of it, will improve their position and will come back to credit-worthiness.' Years on, such predictions have proved to have been hopelessly optimistic.

It is the poor who are the chief victims of debt. And within their ranks, women and children suffer most. Women have to cope and devise survival strategies when the country's debt-stricken economy means that household incomes fall and prices rise. Richard Jolly, Deputy Director of the United Nations Children's Fund (UNICEF) believes that the debt crisis is costing the lives of an additional half a million children a year. Despite the horrific human toll, debt only appears on the financial pages, not the front pages, of our newspapers. Unlike famine or drought, this crisis cannot easily be captured by TV cameras. Nor, says UNICEF, is it happening because of 'any one visible cause, but because of an unfolding economic drama in which the industrialised countries play a leading part.'

The burden of debt has also obliged developing countries to over-exploit their natural resources. Friends of the Earth report in *Rainforest Destruction and Third World Debt, 1991* that, 'in order to earn foreign exchange for debt repayments, agriculture for export rather than agriculture for local needs has been encouraged. Forests have been cleared for their timber or to make way for plantations. Peasant farmers, displaced from fertile lands needed to grow export crops, have been forced to clear forest to grow food, thus adding to the destructive pressures. The intensity of this exploitation not only threatens our global environment, but seriously weakens the ability of the indebted nations to achieve sustainable economic recovery.'

A Philippines grass-roots network, the Freedom from Debt Coalition, says that debt is being paid by '. . . tearing down more of our forests for lumber exports, destroying more of our coral reefs for fish exports, and depleting more of our soil through heavy pesticides and fertilizers used for cash crops.' A similar scenario is being played out across the southern hemisphere.

Passing the buck

The international strategy for dealing with the debt crisis has been dominated by northern governments and the IMF and World Bank. However, the strategy has always depended heavily on the voluntary participation of the banks, making a coherent plan difficult to implement. The 1986 'Baker Plan', calling for new lending to debtor countries, was undermined simply by banks refusing to lend.

The Baker Plan is one of a number of initiatives that have left the North fiddling (a new loan here, a rescheduled debt there) while the third world burns. Each has failed to end the debt crisis. But the governments, who lent more to Africa than did the banks, have arguably made more concessions than the banks.

Governments have supported the banks in two ways. Firstly they have granted them huge amounts of tax relief (in the UK, well over £1 billion) in advance of any loss they might make if the debts are not repaid. Receiving such support in advance has meant that the banks have had to delay or cancel only the smallest debts. Yet they continue to demand, and get, interest and capital repayments from the third world. Secondly, new loans made by governments and international agencies to debtor countries have often been used to pay back more to the banks, rather than being invested in development.

Over the period of the debt crisis, the 'big four' British banks – **Lloyds, Midland, National Westminster** and **Barclays** – made in total around £16 billion profit. When the crisis started in earnest in 1982, it was also a crisis for the banks. British banks, for example, hold some 12.5% of the total commercial debt outstanding – around $53 billion. This crisis has now passed. Sir Jeremy Morse of **Lloyds**, the UK's leading commercial creditor, told shareholders in February 1990 that 'the worst of this long-running problem is behind us.'

Having ridden out their crisis, the 'big four' are also trying to offload the problem by passing the ownership of the loans to other players in the international financial markets. They sell the debt at a heavy discount (you could buy, for example, £1 million worth of Sudanese debt for £20,000). The person who buys it can still demand full payment unless the country concerned, with its scarce resources, can buy it back itself.

Banks have also exchanged a developing nation's debt for shares in companies or assets within the country; such deals are often reported in the press as 'debt-equity swaps'. One British bank, **Midland**, did a deal with Peru to receive payment in fish and raw iron, and early in 1991 was considering accepting logs from the tropical rainforest in Brazil in place of debt payments in cash. Such swaps have in total, however, only reduced the overall debt by five per cent.

'Debt for nature' swaps have also been considered as another option, aimed at supporting environmental initiatives in debt-burdened countries. However, many people argue that such deals are undesirable. Environmentalists in Brazil, where these swaps are being considered, believe that they do little more than legitimise the external debt. They contribute to inflation, lead to a loss of sovereignty over natural resources, and fail to address the real issues behind the loss of forest and the problems of the indigenous people.

Although it was often undemocratic or even military governments in the third world which struck the loan deals, many of those governments have now been replaced by more democratic ones, who remain saddled with the debt. In the Philippines, for example, British banks were involved in ill-fated lending to the corrupt dictatorship of President Marcos. Since the Aquino government came to power in 1986, British banks have allegedly insisted that it also takes responsibility for loans to a private company, Planters Products, that went bust.

If a company goes bankrupt in the UK, any remaining debts are cancelled. But banks argue that loans taken out by countries should not be open to cancellation, even if the issue for the people of the country is one not of bankruptcy but life and death. For all the evidence of poverty and environmental degradation resulting from the debt crisis, banks have refused to accept that writing off the debt will help. 'I cannot agree with the view,' wrote Robin Ibbs, Deputy Chairman of **Lloyds**, in March 1990, 'that cancellation of debt would improve the living standards of the poor.' But there are now enough authoritative studies contradicting this view to indicate that while debt cancellation will not in itself be a complete solution, it is an essential part of one.

In 1988 Percy Mistry, a former senior World Bank official, estimated that sub-Saharan Africa, in the face of worsening poverty, would need to cease all debt payments to be able to restart the development process. In 1989 the World Bank itself estimated that the 17 most indebted countries would need either new aid to the tune of $8 billion a year, or an equivalent cut in their debt payments. In 1990 David Knox, former Vice-President of the World Bank for Latin America, estimated that Latin America needed to have its annual debt payments cut by 50–60%. In 1991 governments agreed to cancel between 50 and 70% of the debt of Poland, a country far better off than most third world debtors.

Addressing the issues

Like the Roman god Janus, banks need to look forward and they need to look back. For the moment, governments bear the main responsibility for ensuring that new finance is made available to third world countries. But banks will lend anew when there is hope of a profit and debt relief will help countries return to 'credit worthiness'. Looking forward, banks must accept the need to consider the environmental impact of new loans, as well as ensuring that the projects for which they are lending the money are economically viable.

Looking back, they need to accept that it was partly their imprudent lending that led to the debt crisis, and that the price has been paid by the world's poorest people and by our global environment. They should now play their part in a resolution of the crisis. In some countries, a reduction of bank debt will be the critical factor; in others the reduction must be shared equally with the governments and international agencies who lend to the poorer countries. Even in the very poorest countries, bank debt reduction will be a small but important complement to the actions that official creditors are now starting to take.

Only with such actions will poor countries be able to start on the road towards economic recovery – thus making it more likely that remaining loans will be serviced in full. But, in addition, only by participating in the resolution of the debt crisis will banks be fulfilling their wider social and environmental responsibilities.

Due to the provisions set aside by the banks against defaults and the considerable sums of public money given them in the form of tax relief, they can afford to agree to cancel all the debts owed by the world's very poorest countries and reduce by at least a half debts owed by the major debtor countries.

As the first steps in this process, the banks, as well as cancelling outright the relatively small number of remaining debts to the poorest countries, notably in sub-Saharan Africa, should support the call for an international agreement over governments coordinating the reduction of commercial bank loans and doing everything within their power to limit the burden placed on third world debtor countries, their people and their environment.

CONSUMER CHOICES

Not all banks in the UK have participated in loans to third world countries. Nor have the building societies, though they will have deposited some money with those banks that have. These organisations can be considered 'ethically neutral' on the matter. The major British banks involved in the debt are **Lloyds, Midland, Barclays, National Westminster, Standard Chartered** and, to a lesser extent, **Bank of Scotland** and **Royal Bank of Scotland**. American banks, such as **Citibank**, also tend to be heavily involved.

In encouraging the banks to address the issues, you do not need to go as far as a group of Swiss consumers went. They took out a joint loan from a Swiss bank involved with third world debt and ceremoniously refused to pay it back until the bank cancelled loans to developing countries. As a consumer, you clearly have a choice of which bank or building society you deal with and you can choose one with no involvement in the debt crisis.

However, the World Development Movement's campaign is specifically aimed at consumers. If your bank is involved in third world debt, says WDM, so are you. It has called on consumers to take action on the issue and its suggestions form the basis of the following recommendations.

✔ Changing your credit card is a lot simpler than transferring your account, and the main profits go to the issuing bank, not Access or Visa. So if you have a credit card issued by **Lloyds**, **Midland**, **Barclays**, **National Westminster**, or **Standard Chartered**, join the campaign by cutting it up and changing to a card issued by a neutral bank or building society.

✔ For a BEST BUY, swap to an affinity card, such as **GiroBank's** Oxfam card. These release money to good causes every time you use them. Send your old card back to your bank.

✔ You might consider also changing your bank account to a neutral bank or building society.

Beyond the shopping trip:

Contact WDM and find out more about the debt campaign.

Write to your bank asking them to take action on third world debt; tell them of your action in changing your credit card. Tell them that you're supporting WDM's campaign, too.

Write to your MP: ask her/him to encourage the government to play its part in relieving the third world of its burden of debt, and especially the poorest countries of Africa. One breakthrough proposal, prepared by a leading debt academic, Stephanie Griffith-Jones, has been that the government should withhold or reclaim tax concessions granted to banks involved in the debt crisis. This, she argued, would act as a carrot and stick method of getting the banks to write off the debt.

DIY

The last decade has seen an explosion of interest in DIY which now clocks up £5 billion in the UK every year. Wood and wooden products such as doors and shelves are one of the main elements of the trade, totalling some £600 million of sales. But as we struggle to fit that hardwood door or shelf unit, how many of us reflect that it may have been part of a rainforest tree?

The chief consideration in this chapter is tropical deforestation and our contribution to it. The UK is the fourth biggest importer of hardwoods, so it is an issue in which we are closely involved. The major questions to be asked here are: to what extent can the logging business be held responsible for the crisis we see developing; and to what extent is the business responding, not only to the ecological imperatives, but also to the equally pressing human issues?

The bulk of our tropical timber comes from Asia. Of the $6.7 billion of wood and wood products that the third world exports, Malaysia alone accounts for nearly $2 billion. The vast bulk of Malaysia's exports are in the form of rough wood – 60% of total third world exports of rough wood and 25% of the entire world's trade! – while Indonesia exports $1 billion of veneer and plywood; nearly half the third world total. Myanmar (Burma) is a major rough wood exporter too, earning over 40% of its income from the trade in 1986. Other significant exporters are Côte d'Ivoire and Gabon in West Africa, Brazil and, perhaps surprisingly, since neither have significant forests, Singapore and Taiwan. These last two countries import rough timber to process and sell on.

Nigeria and Thailand, once major exporters of timber, now have to import wood to meet their needs. Thailand, once almost three quarters covered in forest, now has less than a half of it left and in 1989 it took the difficult step of banning logging. Côte d'Ivoire, too, will soon stop exporting; its primary forest cover is down to 10% of its former glory. But banning exports is a difficult step for two reasons. First, because it cannot really be enforced by poor nations, unable to afford the necessary policing (it is estimated that even in Brazil, only 10% of the business is authorised).

Secondly, the forest is used to help pay the debts of many third world nations. Caught in the debt trap, and unable to meet the repayments from the revenue brought in by cash crops, the obvious course is to sell off their assets. But some countries are now still indebted, and without one of their most important resources which, unlike oil, could have been tapped for ever.

It is inevitable and entirely right that third world countries utilise their forest resources; it is the unsustainable exploitation that has become a focus for international concern. The likely consequences of tropical deforestation have been well rehearsed – climate change, rising sea levels, species extinction and the decimation of indigenous peoples. But the answer is not to boycott timber from the forests. By refusing to buy tropical hardwoods altogether we would not be helping to relieve the underlying causes of deforestation. What we *can* do is to encourage wherever possible controlled logging and sustainable management.

Logging for the future

But what is sustainable management? As yet there is no widely-accepted definition; those interested in the survival of the forest tend to use a tighter one than those responsible for encouraging its exploitation. It is important to distinguish between *management* and *sustainability*; the first does not imply the second. Governments designate and manage their forests in different ways, many of which can be sustainable at least in principle.

Of the huge forested areas still left, some are designated for preservation, but there are enormous areas designated as permanent production forest. Many of these are 'managed' in the sense that they are logged over and left to recover naturally. This can be sustainable if enough small trees are left, and if the logged area is protected until regrowth has reached an economic level. The cutting cycle may typically take from 30 to 60 years, depending on the size of the trees left.

More interventionist management practices also exist, encouraging the growth of wanted species by weeding, killing of unwanted plants or the planting of desirable trees where insufficient stocks are left. This is known as 'enrichment planting'. Any kind of management system is potentially sustainable, providing it is planned and controlled – and adhered to.

However, permanent forest is only one source of tropical timber; forest may be logged in the process of changing its use to agricultural or plantation land (timber or rubber, for example); and wood may come from a timber plantation, or from trees on non-forest land. Statistics are unreliable, but it seems that the bulk of tropical timber currently comes from previously unlogged forest, with significant amounts both from forest being logged for a second time, and from forest undergoing conversion to another use. It is precisely these three categories which give cause for concern.

One of the keys to the sustainable management of forests is for each country to have a coordinated plan ensuring that, where forest is logged, replanting and management guarantee a sustainable supply of timber from the logged area; subsequent use of converted forest protects the soil and maintains the water cycle; and that enough protected forest is retained to preserve biological diversity, the future of the indigenous people and scientific study.

The issue is a complicated one, but there are some initiatives underway which indicate that sustainable logging is possible, even though the examples are few and far between. Certain woods are more sustainably felled than others, too. For example, Malaysia is a major producer of rubber. The trees, once past their productive latex-yielding life, are still useful as a source of timber, and this wood is available on the world market. Some woods are less in demand than others, to give another example; forests may be cleared of popular trees while less favoured trees are left to rot, having been felled in the mêlée. In sustainably-managed forests, it is important to take all commercially viable timber, to relieve the pressure on popular species.

In many countries, there are concessions that are at least managed with long term productivity in mind: trees marked for cutting, rather than whole areas cleared; logged areas protected and re-logging delayed until regrowth has occurred; watersheds protected to minimise soil loss and damage to rivers. But these are very much in a minority, and few go far enough to qualify as sustainable.

One promising example, however, is a forestry project in Quintana Roo State, Mexico. Ten peasant-run 'farms' have been established, each consisting of 25 plots to be cut annually in rotation. Only the largest trees are to be taken. The peasants, with an eye to their future, are better judges of size than the commercial loggers who can move on to new areas when they've finished. The local nature of the project ensures that the money earned stays in the local economy; since 1982, the community has benefited from schools, a health clinic and clean water. They are now looking to Europe for markets, especially for less exploited woods; everyone wants mahogany at present. This kind of project can be a part of the answer: well-managed plantation or secondary forest schemes to take the pressure off the irreplaceable primary forest.

Around the world

So the potential for sustainable management is there but the reality of the situation is difficult to assess. This is partly because, while many governments have designated areas of forest for preservation, permanent forest estate or conversion forest, it is too easy for the designation to change, officially or by default.

A logged area designated for protection may in fact be cleared for cultivation very quickly in response to local pressure rather than protected for 60 years for regeneration. It is much easier to mortgage the future by logging new forest instead; somebody else will have to pay. Since the major 'management system' is this log-and-leave policy, it will take another 30–60 years to see whether it can be maintained. Sustainability of such forests is a fragile thing; at any time they could be relogged or cleared.

More interventionist management systems have really only been attempted on a small scale, and almost insignificant amounts of timber are sourced from such schemes.

In **Africa**, there are no large scale sustainable systems in the main producer countries. Severe depletion of forest in Côte d'Ivoire and Ghana is evidence not only of extraction proceeding faster than regrowth, but the fact that the potential yield is declining as the forest cover is degraded. Such countries are eating into their 'forest capital' to the extent that they will soon cease to export.

Brazil, with its huge forest cover, has a small amount under some management system, though none of this qualifies as a complete sustainable plan. There is some research into sustainable systems, but the few attempts to sell concessions on a sustainable basis have been undercut by the existence of much cheaper operations in other areas. Sustainability has its price.

In **Asia**, where the bulk of our tropical timber is grown, most governments have a policy of reservation of forest land for protection or preservation. It has to be said, though, that they also have a well-used facility for 'dereservation', especially in Malaysia. Government policy provides for sustained-yield management, but does not define the amount of yield that it is intended to sustain. In practice, once the infrastructure for logging is in place, there is enormous pressure to continue production until resources are exhausted.This is sometimes enshrined in policy; the Philippine government's five year plan of 1978–82 aimed to continue production until the islands of Mindanao and Luzon were completely 'logged off' in the mid 1990s. Even officially, one tree is planted for every 21 taken.

Indonesia has by far the largest forests of the region, and ecologically the most important. Large areas of primary forest remain untouched, though the bulk of its designated production forest is already under concession. Legislation requires most concessions to replant, but this happens only minimally and mostly on Java. In practice, most replanting is with softwoods.

Timber extraction is in theory controlled by felling only trees of a minimum size and by enrichment planting if too few 'mother trees' are left. In fact, this is rarely enforced, and in some areas up to 70% of non-target trees are damaged during extraction. Just four species, Meranti, Ramin, Keruing and Agathis, account for 75% of Indonesia's timber exports; the pressure to find them results in over-cutting, though Indonesia derives only 7% of its export income from timber, much of the rest coming from crude petroleum, gas, rubber and coffee.

Indonesia has some impressive laws relating to forest areas, including national parks and forest protection reserves, classified by the forest department. But in practice logging goes on in protected zones, and other departments have their own classification system, and a dual use may exist for an area, resulting in conflict on the ground.

There are some good social forestry schemes, in which teak seedlings are grown with food crops. Once the trees are large enough, the land becomes 'forest estate' for felling and the farmers move on. Softwood groves for firewood protect the hardwood area from the attention of the villagers. These are encouraging moves, but too small as yet to be significant in terms of world trade.

Indonesia has a relatively low GNP of $450 and, despite a comparatively good HDI v GNP rating, income inequality is serious (the richest 10% of people earning as much as the poorest 60%). Since 10% of landowners account for nearly half the land, there is great pressure to open up new areas. This has led to serious human rights, social and environmental problems associated with forest policy in Indonesia, centred on the government's policy of colonising the outlying islands. Plans were for up to one million people to be settled on Irian Jaya and Kalimantan by 1990 to relieve the pressure of its 175 millon people on the more populous islands. Indigenous people have been cleared from the land to make way for the migrants, amid many clashes with the armed forces. Land cleared for smallholdings rapidly deteriorates to yield only scrubby grasses, putting further pressure on the forest, and contributing to the 20 million hectares of 'critical land' – spreading as a result of forest clearance.

Malaysia has two basic systems of forest management; the first involves a log-and-leave policy with a 60 year cycle, the second has a shorter cycle, but leaves half-grown trees to mature. Both are in principle sustainable, with the usual provisos.

In west Malaysia, where the logging situation is somewhat better than in the east, replanting covers only a small proportion of logged area each year. The management system is on too small a scale, relogging occurs too soon and 'collateral damage' during extraction can be as high as 40% of the canopy in addition to the 30% extracted. Most agricultural expansion replaces the forest with oil, palm or rubber plantations, which provide better protection for the soil than annual crops.

Malaysia, though richer than Indonesia, with a GNP of $1810, has a severe problem of income inequality (the richest 10% earning as much as the poorest 80%). This distribution of wealth and power is ethnically-biased, with the Chinese controlling commercial life and the Malays having political domination. The indigenous people – those living in the forest – are the poorest, most isolated and with very little power. This is reflected in the issues surrounding the management of Malaysia's forests.

Sarawak and Sabah together produce most of Malaysia's timber and most of the world's tropical logs. The vast bulk of forest designated for production is already under concession, and extraction exceeds estimated levels of sustainability by almost two to one. The logged land is inadequately protected and cultivators rapidly move in.

Since logs account for much of the state government's incomes there is additional pressure to exploit the forests.

Indications are that most of Malaysia's primary forest has been logged. By the mid-1990s, as much as 60% of Sarawak's forest will have been logged over or severely degraded. The state governments have declared that logging is managed and sustainable, but the logging cycles are too short to allow recovery. Local, less intensive operations may be sustainable, but apply to only 1% of the logged area.

There is clearly a long way to go for governments in defining sustainability and adhering to proper management but there are other important ways to encourage forest preservation which would also encourage sustainable development.

For example, the genetic resources that we have drawn from the forests to make many of the pharmaceutical products we buy were taken freely; they could have yielded an income. Biotechnologists argue that companies should be able to patent the results of their work, but the countries that yielded the genetic material underlying the work should share the proceeds too.

Other examples are the harvesting of brazil nuts which, though the work is poorly-paid, is a sustainable means of income. And rubber: the alliance of rubber tappers and Indians in Brazil speaks of a common interest in the forest. There is nothing wrong with the extraction and exporting of forest products; on the contrary, further work is needed to find more. The problem is the manner and rate of extraction. And the distribution of benefits.

The extraction of minor forest products, such as fruits, game animals and rattan causes minimal damage and is more labour intensive. Uncontrolled timber extraction tends to destroy the minor products industry.

Adding value

On a wider scale, the local processing of timber can help relieve pressure on the forests. Adding value to the timber by making it into doors or furniture, for example, can mean earning much more foreign exchange with far fewer trees felled and with much-needed jobs generated into the bargain. Compare Malaysia with Indonesia, and again with Taiwan. Over 60% of Malaysia's timber is exported as rough wood. Indonesia's exports consist almost entirely of veneer, ply and shaped wood. Taiwan exports $1 billion of furniture, with a little veneer and ply.

But instead of Malaysia maximising its assets, most of Sarawak's precious timber goes to Taiwan and South Korea, where value is added and furniture exports yield good income. Local processing has to be carefully planned too, however. Indonesia's shift to plywood exports by government decree resulted in huge overcapacity – greater than the entire world demand. Although Indonesia now accounts for the bulk of world trade, it has found prices pushed down by over production to below cost in some cases.

A question of interest

At one level, the issue is an economic one; the country needs the income to pay its way (or at least the interest on its debts) and the forest is a means towards this end. But we need to look a little more closely at whose interests are being served by the destruction of the forests. It is widely accepted now that forest destruction is at best a short term palliative with a long term price. But do those who pay the price reap any benefits?

The building of dams, for example, is a major cause of forest loss, and it can be convincingly argued that it has more to do with government prestige than with the needs of the poor. But our concern here is with logging projects. Whose interests do they serve? And why are sustainable practices so rare?

For the people who depend on the survival of the forest, sustainability is crucial; they know their future is bound up with the forest's. But to a concession-holder, with plans already in place to move on to new areas in a year or two, sustainability is just a burden; trees 'wasted', resources tied up in replanting.

Long Lellang

Long Lellang is a Kelabit village in the eastern highlands of Sarawak. Its experience is far from unique. Fewer than 300 people live here, making a simple living – growing rice and vegetables, collecting fruit from the forest, hunting and fishing. While younger people have left for town in search of work, the community has remained their home base, though it can only be reached by a long and risky river journey or the twice weekly local flight.

The major local trade has for many years been the production of mats made from wild rattan, mainly for sale within the extended family. Long Lellang is widely recognised as being the source of the best *tikar lampit* mats in Sarawak. For most of the villagers, trade is a foreign concept; if one person has a good week's hunting or a good day's fishing, the spoils are shared around the village. Money has not been a significant means of exchange in village life.

Recently, however, things have begun to change. And change will have to come faster still, if the village is to survive. For the loggers have arrived. Working their way up towards the Indonesian border, laying waste the forest, they have now reached the Western edge of the village. The village has its own land, of course, and they retain the rights to gather fruit from the forest land after the logging, so all, officially, at least, is well.

As the logging operation drew close to the village, the impact was first noticed by those fishing; the river has become turbid with soil washed from the denuded slopes.

Added to this, there is plain and simple corruption. In Sarawak for instance, local politicians are widely seen to be in league with the logging companies, since they control the logging concessions. And confidence in central government is similarly undermined; concessions are owned by officials and ministers – even the minister for tourism. The incentive

Fish catches have dropped to a fraction of the quantity they rely on. Further down stream, the river has silted up so badly that the ferry serving the villages is regularly grounded and will have to stop running if the river is not dredged. The village now depends on drinking water fed from a nearby stream; the logging company hopes to log the catchment area for this and pay compensation.

The forest animals are so depleted that hunting has been badly affected too; local studies indicate that average catches of 54 kg per person each year have declined to just 3 kg in the past twelve years. A threefold increase in malnutrition has resulted in other logged areas. As the logging companies extract the trees they want, so much damage is caused to surrounding areas by the roads and the felling operation itself that the villagers are unable to gather food from the forest. Traditional slash and burn agriculture is impossible, so the same land is used for crops year after year and yields will inevitably drop. Even the rattan is disappearing, and the rattan mat business is dying out. Yet, as the ability of the village to support itself from hunting, fishing and agriculture is threatened, alternative employment is vital.

With no way into or out of the village, save the light aircraft landing at the airstrip twice a week, trade with the towns is very difficult. The logging operation has made economic 'development' of some sort essential, no matter how foreign to the culture of the Kelabit people. But it has also made it all but impossible.

here is to get the maximum return as soon as possible. The willingness of logging companies to connive in corruption is a major stumbling block in many countries.

But more fundamental is the position of forest communities in society at large. The land that was once assumed to belong to the white people who 'discovered' the country is now owned by the state, which can sell rights over its management without reference to those who live there. It has been too easy for governments to sacrifice the rights of tribal people to the needs of the economy.

Protests by the tribal communities, such as the Penan of Malaysia, against the logging operations are frequent. Indigenous people have no access to areas classed as forest reserves, but they can hunt, fish and gather food, medicines and building materials in protected forest, and farm in the tiny communal forest areas. However, logging companies are awarded contracts to clear land the local people depend on and productivity is much reduced for years after logging.

Traditional shifting cultivation in Sarawak now has a cycle reduced from 20 to 3–10 years as the land the locals can farm has been restricted. This results in the over use of the land. The logging operations silt up the rivers used for fishing; the soil on the cleared watershed is exposed to the rain and washed into the rivers. Claims made by local communities for compensation for damage to their land are ignored. The people have many times resorted to blockades but have gained only media attention so far; even blockading of one's own land is now forbidden.

Poor people from the dominant ethnic groups also number among those dependent on the forest. Common cause has at last been found between the rubber tappers of Brazil and the Indian communities of the Amazon Basin. Together they have drawn world attention to the vulnerable situation of the people as well as to the forest.

This key aspect of sustainability – the issue of control – is seldom addressed. Until people living in or dependent on the forest have some control over its future, sustainability will be hard to ensure. Until those with power over the forest have a long term interest in its future, short term gains will dominate. Few concessions worldwide make any reference to the indigenous people, far less ensure that they benefit.

What can be done?

The governments of the third world nations exporting tropical timbers have a lot to do; rooting out corruption, encouraging the local processing of wood to add value, developing other forest products, involving local people in planning forest developments and much else. But equally, the timber business has to shoulder its share of the responsibility; stopping illegal payments to officials, conforming to management plans to protect smaller trees, replanting and protecting logged areas, labelling wood so that traders know the source.

Retailers, too, share the responsibility. They should check that all their tropical wood products are sourced in accordance with government regulations and in accordance with a sustainable and just management plan. (And they need to adopt careful monitoring policies since governments are frequently prone to highly exaggerated claims of sustainability.) They should increasingly buy wooden products made in the country of origin, rather than from exported raw timber, and favour alternative timbers (especially rubberwood) to the long standing favourites. In addition they should label all woods and wooden products with country of origin and source information. Finally, they should try to read and adopt the Code of Practice for the timber trade proposed by Friends of the Earth (published in their Good Wood Guide). Although this publication is no longer in print, it is relevant and helpful.

The DIY superstore

The bulk of tropical timber imported into the UK comes from South East Asia, where there is, in theory, control of logging. But the vested interests of politicians and officials in forestry concessions make such controls ineffective. Timber and wood products from West Malaysia (where some concessions are said to be long term managed) or from countries such as Taiwan, Singapore or South Korea, are in reality frequently sourced from Sabah or Sarawak, where some of the worst abuses are taking place. The more lucrative processing occurs in the 'country of origin' described on the label.

The UK DIY business is dominated by a few companies: we are all familiar with the big out-of-town sheds that over the last few years have sprung up all over the country: 80% of DIY goods are sold through the large companies, with the rest being sold through the small independent hardware stores. The manufacturing end of the industry is fragmented, with hundreds of small concerns supplying the retailers.

This gives the retailers the major responsibility for the operations of the trade, just as in the clothing business. There are some familiar, though unexpected names: the leading company, *B&Q*, is part of the **Kingfisher** group (formerly Woolworth, and owning Comet and Superdrug, as well). B&Q accounts for 16% of market share. With 13% of the market are *Payless* and *Do-it-all*, now a joint venture between **W H Smith** and **Boots** (which also owns the high street based *FADS* chain, as well as being a major retailer of health foods and manufacturer of pharmaceuticals). The next largest retailer, on 9%, is *Texas* (part of the **Ladbroke** hotels' betting, retail and property group), followed by **Jewson**, **Wickes**, **Great Mills** and **Sainsbury's** *Homebase*.

The combined **Boots/W H Smith** DIY outlet *Payless/Do It All* has given no indication of social and environmental policies – nor does W. H Smith's annual report make any mention of the environmental or social impact of these operations. The company's general environmental statement claims that hardwood products sold by the DIY subsidiary are from sustainably managed forests. This assertion is not backed up by any detail, however, and seems to conflict with the fact that Malaysia and Indonesia are quoted as source countries. There is no indication of the means by which sourcing is monitored, nor of any independent certification.

W H Smith declined to complete the questionnaire and **Boots** did not respond. The latter claims, however, that hardwood doors at *Payless* are sourced from reputable suppliers dealing through proper forestry plantations and not from endangered areas. No further information is available about the source of supply and how it is monitored, nor about the source of other hardwood products.

Other companies are a little more forthcoming:

Texas states that 'we are actively encouraging our suppliers only to source timber and timber products from properly managed and accredited sources. We have an office in Taiwan with a brief to develop good relationships with suppliers throughout the Pacific Basin and to source products from environmentally sound, ethical manufacturers.' Texas also has a subsidiary in Hong Kong – Texas Homecare (Far East) Ltd.

Texas also says that it has 'already taken several steps to ensure that the most environmentally sensitive areas of the business and products are as "green" as possible, where such a move is practicable and cost effective. Texas Homecare . . . as part of its own policy, makes a determined effort to obtain details of the source of every wood product sold in the stores. Part of this campaign has been to gain written confirmation from countries that supply Texas, that their governments have an active policy of reforestation, thus ensuring that Texas Homecare only uses products from a sustainable source.' Texas states that it insists on seeing a copy of any 'accreditation certificates', though it is not clear what happens when these are not forthcoming, nor who issues them. The company also says that its staff visit suppliers, plantations and processing factories for themselves.

On the issue of encouraging the local processing of timber, Texas imports finished products such as hand tools, hardware and furniture from a number of third world countries in Latin America and Asia. The company is actively seeking new suppliers in the third world. (Taiwan is currently its largest supplier, for which Malaysia is probably the original source.)

B&Q has a written environmental policy covering the procurement of tropical hardwoods, among other issues of concern. The company indicates that it will continue to sell tropical timber from sustainable sources, as it believes that by creating a market for such timber it provides an incentive for reafforestation. B&Q, using environmental consultants, 'audited those companies who supply the bulk of our timber and timber products.' It has set up a checking mechanism and asked suppliers to complete a full-scale questionnaire covering use of tropical hardwoods. They expect suppliers to 'be able to certify and demonstrate to our satisfaction that these products have been derived from sustainable sources.'

B&Q's statement continues: 'we have a programme of inspection of felling and processing locations in the tropics to test the validity of suppliers' claims, which also takes into account efficiency of processing.' The company points out that doors have to be made from something, and that there are also environmental problems related to alternatives such as aluminium and plastics. B&Q appear to have no policy addressing the issue of adding value to the timber in order to provide incentives for reafforestation.

In respect of the social impact of forestry, it appears that none of the retailers have begun to address the issues, although Texas does at least refer to concern for 'fair' treatment of employees at its suppliers' operations.

On the question of labelling, none of the retailers surveyed have plans to introduce it. B&Q, for example, states

---

Recycled paper

One issue that might seem at home in a chapter looking at deforestation is the impact of paper use on tropical forests. Indeed, it is true that tropical hardwoods are turned into pulp in a quite unjustified operation. But this paper finds its way into the UK in tiny amounts, if at all. The bulk of our paper is sourced from trees grown specifically for papermaking; but it is here that the problem lies. Increasing demand for softwoods has led to more land in the UK and other temperate countries being turned into forestry plantation. In some cases, a valuable native ecosystem has been destroyed. So recycled paper is a good thing to buy, but not to save trees; rather to prevent them being planted. As has been well put, buying recycled paper to save trees is like cutting down on sandwiches to save wheat.

that it is not intending to label all the wood it sells, 'because it is difficult to be sure, whatever measures you take and whoever you are, exactly where any piece of wood comes from.' This would indicate that the company is not totally confident about its monitoring process, which, in view of the fact that truly sustainable sources of tropical hardwoods are so few, is probably a realistic position. However, it is not enough for companies merely to leave it at that; they must exert pressure for change and take responsibility for their sourcing. In relation to relieving the pressure on scarcer woods, none of the companies in the survey have given any indication that they are actively sourcing alternative timber (eg rubber wood), or products made from such timber.

CONSUMER CHOICES

Since hardwoods are a valuable resource which take years to replace, one way to decide whether or not to buy them is to consider the use to which they are being put. Hardwoods have sought-after qualities; do their uses do them justice?

Most importantly, consumers can buy from retailers whose policies are most likely to encourage a sustainable use of the forest. A word of warning on sustainability: since no agreed definition exists, a veritable forest of claims from retailers is inevitable. Questions: are sources given? is a sustainability claim backed up by information about management plan, local control and verification? Most governments and forestry departments claim sustainability, yet clearly most are not sustainable in any global sense. To some, 'sustainability' means purely the continuity of supply; when one forest is exhausted, another will be logged over. Significantly, none of the major retailers was recommended in the Friends of the Earth Good Wood Guide.

A specialist tropical timber importer, the Ecological Trading Company, is offering a real alternative to the normal channels. ETC sources only from independently-verified sustainable sources under local control. The company also gives preference to 'secondary timbers', relieving pressure on the popular varieties. Examples of current sources include the Quintana Roo project mentioned earlier. ETC also purchases from a project in Papua New Guinea. Here a portable sawmill is being used by the Village Development Trust to enable local people to gain access to timber, without great environmental damage. Over 90% of the land in PNG is communally-owned.

✔ BEST BUY timber is available from **Milland Fine Timbers**, imported by **ETC**.

✔ Of the major retailers, **B&Q** and **Texas** seem to have gone furthest in developing a policy on hardwood sourcing; go there for preference.

✔ Think carefully about the use of tropical hardwood; does the use it is put to do it justice?

✔ Try to buy hardwood (or softwood) products manufactured in the timber-exporting nations of the third world; the 'country of origin' label refers to the processing nation.

Beyond the shopping trip:

Ask Friends of the Earth for information about their Tropical Rainforest Campaign, and how you can support it.

Write to B&Q and Texas with words of encouragement and asking for a copy of their policy on hardwood sourcing (say you have heard about it from this book!). At the same time ask them how they go about monitoring the success of the policy.

Write to the other companies, asking whether they have developed a policy on the sourcing of hardwoods.

Ask companies to label products with country of origin.

Furniture

One aspect of the British colonial past that is still with us is the existence in houses up and down the country of chests, inlaid tables and carved chairs imported from colonial outposts the world over. Such furniture is testimony to the craftsmanship that was, and still is, a feature of many traditional communities. It is, however, an exception to the rule as far as modern furniture goes.

Household furniture is a huge market, though one that suffers badly from recession. In the UK, we spend some £3.5 billion on household furniture every year and, according to recent surveys, **MFI**, inventor of the flatpack concept, is the market leader both as a retailer and as a manufacturer of kitchen furniture through *Hygena*. **Lowndes Queensway** was next until its demise in 1990, with **Magnet** and *Habitat* (**Storehouse**) also significant. **Asda** is a recent entrant into the fray, since it bought *Waring and Gillow/Maples*. **Hillsdown Holdings** has wide ranging interests in food processing, housebuilding, insurance and also manufactures furniture and furnishings under the *Christie-Tyler* name and for retailers such as M&S.

To the extent that wood from the third world is used in furniture, the trade presents us with many of the same issues as those looked at in the DIY business. However, one obvious difference is the potential for value added in the country of origin. Currently, very little of our furniture is made in the third world. Some $2 billion worth is exported by third world countries each year; about 15% of the world's trade. But the UK imports tiny amounts of this – only 8% of our imports come from third world countries.

Cane, bamboo and rattan furniture is mostly third world sourced – in the main from the Philippines, Thailand, Malaysia and Singapore. Deforestation has taken its toll on rattan furniture. Gathered from natural forest, rattan is in increasingly short supply in the Philippines and probably other countries, too. Taiwan is the UK's major source of wooden furniture; nearly £30 million worth in 1990. We also import smaller quantities from China, Malaysia, Singapore, Hong Kong and Indonesia. But the bulk of the furniture that is 'third world sourced' is merely grown there, exported as timber, and made up in the EC and other rich countries. The two methods of sourcing present us with quite different issues.

If tropical forests are to be conserved, then they must be given an economic value; it seems to be a paradox, but the export of forest products is part of the answer. It is also part of the problem, however, because of the unsustainable way in which timber is extracted. If the countries that are stewards of the forest are to put serious efforts into its survival, they must have the means to do so; an income from the forest that fairly reflects its importance is a step in the right direction. Governments also need the incentive; the forest must be worth preserving, as an economic as well as ecological asset. Added to this is the potential social benefit of jobs created in manufacturing wooden products. Often small scale and labour intensive, such work can be a valuable contribution to the process of development.

In this light, the tiny proportion of furniture sourced in the producing countries is important; firms importing and selling it need encouragement. But the export of timber for manufacture in another country risks compounding the problem; such products are very much a second best. The fact that the bulk of our furniture is imported from Taiwan is little comfort, since most of the timber used is likely to have been exported from countries such as Malaysia, where the controls on logging are widely flouted.

Retailers are the dominant link in the chain. Manufacturers tend to be not only mainly small and fragmented, but they are only in a position to avoid third world sourced wood; they can have little interest in buying furniture made in the third world themselves. Retailers, on the other hand, are able to choose the source of both timber and furniture itself.

The retailers are certainly in a position to influence the trade in hardwoods, not only ensuring that unsustainably extracted wood finds no market in the UK, but that positive alternatives are encouraged. These range from locally controlled logging concessions with an eye to the future through to the use of alternative woods, such as rubberwood.

Retailers should set targets for the increasing purchase of tropical wood-based furniture made in the country of origin, rather than from exported raw timber, and check that the tropical timber used in their products is sourced in accordance with government regulations and a sustainable management plan. They should also favour alternative timbers (rubberwood especially) and label all woods and wooden products with country of origin and source information. It would be a good start were they to read and set targets for the adoption of the Code of Practice for the timber trade proposed by Friends of the Earth. Such a code gives retailers, as well as the rest of the trade, something to aim at.

Asda states that it stocks a very limited range of furniture using tropical hardwoods in thirty of its Allied Maples stores, and that the policy was recently under review. It is not known what the result of the review was.

Storehouse sells furniture made from tropical hardwoods through Habitat. It is reported that Habitat had a policy to replace mahogany with dark stained poplar, but it is not known to what extent this has affected the range in the shops. The company stated that little tropical hardwood was used, and what was used came from 'government-approved renewable' sources, principally in Indonesia.

Neither **Magnet** nor **MFI** filled in the questionnaire. However, MFI stated that none of its furniture came from, or used wood from, the third world. While much of the furniture retailed by MFI and Magnet is made no doubt from pine or chip board, it is likely that veneers and cane, bamboo or rattan furniture will be sourced in the Far East or the Philippines. MFI has not confirmed this and makes no reference in its literature to policies addressing the social and environmental impact of sourcing wood or furniture in the third world. Neither is there any indication that Magnet has developed such policies.

The existence of a well thought out code of practice, such as FoE's, gives retailers, as well as the rest of the trade, something specific to aim at. None of the furniture retailers appear to have developed such a code.

CONSUMER CHOICES

Check the source details of all wooden furniture before purchase. If it contains tropical hardwoods, such as teak or mahogany, then it should preferably be made in the third world, too. Most of our furniture is made from temperate woods such as pine, ash, beech and sycamore, and that should continue; it is a more sustainable alternative, after all, and our own furniture industry needs a supply of wood, too.

Most importantly, buy from retailers whose policies are most likely to encourage a sustainable use of the forest. Which ones have developed a policy on this? Which retail third world manufactured products? Which of the companies label products with country of origin?

While environmental issues are seldom top of the agenda with the small community-based suppliers of the 'alternative' trading organisations, at least the control of the money earned is firmly in the hands of local people; the major issue in the long term, if the people of the third world are to gain the benefit of the forests' resources.

✔ BEST BUY furniture, though only a limited range made from hardwood, rattan and cane, is available from **Oxfam Trading**, **Traidcraft** and the smaller 'alternative' third world suppliers.

✔ Go for third world sourced furniture, as a better

alternative to furniture made here from tropical timber. If you are in the market for handcrafted furniture, ask the maker to use tropical wood from Milland Fine Timber.

Beyond the shopping trip:

Write to the furniture retailers; none of them seem to have taken these issues on board with any seriousness and they should set the standards for their suppliers.

It is worth contacting Friends of the Earth and getting the latest information from their Tropical Rainforest Campaign. Their detailed Code of Practice is interesting to read and if you ask them for the names of less popular woods, you can watch out for them and help towards the better management of forests.

Beef

The beef in one burger, if sourced from cattle raised on cleared forest lands in Latin America, would require grazing space equivalent to a medium-sized living room. Eleven square metres that would have been home to trees, undergrowth, insects, monkeys, birds . . . a total biomass of around half a tonne. Food for thought, so to speak. The power of an impulse consumer decision has greater implications than one might think.

Most of the nutrients in a forest ecosystem recycle rapidly between the trees and the forest floor, leaving little in the soil itself; a very efficient process giving great productivity. But when the forest is cleared and the vegetation burned off, the nutrients go with it, leaving poor grassland as a result – and hence the large areas required for the cattle. It doesn't seem to make much sense, but the rainforest is not an 'economic proposition'. The land is cheap, and it is more profitable to clear it and raise cattle even if only for a few years. The meat can then be exported, earning much needed foreign exchange for the government.

There can be few people nowadays who don't automatically connect burgers with the rainforest. The burger has come in for some bad press – from global warming caused by the destruction of the forest to ozone depletion caused by the CFCs used in the manufacture of its throwaway container – but our concern extends beyond these issues to the wider implications of the way beef is raised and consumed.

British beef?

In the UK, we spend some £9 billion a year on meat and meat products, a quarter of it on beef. Beef's popularity is on the wane – due initially to the price, but more recent health concerns over its saturated fat content, hormones used in the raising of cattle and BSE ('mad cow disease') have dented sales further. The notorious fast food burger accounts for £1 billion a year – just under a quarter of the beef we eat.

Most of the beef consumed in the UK is actually produced in the EC and the big burger chains claim to use only EC beef. However, despite taxes imposed on beef from Latin America, we import some £164 million worth of meat from there every year – between 5% and 10% of the beef we eat. The most significant countries are Brazil, Argentina and Uruguay as well as Zimbabwe and Botswana in Africa.

Brazil accounts for more than a quarter of the third world's total trade in fresh and frozen beef. Argentina holds the same proportion of the trade in tinned beef and earns over 5% of its income from the beef trade. The UK imports meat, fish and leather from Argentina. Its other major exports include unmilled wheat, vegetable oils and oil seeds, unmilled maize, animal feed and petroleum, which between them account for around 50% of total exports – providing for a reasonable degree of diversification compared to many other third world countries. However, Argentina's heavy debt service repayments will have eaten up a quarter of its export earnings in 1991, and hyperinflation in 1990 increased prices by 1800%! Argentina is relatively urbanised with 86% of its 32 million people living in towns and cities. With a GNP of $2,390 it is wealthier than most of the third world countries the UK imports from, and yet, income distribution is seriously unequal with the top 10% of the population earning as much as the poorest 60% of the population. The poorest 40% earn just 14% of the total income. Despite this, its HDI v GNP rating is +10. In terms of human rights, the situation has improved since the days of military rule but still gives cause for concern.

Zimbabwe and Botswana are far less important in world

trade, though still earning 2% of their income from beef.

We buy our meat in two major forms: as unbranded raw meat and as branded meat products. In the first case, the supermarkets dominate the trade, taking 42% of the business. The major manufacturers of meat products are **Associated British Foods** (own label ready meals), **Gerber Foods International Ltd** (own label canned foods and frozen ready meals), **H J Heinz Ltd**, **CPC International Ltd** (*Knorr* and *Napolina*), **Ranks Hovis McDougall plc** (*Atora*, *Bisto* and *Sharwoods* brand ready meals), **Unilever** (*Menumaster* and *Healthy Options* frozen foods, *Fray Bentos*, *Walls*, *Mattesons*) and **United Biscuits (Holdings) plc** (*Ross* chilled and frozen foods).

Two major distributors of fresh and cooked meats are **Hillsdown Holdings plc** under the brand names *Wirral*, *Beechwood* and *Culrose* and **Booker plc**. Hillsdown, now one of the largest food manufacturing companies in the UK, is also a major supplier of own label products to retail outlets, and Booker supplies the catering trade with its brand *Stocks Lovell*. One name not well known to consumers is **Union International**, the company controlled by the Vestey family and behind the 1200-strong *Dewhurst* chain of butchers. The company ranches cattle in Brazil and Venezuela and markets canned steak and corned beef in the US, Europe and Japan.

Beef production – land and labour

What is the impact of our beef purchases on the third world, and the environment? And, more importantly, what can we do about it?

There is no doubt that increasing exports of beef from Brazil and Argentina have contributed to the depletion of rainforest. According to one survey, the declining availability of brazil nuts (gathered from the forest) is attributable to the creation of cattle pastures in Brazil. The ranching was in many cases merely a cover for land speculation. Government incentives coupled with the value of land as a hedge against rampant inflation have proved sufficient to secure the clearing of forest land. Meat is almost a by-product.

Brazil probably has the most unequal distribution of land in the world; 69% of the land is owned by just 2% of the landowners, while 70% of the agricultural workers have no land of their own to grow food. In that context, the existence of large farms of any kind is a significant cause of poverty. Due to the massive scale of these operations, agricultural production is actually quite inefficient and hunger widespread.

This is a classic example of the need for land reform, both to ensure that agricultural priorities reflect the needs of ordinary people and to improve productivity. But repeated attempts over the past three decades have been derailed by the landowners, whose wealth carries with it great political and even paramilitary power. A movement of landless rural workers has grown up, addressing the situation by occupying unused portions of large land holdings and growing crops for the benefit of the poor, but human rights abuses are rife, including the torture and murder of prominent rural, landless workers' leaders fighting for redistribution of land. The murders (often perpetrated by ranchers) continue unabated, though the murderers of Chico Mendes, the rubber tappers' leader, were convicted and sentenced in late 1990. In Brazil it is difficult to escape the conclusion that the production and export of beef helps nobody but the wealthy.

An interesting insight into beef production is given by the example of Central America. Here the production of beef has been promoted by the World Bank as a way of increasing exports; the beef goes mainly to North America. However, the US has for many years been exporting harmful pesticides (the so-called 'dirty dozen' in particular) to Central America. These have ended up in the beef, which has subsequently been banned in the US itself. Consequently, the ranches have been moved to uncontaminated land – the forest. Recently the US also banned Brazilian beef imports due to inadequate testing for contaminants such as medicinal residues.

Large areas of land in many countries are under beef, though not always the poor forest soils. The question is, what is the alternative? How does beef compare to other agricultural products?

The ranching of cattle provides very little work for rural people, compared to the sowing, nurturing and harvesting of crops, so little money is fed into the local economy through that linkage. Similarly, the large scale of the production means that the local economy is by-passed; the wealthy landowners who derive most of the income spend a large proportion of it on imported goods. The processing of the meat is more labour intensive, however, and there is an element of value-added, so some benefit arises here, but overall the picture is not impressive. In all countries, though particularly in Latin America, ranching displaces peasants and hunter-gatherers from the land. In Botswana, with its low population and large land area, this is likely to be less of a problem.

Environmentally, the ranching system threatens the soil, since it is characteristically a user of new land. Such land is frequently fragile, arid (Africa) or forest margin (Latin America), and its exploitation is risky at best. Since the land is cheap and it is easy to open up new land when production falters, there is, paradoxically, an inducement to over exploit it. There is no incentive to ensure its long term future by more difficult and costly sustainable management when the whole community shares the cost of unsustainable practices; the tragedy of the commons.

As far as the economy of the beef producing country is concerned, other factors come into play. Most countries entering the beef market gradually find themselves export- ing less, as demand in the country grows, and eventually they become net importers. In order to boost production, it eventually becomes necessary to devote more land to the growing of fodder crops for the animals (or to put further pressure on the marginal land). Besides the competition this represents for other crops (for food or cash), it also under- cuts the major advantage of beef farming: its utilisation of rough grazing land. While raising beef for the local market may not be a bad thing, trying to achieve export production as well can put too much pressure on the land.

The experience of Botswana is a case in point; its exports of beef have declined from 29,000 tonnes in 1983 to just a quarter of that by 1988. During the same period, beef consumption increased by 50%. In Zimbabwe, beef consumption has more than doubled while exports have remained static as more land has been devoted to beef production; food production as a whole has risen four fold in ten years.

Unilever, one of Europe's largest consumer goods companies, with substantial involvement in agribusiness in the third world, has a cattle breeding operation in Zimbabwe, which it states is located in an area unsuitable for intensive communal farming due to water shortage. Unilever says it actively seeks to conserve the wildlife on the ranch, and carries out regular game counts to check on this. The company does not have its own meat production facilities, but seeks and obtains assurances from producers that processed meats it uses (which include corned beef raised on traditional ranching lands in Brazil) are not from sources that raise or graze stock on land cleared of forest for this purpose.

United Biscuits uses third world beef in its products, but this is apparently sourced in Botswana. It is unaware of any environmental problems arising from this. UB also stated that where possible, it only purchased raw materials from countries with an excess of supply.

The US company **CPC**, a worldwide processor of packaged foods, made no mention of its policy on sourcing meat, but stated that it does not operate farms in the third world.

None of the other manufacturers responded to our questionnaire, though **Gerber**, which principally manufactures own label food products for retailers and markets a range of canned, frozen and other foods, sources beef from South America. **Hillsdown** sources beef from Argentina. The company is a major wholesale distributor of meat and the hides and skins that are by-products from its abattoirs. There is no indication that these or the other manufacturing companies have policies addressing the social and environmental implications of their sourcing of meat and meat products. The same is true of all bar one of the supermarkets in the survey. Of the supermarkets, only the **Co-op** states that it does not source own brand canned meat products from Latin America, though it does not seem to make any such stipulation of other manufacturers from whom it buys.

Subsidies and surpluses

It is the very inefficiency of beef that was its major attraction not so long ago. The great farms of the American mid West produced (and still produce) a huge amount of cereal food, largely due to the inputs of fertiliser, pesticides and energy. They produce far more than the US could possibly eat, and pressure has long been felt to reduce production. However, big US farmers (many of them large corporations) are a powerful lobby, despite their tiny numbers, and such a move would be politically unacceptable.

The answer that met this need a few decades ago was the burger. By simple mathematics, a grain surplus could be eaten, since it takes several kilos of grain to produce a kilo of meat. This system might well meet the political needs of a government, but it does little to help a world where people go hungry while scratching at some land on the edge of the encroaching desert. One burger more or less at McDonald's doesn't mean more or less food in Ethiopia, of course. But the subsidised agricultural surpluses in the rich countries are causing major problems for the poor farmers of the third world, who do not enjoy the same subsidies.

The dumping of surplus agricultural production on world markets has forced down the price of many products, including beef, to below the costs of production. This inevitably drives small farmers in the third world out of business, compounding the problems of food availability. Similarly, the subsidised availability of such surpluses (often called 'food aid') in third world countries puts pressure on local farmers once again. Such factors are major contributors to food shortages in poor countries.

The third world and beef production

The production of meat of all kinds in the EC relies increasingly on a feedlot system, in which the animals are raised in sheds and fed on processed foodstuffs. The great ecological advantage of meat animals is lost; whereas animals such as cattle have a useful function in turning poor grassland into food, this is not used in the modern system.

The UK imported £600 million of animal feedstuffs in 1989, of which around 13% came directly from the third world. India, China, Brazil and Thailand are among the major suppliers of animal feedstuffs direct to the UK, though more comes in via the EC. In the case of Thailand, tapioca – made from cassava – provides a major export with over five million people dependent on it.

So too much beef is being produced (due largely to the subsidising of production in the rich countries), health concerns are reducing demand in the rich countries, and the lunacy of feeding surplus grain to unwanted animals strikes more and more people. In this context it is difficult to feel enthusiastic about the third world going into beef production at all. As a business it seems more part of the problem than the answer; certainly not addressing the issues, and probably ultimately flawed as an income earner. Meat produced in the EC raises many of the same issues, leading increasing numbers of people to reduce or avoid meat consumption generally.

CONSUMER CHOICES

The clearest issue at stake here is the importing of beef from the third world. Avoiding third world beef is certainly a recommended action for those who value the meat component of their diet. It is not often this book will advocate not trading with the third world, but in this case the benefits are more than outweighed by the risks and costs. In particular, beef from Central and South America seems to have little to commend it.

In the event that companies do buy beef from the third world, or products containing it, they should certainly check that the land on which it was produced was not forest land, nor land from which small farmers have been forced.

Botswana is the source of only a small proportion of our imports but probably constitutes a lesser evil (though still highly questionable), since the cattle are ranched on a smaller scale than in Latin America.

It is also of relevance to consider the inefficiency of beef production generally. Beef produced in the UK is increasingly fed on grain products rather than grassland, and it takes several kilos of grain and non-grain protein to make one kilo of beef protein. This makes very little sense in a world that is now experiencing a global shortage of grain for human food.

The fast food burger, while alone not a major disaster for the rainforest, is nonetheless a child of the throwaway society. Rather than merely offering a useful service for those busy occasions, the burger has become a symbol of a fundamental change in the way we eat – even the way we think about eating. It is wasteful, sanitised, uniform and creates a culture that is literally taking over the world; it is even found in many third world cities. As a system of food distribution, it has little to recommend it in the context of the concerns of the Global Consumer. Environment-friendly containers just don't address the problem.

✔ If you do buy products containing beef, go for **Co-op** brands and **United Biscuits** brands (*Ross, Youngs*) as a first choice.

✔ Don't buy beef, if you can't tell where it comes from. Lamb makes more sense economically where it is grown on temperate marginal pasture, such as Northern England or the Scottish Highlands.

Beyond the shopping trip

Write to the Co-op and UB and tell them that you have discovered from this book that their brands do not contain Latin American beef. Ask them if they are considering addressing other social issues in their sourcing of food products in the third world.

Write to the other supermarkets and manufacturers and state your concerns about the social and environmental implications of purchasing meat from the third world.

Fish

There is always the danger that an industry will seriously damage the environment. We are accustomed to hearing the term 'sustainability'. This is often taken to mean the likelihood of an industry being able to continue, measured in terms of its long term impact on the environment. In the fishing industry, like the timber trade, the environmental damage it wreaks can destroy the very foundation of the business.

Like the timber trade, the human problem is equally pressing; communities reliant on fishing for generations are the first exposed to the negative impact of the global fishing industry. When the environment suffers, it is the poor who suffer with it.

A trade which exemplifies three of the major issues arising from the globalisation of tropical fishing is that of tuna fishing. Yellow Fin Tuna in the Eastern Tropical Pacific associates closely with dolphin schools. For the fishworkers, the surface-living dolphins are a useful indicator of the presence of tuna. But the purse seine nets used in large scale operations to encircle and trap the fish are equally effective at trapping the dolphins and other forms of marine life. Not only is environmental damage affecting entire ecosystems, but large scale fishing is also displacing local fishing communities. The problem most retailers have in establishing the 'green' credentials of their tuna (despite the fact that only a small proportion of the catch is implicated at all) is due to the difficulty of tracing fish to their source; a third significant issue.

The fish market

While the UK has its own fishing fleets, and the focus of attention is usually on the North Sea, a surprisingly large quantity of our fish actually comes from the third world. Each year, we import £200 million worth of fish from countries such as Thailand, Bangladesh and Fiji. More than half the preserved (mainly canned) fish imported into the EC comes from the third world, with Thailand as the major source. A large and increasing proportion of the catch is for the luxury market, items such as crustacea (prawns and shrimps), sold frozen or preserved.

Most of the fish we eat is in various processed forms; canned fish, convenience foods, frozen fish products. Only about a quarter is the traditional fresh fish from the fishmonger's slab (though half the sales of this are actually through supermarkets, markets and mobile shops).

The market leader in canned fish is *John West* (**Unilever**), taking a third of the market. *Princes* (a subsidiary of **Mitsubishi Corporation**) accounts for a quarter of the market. Supermarkets 'own label' products take another 30%. In the fish products sector (including crustacea), *Birds Eye* (**Unilever** again) is the main brand, but *Ross* (a subsidiary of the leading biscuit manufacturer **United Biscuits**) is significant and *Princes* is expanding.

The global fishery

Altogether the third world accounts for over 40% of the world's fish market, having grown by more than a third in 15 years. This reflects the extent to which the industry has developed from being one primarily serving local dietary needs. Fresh fish now accounts for nearly $7 billion of third world trade, making it the most important food export apart from coffee and sugar.

Tuna fish accounts for the largest part of the UK's total third world range of fish imports; over £50 million worth comes from Thailand, with Fiji, the Maldives, Mauritius and the Philippines also exporting large quantities to the UK.

The trade in crustacea is very different. To meet the demand for this food, which fetches high prices in the rich countries, and to meet their own export aspirations, many third world countries are turning to the farming of shrimps and prawns. These farms are developed in coastal areas, where the right mix of sea water and fresh water is available for the growing larvae. In Bangladesh, this industry has taken off in the last 10 years; some estimates put current earnings at nearly £90 million, making fish as a whole the fourth most valuable export. The long term effect on this new industry of the cyclone in April 1991 is difficult to predict; certainly production will be decimated in the short term.

Other countries, such as Thailand, Pakistan and India, are major suppliers. The attraction of these farming developments is the high productivity that can be achieved in coastal waters. It can be a lucrative market to move into. Indeed, such 'aquaculture' projects are increasingly being engaged in by TNCs; **Unilever**, for example, has invested in prawn farming in all the countries from which we import significant quantities. Yet, despite this, the prawn and shrimp trade still involves local people too. The catch is collected at village level, where much of the processing may also take place before shipment to packing factories, usually in the same country.

Both crustacea and tuna are rapidly increasing in popularity in the UK – more than doubling in value terms during the 80s. The trend is reflected in the importance of both products to the third world.

Source and sustainability

In the highly productive coastal waters of third world nations the local fishing fleet, with its small boats, some with outboard motors to extend their range, competes with the large commercial fleets. Fish from both kinds of vessel will find their way to our shops. Tuna is frozen before selling on the world market as a commodity. Much of it is then processed, cooked and canned in Thailand, the leading third world exporter of canned tuna – most of it from other nations. Thailand accounts for 10% of the world's canned fish exports.

It is difficult to trace back the source of canned fish, since that labelled 'produce of Thailand' may have been caught off the coast of Africa.

Without knowledge about the source of the fish used in the products we buy, there is little consumers or the industry itself can do to address the social or environmental problems that arise. However, the Whale and Dolphin Conservation Society's campaign to draw people's attention to the plight of the dolphins is a useful illustration of how consumer pressure can be brought to bear when the information is available. But there are much wider issues at stake than the fate of dolphins.

One of these is the sustainability of the trade. In the case of tuna, sustainability can be measured directly in terms of fish catches. If more is taken than is reproduced each year, then numbers decline at an increasing rate, since fewer adults are left to breed at all. In this regard, fish are quite forgiving, since so many young die anyway before maturity. But even so, there is concern about the over-exploitation of fish stocks. The use of drift nets, sometimes up to 50 km long, can have enormous impact on fish stocks – and all forms of marine life – if unregulated. Thailand, its own fisheries already depleted, has negotiated with Malaysia to allow its boats to do the same in its neighbour's waters. 100,000 Malaysian fishworkers, three quarters of whom are already below the poverty line, no doubt view the move with some concern.

As the large scale fleets of countries such as Japan, Taiwan and South Korea look further and further afield for fish stocks, they come up against barriers. Fishing countries, anxious to conserve their own fish stocks, have set exclusion zones around their shores. Within these, they attempt to control the activities of their own fishermen, through the recording of catches. One imaginative way around this has been adopted by the South Korean fleets.

Korean boats pick up the artisan fishworkers, boats and

all, from Senegal and transport them to a third country, such as Liberia, where the fishing is productive. The small boats fish, just as the locals do, but their catch is taken on to the large Korean vessels for sale elsewhere instead of being landed for sale in the local market. This raises a number of important issues for the fishworkers and for the country whose waters are exploited in this way.

The trade is unregistered and the catches unrecorded, making the assessment and conservation of fish stocks impossible. Sometimes, the fishworkers in their small boats are arrested, while the large ships turn and run. The local fish market, in which the women are often the first link, is denied its catch, creating employment problems. And the fish find their way on to the international market instead of being available as a local food.

Manufacturers and retailers need to push for the proper recording and labelling of source information to ensure that the fish catches are registered properly. Some companies claim that tracing is possible with the use of coding on the can itself, though it seems unlikely that this method can isolate the fishing ground.

Unilever purchases tuna from Thailand, Indonesia, Philippines, Fiji, Maldives and Côte d'Ivoire; shrimps, prawns, crabs and oysters from Thailand and oysters and mussels from South Korea. They are purchased, and packed by third party packers selected by the company after rigorous checking, mainly of operational factors. Unilever's *John West* subsidiary takes the environmental issues arising from its sourcing of fish very seriously, having independent inspectors in all Thai canners used. The company states that it is taking the lead in identifying other possible environmental problems.

United Biscuits relies on the industry association's monitoring to ensure that its third world catches are properly reported, but no initiatives addressing the social and environmental impact of the operations were reported.

Mitsubishi Corporation, Princes' parent company, did not respond to the questionnaire, though it is a signatory to the agreement between the industry and the Whale and

Dolphin Conservation Society to ban the processing of tuna caught with drift nets.

The **Co-op** was the first retailer to sign the WDCS agreement. **Sainsbury's** was the first supermarket to respond to concern about the killing of dolphins by tuna fishing, though it subsequently declined to sign the agreement with the Whale and Dolphin Conservation Society, as it would mean 'signing a separate series of agreements with lobby groups throughout the world and this cannot be in the customers' best interests'.

The WDCS is co-funding an independent inspection programme of Thailand's canning operation with the US conservation organisation Earth Island Institute. Thailand's largest cannery, a supplier of *Princes*, has employed an independent inspector recommended by Earth Island Institute to oversee its operations. Inspectors are free to conduct wide-ranging checks with unlimited access to records of fishing vessels, shipment, on-shore production and fish. The WDCS is worried by the speed at which the companies identify their tuna products as dolphin-friendly while 'remaining obstinate about placing an independent verification procedure in place as agreed'.

While the above initiatives are important and welcomed, they do little to address the broad sustainability question. If the fish is traded around the world before canning, there seems little individual countries can do to ensure that stocks are protected. The role of Thailand as canner to the world is crucial here. There are smaller countries, such as Fiji and Mauritius, dependent on the fish trade, that do their own canning; that is the direction the trade should move in, so that there is at least the chance of effective monitoring.

Fishworkers and the future

Fishing communities are almost universally among the poorest and most marginalised sectors of society, particularly in the third world. Not only can the work be highly dangerous, but at the mercy of the weather, it is also highly unpredictable. Having to compete with the large fishing fleets, the small fishing communities cannot predict what sort of catch they will return with. If they do not return with sufficient, they simply do not eat. It is a cruel irony that as a rule fishing communities are among the most malnourished.

The involvement of 'artisan' fishworkers in the international fish trade is not necessarily a bad thing, since they may in this way get access to credit and equipment not available locally. But the trade is in the end environmentally and socially unsustainable unless the catches are recorded and controlled and the local people are gaining a fair return for their catch. The fragmented and sometimes illegal nature of the trade makes this difficult to assess.

None of the companies surveyed indicated policies to monitor the impact of fishing operations on traditional independent fishworkers' communities. **Unilever**, however, states that the canneries used by the company source material locally, so that traditional fishing communities still have an outlet. It also states that staff welfare is included in its assessment of the canneries.

The mighty shrimp

Prawn and shrimp farming present a different set of issues, though again sustainability is the key. There is the need to ensure that the natural environment, and the livelihoods of local farmers and fishing communities, are safeguarded. The rapid growth of shrimp and prawn farming is of great concern to coastal communities (the World Bank, for example, plans to invest $75 million to promote shrimp farming in India) as the precise environmental conditions it needs are only found at the margins of sea and fresh water. This combination of capital intensive, low labour industry creates additional and often devastating economic and social problems for fishing and rural communities that are already marginalised.

There are enormous environmental implications too. The salt water needed for the prawn farms leaks out into the surrounding farmland, raising the salinity of the soil. Few crops can stand the increasing levels of salinity. In Thailand, thousands of local farmers depend on rice growing and a bit of fishing for their living, but both are affected by the growth of prawn farming. The farms pump sea water into inland ponds, causing salinity problems in the neighbouring rice fields. Conversely, if the salt level rises too high, fresh water is pumped in, depriving farmers of the irrigation they need. Rice yields have fallen and indebtedness is driving small farmers to sell their degraded land.

Beel Dhakatia, the 'swamp of the bandits' in south west Bangladesh, supports 100,000 Namasudras, a low caste Hindu community. They farm the land when the annual floods disperse, leaving fertile silt behind. Dykes erected by the rich shrimp farmers block the natural drainage, and during the severe floods of 1988, the Namasudras had to demolish the dykes to save their lives and property. Reprisals followed, in which private guards were used.

In Thailand, mangroves are becoming deforested, and damaged by the toxic outfall from the prawn farms. This is diminishing local catches of shrimps and coastal fish, further damaging the future of local people. The Thai government is concerned about declining catches, but blames the problem on overfishing; an example of the way sustainability needs to be a broader concept than is commonly understood. Overfishing is a function of the rate at which the fish reproduce themselves as much as the rate at which they are caught, and the loss of mangrove badly affects the first.

On Negros island in the Philippines, sugar farmers are turning to prawn farming as an answer to declining prices in the face of declining trade with the US. The big US fruit company, **Dole**, is moving into prawns in case it loses its plantation lands in the impending land reform programme. Naturally rich mangrove swamps fringe the land, providing a nursery for many forms of marine life. Estimates suggest that 90% of the mangrove has now gone to make way for prawn farms, such is the economic power of the trade.

This, while ensuring huge productivity (and profitability) in the farms themselves, also ensures that the 'wild' shrimps are lost; there is nowhere for the larvae to grow and mature. Local fishworkers relying on the natural populations for their livelihood face ruin. Fishworker organisations have called for the involvement of local communities in the development of prawn farms, so great is concern about their impact. Companies should ensure that local community representatives are consulted about the development of prawn and shrimp farms.

Unilever, which has set up pilot prawn farming projects in Malaysia, Côte d'Ivoire, India and Sri Lanka, was the only manufacturer indicating a response to the environmental issues surrounding prawn farming. Its policy is to minimise the environmental effects. It states that water quality has to be very high and, though this may actually be the cause of pollution in the surrounding area, the farms are not intensive operations; this would indicate less effect on the water quality in the surrounding area. Assessment of social impact is not mentioned.

Local action

Faced with this multitude of threats fishworkers may have little power, but they are taking action. There are local initiatives through which fishworkers visit fishing communities in other countries to learn new techniques. Local fishing communities faced with declining catches are attempting to start their own low-capital prawn farming. There are also international federations representing small scale fishworkers. These develop strategies for lobbying governments and recommendations for more appropriate ways to exploit the harvest of the sea.

But the power of the market is very great and consumers, whose money creates this power, can help to create changes too.

CONSUMER CHOICES

There are a number of critical issues here – the effect that modern fishing methods have on traditional fishing communities and the environmental problems experienced in the fishing grounds. By pressurising the supermarkets and manufacturers, consumers can begin to influence the links further back down the complicated chain and foster changes to the damaging way the industry operates.

✔ Buy tuna that is canned where it is fished – for example, tuna from Mauritius, Fiji or the Solomon Islands, rather than Thailand.

✔ Buy tuna from supermarkets and manufacturers that have signed the agreement of the Dolphin and Whale Conservation Society.

✔ Buy prawns and shrimps from **Unilever**'s *John West*; while there are serious questions still about the social impact of its operations, Unilever is at least monitoring the environmental impact.

Beyond the shopping trip:

The issue of dolphins (and other creatures) is important. Keep up to date with developments in the industry; obtain up-to-date information from WDCS and Greenpeace.

Write to the companies that have signed the WDCS agreement and congratulate them. Ask them to push for effective monitoring of the fishing as well as the canning; that is where the pressing social issues arise.

Write to companies that have not signed the agreement and tell them of your concerns.

Write to the companies marketing prawns and shrimps: ask them to develop systems to monitor the social and environmental impact of the sourcing.

Coffee and Tea

There is an apocryphal story of an old lady (always an old lady, of course) who asked for a packet of English Breakfast Blend tea, on the grounds that she didn't like 'that nasty foreign rubbish'. The truth is, though, that as we gaze along the supermarket shelves, looking for a jar of coffee or a packet of tea, the country of origin is seldom on our minds. While many of us automatically assume that our tea comes from India and Sri Lanka and our coffee from Brazil, in fact Uganda, Kenya, Malawi and Indonesia are important sources, too.

Tea and coffee present consumers with a number of important issues. Much of the production takes place on plantations where working conditions can be very poor, from low wages to high levels of pesticide use. Smallholders, who also grow a significant proportion of our tea and coffee, bear a great deal of the risks; they are dependent on the crop, but powerless to influence the price they get. Consumers cannot ignore the fact that exports of the crops represent a vital source of income for many countries too, dependent on the growing of commodities since colonial times.

The beverage business

Coffee and tea are a vital part of life here, too. We may not make our living growing them, nor exactly measure out our lives in coffee spoons, but these drinks have been an important part of our social lives for many years. During 1989, 32 billion cups of coffee and 70 billion cups of tea were consumed in the UK – enough to fill around 40,000 average-sized swimming pools. Together, we spent £1.3 billion on hot beverages in 1989, approximately half on tea. The remainder was spent on coffee, and a small proportion on food drinks, such as cocoa, malted milk and instant hot drinks.

This chapter is primarily about tea and coffee; cocoa is the subject of the section on confectionery. This is because the majority of cocoa and cocoa derivatives are used in the production of confectionery, biscuits and cakes. Cocoa and drinking chocolate sales are falling and currently account for only 28% of the food drinks market.

As with most of the food industry, there has over the years been a concentration in numbers of companies involved in tea and coffee. There are now four companies that supply three quarters of the tea we drink in the UK. *Brooke Bond* (a subsidiary of **Unilever**) has 33% of the market, *Lyons Tetley* (**Allied-Lyons**, which also makes own label teas) has 22%, **Hillsdown** (*Ty-Phoo*, *Ridgways*, *Fresh Brew* and some supermarkets' own brands) and the **Co-operative Wholesale Society** each have 10%. Own label teas account for 16% of the market. Speciality teas are a small proportion of the total (5%), the major brands being *Twinings* (**ABF**), *Ridgways* and own labels.

The big companies have achieved a high degree of vertical integration, which means that, through their subsidiaries around the world, they control just about every aspect of the tea industry from production through to marketing.

The coffee market is similarly structured with a small number of major companies owning the majority of the brands we see on our supermarket shelves. About 90% of the coffee consumed in the UK is in the form of soluble (instant) coffee. In 1989, **Nestlé** had 54% of the market in instant coffee, while **Philip Morris** had 22%, through its subsidiary Kraft General Foods, which makes Maxwell House. Supermarkets' own labels account for a declining share – currently 15%. One brand alone – *Nescafé* – accounted for 40% of the brand share in 1987. The roast and ground market is a little more diversified, but still led by two companies – Lyons, a subsidiary of **Allied-Lyons** with 17% of the market, and Kenco (**Philip Morris**) with 15%.

A world trade

World trade in coffee was worth US$ 15 billion in 1989, making it the most important third world export after petroleum, gas and clothing. Coffee is produced in over 40 third world countries, and most is traded on the world market. Thirteen countries derive over 30% of their foreign exchange earnings from its export, some depending almost exclusively on it for their economic survival. Uganda for instance derives a staggering 97% of its export earnings from coffee, though prior to the devastation of the Idi Amin years, it had been an exporter of cotton, tea and tobacco. With a per capita GNP of just $260, and 90% of the population living in rural areas, Uganda is now one of the world's poorest countries. Colombia and Ethiopia also earn over half their foreign exchange from coffee.

Coffee accounts for 35% of Costa Rica's export earnings and together with bananas, its other major export, it is highly dependent on a small number of commodities for a large proportion of its income. Surrounded by highly volatile and very poor countries in Central America, Costa Rica is comparatively peaceful and wealthy with a per capita GNP of $1610 and has a good HDI v GNP rating. It does, however, have a severely unequal distribution of income with the top 10% of the population earning as much as the poorest 80%, and the poorest 40% sharing just 12% of the total income. Because Costa Rica spends very little on defence (technically it has no army), its 2.9 million inhabitants enjoy relatively high education standards and good health care.

The UK imported around 111,420 tonnes of coffee beans in 1989, of which 16,320 tonnes came from Uganda, our biggest supplier, followed by Colombia, Costa Rica, Brazil, Côte d'Ivoire, Indonesia, Kenya and the EC. The EC? Several EC countries are major re-exporters of coffee imported from producer countries.

Tea is also grown mainly in the third world, though until the Chernobyl disaster, the Soviet Union was a major producer. Unlike coffee, only 40% of tea production is traded internationally, the rest is consumed in the country of origin. While no country is quite as dependent on tea as Uganda is on coffee, Sri Lanka is around 40% dependent on tea exports, while Kenya and Malawi also earn a significant proportion of their income from its sale.

Surprisingly, around half the tea we import now comes from Kenya. In 1988, we imported 91,000 tonnes from Kenya, 31,000 tonnes from India, 19,000 tonnes from Malawi, and 13,000 tonnes from Sri Lanka. This is a recent phenomenon. Only eight years earlier, India had taken the lead, followed by Kenya and Sri Lanka. India now has a job supplying its own massive domestic market, let alone exporting as well, and its major exports are in fact precious stones, pearls and clothing. Sri Lanka's tea industry has been jeopardised by the civil war and the emergence of African producing countries.

Tea and coffee on the ground

The way in which coffee and tea are grown around the world varies widely; even different regions within a country will have different patterns of land ownership and different systems of marketing. Coffee from Africa is grown by peasant farmers primarily on smallholdings, usually less than two hectares. In South America, it tends to be grown on larger estates of anything from 10 to 300 hectares, using family and waged labour. Coffee growing is highly labour intensive, but there is an uneven demand for labour. The four months' harvesting period accounts for around 50% of the labour requirements.

For plantation workers, wages and conditions vary from country to country, but in spite of legislation that may exist, agricultural wages are generally poor, and nearly always lower than industrial wages. Establishing effective independent unions is more difficult than in industrial workplaces, since communication is poor between rural communities and lack of alternative employment makes workers vulnerable. Working and living conditions on estates vary from almost acceptable to appalling.

The plantation system itself is in part a reflection of a society with extremes of wealth and poverty, in part its cause. In Central America, during the late 19th century, there developed a need to boost agricultural exports. A policy of privatising communally-owned lands was established; this not only released land, but provided a ready supply of labour - the newly-landless peasants.

As commodity prices increased, this process continued, with more and more land coming into private ownership, and an oligarchy of powerful families began to control the economy. The repressive social systems of Central America can be traced to the coffee-based economy. The private and state armies needed to keep control of the privatisation process grew into the tools of repression used to control the growing unrest as the expectations of the ordinary people went unmet.

A more recent trend that is observable in many countries is an increase in the number of workers on temporary contracts. This is cheaper for the plantation, since employers have fewer responsibilities towards temporary workers who are often not covered under employment legislation, and have few of the rights and benefits that permanent workers are in theory supposed to enjoy. There is very little comparable information documented on variations in wages and conditions on different estates, but generally larger estates tend to be better than smaller ones.

The International Labour Organisation (ILO) has produced a set of Conventions and Recommendations for international standards for rural workers covering wages, working conditions, hours, holidays and welfare facilities, freedom of association, collective bargaining, training and social security. These should be taken as a reference point against which to judge the performance of individual plantations.

The main concern for peasant farmers is lack of security. They may in theory have a choice about what is grown, and at least can grow enough food for a subsistence living. However, in practice, many are locked into a production system in which they eke out a precarious living, and have no control over how much they are paid for their crop. At one level that is not surprising, since their governments too are heavily dependent on world commodity prices. In Colombia, peasant farmers have found that there is one viable alternative; to start growing coca for cocaine production. The drugs industry has led to escalating violence, kidnappings and murders in an already violent country.

According to the principle of the free market, if the price is too low, coffee growers will stop producing. Many, however, cannot afford to uproot their lifelong investments – their coffee bushes, which take several years to even begin to produce coffee beans. They must accept whatever price is offered – even if it is below cost.

Peasant farmers have little control over the sale of alternative crops for domestic consumption either, as government policy will frequently control prices at a low level to ensure a cheap supply of food to the cities. This is a way of avoiding political unrest, which is potentially more damaging to a government than unrest and poverty in rural areas. The peasant farmers lose out again.

Tea is also labour intensive, but in most countries, the labour requirements are more evenly spread throughout the year, as harvesting takes place on an almost continuous basis. Most tea is grown on a plantation system; Kenya is the only major exporting country that grows a substantial amount under a smallholder system. 50% of the tea it produces is grown by smallholders who sell their crop through the Kenya Tea Development Authority.

Patterns of ownership of tea plantations vary from country to country. In Sri Lanka for instance, all plantations over 20 acres were nationalised in 1975, but this did not lead to the hoped-for improvements in conditions.

Many tea pickers in Sri Lanka are Tamils, a Hindu minority group, in a largely Sinhalese Buddhist country. Like Tamils in many other countries in Asia, their ancestors were brought over from South India to work the then British-run plantations. Owing partly to the divisions created during British colonial rule, they are now considered to be foreigners and treated like second-class citizens, for years denied even a vote, though born there. Many have been 'repatriated' to India, where they experience the same attitudes towards them; 'Indian Tamils' find themselves labelled as 'Sri Lankans' overnight. In South India, most of the tea pickers are employed only as casual labour, without the security of the permanent labourers and often bringing home as little as half the wages. The flood of hundreds of thousands of Tamils from the human rights violations and civil war in Sri Lanka has weakened the position of workers and the estate owners take advantage of their desperate need for work.

Sri Lankan workers more commonly have permanent status, though this is gradually changing as Sri Lanka finds other countries competing in tea production and costs are cut. Low wages mean that children often work alongside their parents to boost the days' pickings. Working and living conditions have always been poor, despite a government scheme to improve the quality of the housing, and put in sanitation, water and electricity. Conditions on estates belie the general position of Sri Lanka's people; though one of the poorest countries, with a GNP of just $400, its HDI v GNP rating is the highest, at +45, due to a high level of social spending before the civil war. Serious inequalities still exist, though, with the top 10% earning as much as the poorest 60%.

In Malawi, by contrast, about 80% of the estates in the south (where nearly all the tea is produced) are owned by three transnational companies including **Unilever** and **Lonrho**, which does not itself retail the tea it grows. The remaining 20% are owned by three families, descendants of the European founders of the estates. The Commonwealth Development Corporation is developing estates in the North. In Tanzania, all the estates were nationalised, but the government has recently established joint ventures with companies like Lonrho and Unilever, who now have both acquired 75% stakes in some plantations. Lonrho's Luponde estate grows organic tea available through **Hillsdown**. India and Bangladesh both have substantial numbers of estates owned by domestic companies.

Unilever controls over 72,000 hectares of plantations in 12 developing countries. Tea plantations, most of which are located in Kenya, India, Tanzania and Malawi, account for 23% of the area. Brooke Bond is the tea market leader in the UK, as well as being the major supplier of packaged tea to the Indian market. Unilever has a policy for health and safety at work that applies to all subsidiaries. It claims that such standards are monitored centrally. All employees involved in applying pesticides are trained in safe handling and application; respirators are issued where appropriate, and pesticides are kept secure in appropriate storage facilities.

Wages, while not monitored as part of a central policy, are monitored more closely in certain operations, such as plantations. Each company operates autonomously with regard to wages and hours negotiations, but Unilever policy is that these should be at least what is normal within any business sector and country. While 'normal' can vary from the reasonable to the desperate, Unilever wages are held to compare favourably with other operations. It also states that all the countries in which it operates have legislation regulating employment conditions. Unilever recognises the right of employees to be members of trade unions (most of its workforce are, apparently).

Unilever provides housing and schooling, hospitals and other welfare facilities (in many countries this is a legal requirement). The perennial problem of job security on plantations in general, where temporary labour is increasingly used, is tackled by Unilever, by re-appointing the same seasonal labourers each year. The company also states that the number of temporary workers is declining on its estates, and that they normally have the same conditions as permanent staff.

The **Co-operative Wholesale Society** has a 39% shareholding in CWS (India) Ltd, which owns and manages tea estates. The estates were originally wholly owned by the CWS, but, due to government regulations in 1973, the company became an Indian registered public company. Ultimately, the whole of the capital will revert to Indian nationals. When CWS owned the estates, rates of pay, housing and educational facilities were apparently well above the legal minimum standards.

The other companies surveyed, apart from **Lonrho**, are not major plantation employers and had not formed any policy addressing the issue, preferring to rely on the employers to act fairly. Unlike Unilever, Lonrho makes no mention in its literature of policies and practices regarding the working conditions of those employed on its estates.

None of the companies in the survey gave us any indication that they have specific policies addressing the problems facing peasant farmers. However, **Nestlé** states that it gives investment loans to farmers or guarantees bank loans for them. Advice is provided by Nestlé agro-technical advisers. One exception to its policy of non-involvement in growing is Agro Development Nigeria Ltd, in which Nestlé has a 24% stake. The company rarely has contact directly with the growers and does not seem to recognise any responsibility for initiatives to improve prices, wages or working conditions. It does, however, claim that it encourages the growers to use fewer pesticides by enforcing strict quality control standards.

The trading system

Over the past several decades the *terms of trade* in commodities such as tea and coffee have been declining dramatically; the buying power of the exports of many third world countries has actually reduced over time. In the case of Uganda, for example, its terms of trade declined by 39% in the 10 years to 1988. Kenya's declined by 28%. So third world commodity exporters are having to export more in order to pay for the same (or even a smaller) level of imports.

Tea is sold either through auctions, usually in the country of origin, or through direct forward contracts. Tea is also being increasingly sold ex-garden – at the farm gate, if you like. With so few companies controlling both the buying and selling there is evidence of collusion among buyers and sellers attempting to widen the margin between what they pay the producers and what they charge the customer; 'gentlemanly trade', as it is coyly referred to.

There is no internationally fixed price for tea; brokers control the proceedings, and the price depends on how much tea comes on to the world market. This means that prices can fluctuate wildly. For instance, the price fell from £1.65 a kg at the beginning of January 1990, to £1.35 at the end of February 1990. This makes economic planning for countries dependent on tea for a high proportion of their earnings a real nightmare.

Unlike tea, where large transnational companies have direct control over production, through ownership of plantations, most coffee production is controlled by state run marketing boards, or private merchants. Again countries vary greatly. In some countries like Costa Rica, the processing and marketing channels are fairly straightforward. The beans are delivered to one of a hundred processing units by agents. Producers receive part payment at the time of delivery, and the rest several months later. Processors sell the bulk to the 25 or so exporters, the remaining 15% being sold locally. All transactions between producers, processors and exporters are regulated by law, controlled by the *Oficina del Cafe*.

By contrast, in Indonesia, production is carried out by some 650,000 smallholders, processing is highly decentralised, there are several levels of intermediary, with hundreds of village collectors, regional collectors and agents of the 250 or so exporters. There is minimal government control.

Coffee is sold on the physical or futures markets of London and New York. The physical markets sell actual coffee, but the futures markets buy and sell future contracts, and it is often at that stage that money can be made by speculators who can afford to take risks. It is the futures markets that affect prices. Until July 1989, the International

Coffee Agreement, through an economic clause, set upper and lower price limits for the different grades of coffee sold and bought by its members on the world market. It did so by setting export quotas for all producing members. This was designed to ensure a steady supply and steady prices.

But, like so many of the commodity agreements, it failed in those objectives. The economic clause of the agreement was abandoned and coffee flooded freely on to the market, causing the price to drop by 50% in just three months. The problem is that not only is it in the consuming countries' interests to have low prices, but the producing countries are not sufficiently united to be able to control prices. Brazil, for instance, produces around 30% of the world's traded coffee, but derives only 10% of its foreign exchange earnings from it. Keen to maintain its mammoth share of the trade, it can afford to undercut other producers for a while. At the other end of the scale, Uganda is the sixth largest exporter, but accounts for only about 5% of the world trade in coffee. Its extreme dependence gives it little room for manoeuvre.

A further problem is that when the price of coffee in the shops drops, it does not mean that people will buy more. But when the price goes up, people in the UK will switch – at least in the short term – to tea or other drinks. The coffee manufacturing companies are very powerfully placed to exploit this situation, by passing on price increases while being less prompt at passing on the price decreases.

Allied-Lyons and **Nestlé** both responded directly to this issue in our questionnaire. Allied-Lyons considers that simply by purchasing commodities it assists the third world, through the foreign exchange earned, and that it would be unreasonable for the company to seek to pay higher prices; 'the fairness of trading is the responsibility of the Governments and of GATT.'

Nestlé's annual report mentions concern about the loss in foreign exchange earnings and the consequent hardship for many producing countries, following the collapse of the international coffee agreement. It believes that the long term success of any price stabilisation mechanism depends on both effective quotas and the price being realistically related to actual production costs. The company states that it is a reliable purchaser, promptly paying a fair price, though there is no indication that the company pays more than the currently very low world rates. Like Allied-Lyons, Nestlé does not believe that it should pay in excess of world market prices. 'Is New Consumer seriously suggesting that Nestlé pay in excess of market prices?' Nestlé's annual purchases of coffee beans represent about 11% of the world's coffee production, the company therefore has power and influence over these prices.

Sara Lee, mainly a manufacturer of frozen desserts, but also the owner of *Van Nelle* and *Douwe Egberts* ground coffees, goes a stage further, making a virtue of keeping the prices it *charges* high as the world price it *pays* falls; 'we resisted some of the pressure to lower our prices', resulting in increased margins for the company.

None of the other companies in the survey gave any indication of policies on ensuring better and more stable commodity prices.

Hooked on coffee

For many third world countries, the export of primary agricultural commodities like tea and coffee is vital to the economy; a large proportion of their income depends on the trade. The vast majority of people in developing countries live in rural areas – 70% or more in some of the poorer third world countries – and depend directly or indirectly on agriculture for a living. Countries and people alike are dependent on agricultural crops.

The context in which nations became so dependent on the export of these commodities is closely bound up with their colonial past. Production on such a large scale was often introduced by the colonial power, in order to satisfy its domestic market. Thus crops like sugar, cocoa, palm oil, cotton, tobacco, tropical fruits, spices, as well as tea and coffee, came to be produced in huge quantities to meet the growing demands of the European merchant classes and aristocracy.

When the colonies gained their independence (during the 19th century for most of Latin America, and from the late 1940s onwards for the African and Asian colonies), the structure of agricultural production usually remained the same, though some countries nationalised estates and implemented land reform. These commodities continued to have a market, though many of them were no longer considered to be luxuries. They were now being consumed by a much larger market in the industrialised world. A Good Thing, perhaps? If the crops fetched better prices on the world markets, yes.

Third world countries are, however, striving to diversify and industrialise; by continuing to depend on these exports they will never achieve the level of economic activity required to alleviate poverty. But they depend on getting a reasonable price for them in order to be able to finance the necessary changes. Many people in the third world feel that they are on a treadmill that goes faster each year; as earnings decline, the prospect of self-financed industrialisation recedes further.

In the words of President Museveni of Uganda: 'We not only reject the perpetuation and continuation of a system in which we must ship more and more coffee in order to get fewer and fewer imports, but we also reject an economic system in which the vital economic interests of our population are subjected to the erratic pendulum of commodity markets.' The tragedy is that despite what Museveni says, third world countries do not have the power to reject the international trading systems, and have few choices open to them.

A question of value

As with so many third world primary commodities, the bulk of coffee is exported in its raw form – green beans. Most of the final price paid by the consumer relates to the costs of the processing, packaging, distribution and advertising. Very few producing countries export roasted or instant coffee. Only about 1% of total production exported is in roasted form and only 4% is exported as soluble. Just under half of the 36,000 tonnes of instant coffee consumed in the UK is imported, and the majority of these imports come from European factories.

There are practical problems in processing coffee in the country of origin; different blends are suited to different markets, for example, and shelf life is decreased once processing takes place, unless vacuum sealing or gas-flushed bags are used. However, there is real potential in this development. It not only means that producer countries can earn more from their crops; they also gain a position of greater strength in the market, exporting a consumer product rather than a faceless commodity. The costs of transport are considerably reduced, too, in the case of instant coffee, which is only about a third of the weight of the equivalent green beans.

Buying from companies that have imaginative and beneficial sourcing policies can also be good, ensuring that each pound you spend goes that bit further towards effective development.

Brazil and Colombia both export instant coffee through normal commercial channels. Tanzania and Nicaragua export their own blends through 'alternative' trading organisations. Both are available nationally. The Tanzanian and Nicaraguan blends have the advantage that the production systems are relatively beneficial to the coffee pickers and smallholders; not a claim one would make of either Brazil or Colombia!

Tea by comparison is always processed in the country of origin, though it is subsequently blended nearer the market with teas from different countries. There are, however, teas packed ready for sale in producer countries; the *Indian Summer* range recently-launched is packed in Calcutta by a company part owned by the Indian government. And **Traidcraft** sells blends from specific countries, or even tea gardens. All their teas stipulate a minimum proportion from 'acceptable' sources.

The **Co-op** responded to this concern by stating that 'for commercial as well as ethical reasons, there is an increasing trend towards the import of finished products', though no examples were given of tea or coffee so sourced. **Unilever, Allied-Lyons** and **Nestlé** all have processing plants in the third world, though these are primarily devoted to production for the local market. None of the companies surveyed referred to a policy of adding value in this way.

Changing consumer demands

Two types of coffee are grown throughout the world; countries tend to specialise in one or the other, depending on growing conditions, so changes in the market affect some countries more than others.

Arabica is higher quality, grown at high altitudes, mainly in South America, East and Central Africa, and to some extent in Indonesia. *Robusta,* used primarily as a filler and in the production of instant coffee, is mostly grown in West and Central Africa and in South East Asia. There has always been a market for robusta in the UK, the biggest consumer of instant coffee.

With the increase in popularity of higher quality premium brands of instant, more arabica is being used, in preference to robusta. Robusta growers cannot change over to growing arabica, as the environmental conditions are not always suitable (though this is happening a little in Kenya). Robusta farmers are also suffering because the price advantage they enjoyed has been partially eroded since the general collapse of coffee prices (robusta is cheaper to produce).

CONSUMER CHOICES

Sara Lee, Philip Morris and **Hillsdown** did not respond to our questionnaire, and there is no indication from available information that they have developed any policies addressing the social and environmental issues arising from their sourcing of products in the third world. **Allied-Lyons** clearly regards itself as a good corporate citizen, giving a lot of information about its charitable contributions and community work in the third world. But the company gave no information to indicate that its everyday business runs in accordance with those same values.

Nestlé is clearly aware of some of the issues arising from its involvement in the third world (not surprising, given the publicity it has had to endure for many years over the baby milk campaign – see page 266–7). Its chief executive, Helmut Maucher, is quoted, however, as saying, 'Of course I am not against culture and ethics, but we cannot live on that. The "fighting spirit" should have priority, and not this ethical and social drivel that is so fashionable. What is important is a truly competitive attitude, whereby people really try to attack the opposition and put better products on the market.' He added that he was 'totally in favour of including social and ethical issues in company policy, but it is a matter of getting the proportions right.'

Unilever, with its long term and direct involvement in the third world, and its huge resources, has the most well developed understanding of the issues. It is likely to be the case that, as the company claims, its plantations are among the best in the countries it operates in. However, Unilever, in common with its competitors, has less developed policies to monitor the wider social impact of its sourcing of products from third parties.

While the **Co-op** stands out as having written policy statements on social objectives, which attempt to formalise the practice of social responsibility, it has no written policy on trading with the third world. It recognises its role in raising consumer awareness of social issues as crucial and takes an interest in ethical trading practices, supporting development projects involving cooperatives in several third world countries. These initiatives are not, by and large, matched by awareness of the company's role in development through trade.

Should we buy tea and coffee at all? In the long term, reliance on growing and selling such crops is never going to be a sustainable way to run a country. The need for countries to diversify is clear, and some would argue that a boycott of the product is the best way to stimulate that. It is not, however, a serious option seen from the point of view of the farmers who depend on the crop now.

A change in the terms of trade is really the only hope for improvement, so that countries can finance their development plans. That means consumers paying higher prices. It means the producer countries processing their crops for sale, to add value to them. And it does mean political work, too, to improve the basis upon which third world nations have access to the UK market.

Overall, it is not possible to pick out a 'best buy' from among the major companies as all have fallen significantly short of addressing the real issues. Fortunately, to the rescue come the 'alternative' brands of tea and coffee from organisations founded on the principle of fair trade. Though the companies are small, their brands are available nationally through mail order or voluntary sales reps.

As we go to press, a scheme is being proposed by a consortium of development agencies and discussed with manufacturers to produce a 'people-friendly' brand – one that is more socially and economically sustainable to the people who produce it. A Fair Trade Foundation (see page 315) is being formed to award the seal of approval, along the lines of a similar, successful scheme in the Netherlands.

✔ BEST BUY tea and coffee from organisations like **Traidcraft**, **Oxfam Trading** and **Equal Exchange**.

✔ Look out for the Fair Trade Mark label on products in supermarkets. Trial testing may soon be underway.

If alternative brands are not available, go for Co-op (*99 Rich Leaf, Indian Prince, Canterbury Gold*) or Unilever (*PG Tips, Choicest Blend, Red Mountain, Café Mountain, Choice, Brooke Bond*) brands.

Blends such as *Indian Summer*, packed in the growing country, are worth looking for, too.

Beyond the shopping trip:

Write to the manufacturers of your usual brands and ask them what steps they are taking to find out where exactly they source their tea and coffee. Ask them to check out working and living conditions of the workers.

Or write to your usual supermarket and ask them to put pressure on manufacturers concerning the issues raised in this chapter.

Sugar

Sugar cane, first introduced to the British palate in the 14th century, was regarded as a novelty; too expensive for everyday use. At the end of the 15th century, Columbus introduced it to the Caribbean, and shortly afterwards, the first Caribbean sugar mill began grinding out the refined product at an increasingly affordable price.

Over the next couple of centuries, the colonial powers introduced sugar into so many islands in the region that the Caribbean became the world's sugar centre, accounting for more than 80% of world production. The sugar was destined for the sweetening tooth of the European consumer; in the UK, annual consumption rose from 4lb a head at the beginning of the 18th century to 120lb at its peak in the 1960s; UK consumers were eating their own weight in sugar each year!

In the UK we now spend a little over £300 million each year on sugar for home use, though sales are declining due to the growing awareness of the health risks involved in its overconsumption. We are instead spending more on artificial sweeteners; some £30 million in 1988. But while we have reduced consumption of this 'table top' sugar, from nearly 14kg per year in 1984 to 10 in 1988, this now accounts for only a quarter of the sugar we eat.

The bulk is consumed (often unwittingly) in many drinks and manufactured foods, both sweet and savoury, or through the catering industry. UK consumers' overall sugar consumption is 2.2 million tonnes per year, a figure that is unlikely to decline in the near future, since industrial use is actually on the increase. Of the table top sugar sales, 84% is in the form of white granulated sugar.

Sugar is unique in that an identical product can be produced from two completely different plants. Sugar cane is tropical and grown almost exclusively in developing countries, whilst sugar beet is a temperate crop, grown almost exclusively in the industrialised world. For consumers, the sugar business poses one overall question; do we buy third world cane sugar, or European beet sugar?

Slavery has been abolished and the colonies that produced sugar for the Empire have gained independence, but the sugar trade still perpetuates poverty in the sugar producing countries. Many communities and entire countries, such as Mauritius, Jamaica and Cuba, still depend on the crop for their livelihoods.

A near-monopoly

The sugar market in the UK is controlled by just two companies – **Tate & Lyle** and British Sugar (now a subsidiary of **Associated British Foods**). Tate & Lyle has 27% of the brand share in the retail market, while British Sugar's *Silver Spoon* brand has 55%. **Napier Brown's** *Whitworths* has just 5%, while retailers' own label brand sugar takes 11% of the market (half of this is produced by Tate & Lyle). **Billingtons** produces a specialist range of raw cane sugars and takes the lion's share of the increasingly popular golden granulated sugar market.

Tate & Lyle has a near monopoly on cane refining and British Sugar manufactures all the beet sugar sold in the UK. The UK market is dominated by these two giants to the extent that attempts by Tate & Lyle to buy British Sugar from its previous owners Berisford were referred to the Monopolies and Mergers Commission. If their bid had been successful, one company would have controlled refining and distribution of over 90% of the UK sugar market.

A controlled market

Though sugar is a major internationally traded commodity, unlike coffee and cocoa the majority of global production is consumed domestically. Of the 108 million tonnes of sugar produced throughout the world in 1989, only 26% was exported. Beet production accounts for a little over a third of total production.

Around 60% of the sugar exported is sold on the free market, with no controls on pricing; the resulting price variations were dramatic during the 1980s. Between 1982 and 1989, the annual average world price see-sawed between 12.82 and 4.06 US cents per pound – though these figures ignore daily fluctuations which actually took the price to below three cents! Half way through 1990, the price fell from its peak, to 10.7 cents, because of increased production of both cane and beet.

The remainder of traded sugar is sold through controlled markets. Sometimes a producer nation and a consumer nation will forge an agreement whereby a quantity of sugar is supplied each year at a set price over a given period of time. There are also three special multilateral arrangements:

The US quota system guarantees continuous availability by protecting its own domestic industry, and allowing producers in the Caribbean, Central and South America and the Philippines access to its market. In 1989, the major suppliers were Colombia, Dominican Republic, Philippines and Mexico.

The agreement between Cuba and Eastern Europe allows the world's biggest exporter of sugar a guaranteed market for the product on which it depends for its foreign exchange earnings. Cuba earns 76% of its foreign exchange from the export of sugar. With the changes that have been taking place since the end of the 1980s in Eastern Europe, Cuba will urgently need new markets for its sugar. In 1989, around 70% of its sugar exports went to the Eastern European socialist countries.

The Sugar Protocol of the Lomé Convention is the special arrangement that is of most relevance to consumers in the

UK. Under the Sugar Protocol, the EC guarantees to import no less than 1.3 million tonnes of sugar cane annually from the African, Caribbean and Pacific (ACP) countries at a guaranteed price, which has remained virtually unchanged since 1985–6. In October 1990, the price was 28.51 US cents per pound – nearly three times the current world price (EC consumers pay the difference). However, during that year, the EC was attempting to reduce the price to ACP producers. Under the Lomé Convention, former colonies of EC members are in theory entitled to export raw materials to the EC without constraints, though in practice there are increasing constraints.

The Sugar Protocol is in effect an acceptance that the EC countries bear a responsibility towards ex-colonies developed by them as sugar plantations. It was implemented to protect those ACP countries that had traditionally exported sugar under the former Commonwealth Sugar Agreement. The major beneficiaries of this arrangement are Mauritius, Fiji, Guyana, Jamaica and Swaziland.

Tate & Lyle is both bound by and benefits from the Sugar Protocol. In the UK, it is not free to buy raw cane sugar and sell the refined products in a free market, as the amount of cane sugar that can be imported, and the minimum price that can be paid, are controlled. This means it imports, at a guaranteed price, around 1.1 million tonnes of raw cane (almost the entire quota) into the UK, from Mauritius, Fiji, Jamaica, Guyana and Swaziland.

Tate & Lyle is aware that continued access to the European market is not guaranteed and is using its highly powerful and influential position to lobby the EC to maintain support for the ACP cane producers and increase the quota. Given the advantages to the company of an increased quota, this is not surprising.

Dependence

A major issue in the sugar business is the dependence of growers, and entire countries, on one commodity the value of which is in long term decline.

Mauritius is the largest supplier of cane sugar to the EC, exporting a little over half a million tonnes in 1989/90. The majority of families here depend to some degree on sugar for a living; over 50,000 are employed directly: one fifth of all paid workers. There are approximately 19 large estates and 35,000 smallholdings. Sugar cane occupies 90% of the cultivated land, though there is a policy of promoting food self sufficiency. Attempts to reduce dependence on sugar by diversifying into clothing (now its major export), tea, textiles and tourism have been quite successful, but sugar still represents just over 40% of foreign exchange earnings.

Fiji, Guyana, Jamaica and Swaziland each supplied the EC with between 100,000 and 200,000 tonnes in 1989/90, Guyana and Jamaica depending on the EC for over 90% of their sugar exports. Swaziland is the second largest supplier of cane sugar to the EC, but sells half its exports on the world market, making it particularly vulnerable to price fluctuations. Sugar is currently the largest foreign exchange earner for Swaziland, though diversification into cotton on some estates is aimed at reducing dependency.

In Jamaica, a quarter of the 2.4 million population is directly involved in the growing or processing of sugar cane, half of which is grown on plantations that have their own refining factories. The rest is grown on farms ranging in size from half an acre to 1,500 acres. Cane farmers register with their local factory and provide an annually negotiated amount of cane. They receive two thirds of the price per tonne paid to the factory for sugar. The price is fixed but because prices of inputs such as fertiliser are not, small farmers in particular are vulnerable. There are three government run estates, the bulk being managed by foreign companies, including **Tate & Lyle**.

The level of dependence that these countries have on the EC market is dangerous. While they at least get a guaranteed price that is usually better than selling on the world market, they, like Cuba, are going to have to anticipate a decline in demand if the EC Single Market continues to ensure that its beet farmers are protected. Diversification away from sugar will not be an easy task for an agricultural economy based since colonial times on a single crop. Despite a relatively progressive parliamentary democracy, Jamaica suffers from severe inequality of wealth distribution, with the richest 10% earning as much as the poorest 80%. However, life expectancy and infant mortality statistics, access to sanitation and clean water are all impressive and comparable with richer nations. Its HDI v GNP rating is very high. As well as sugar, Jamaica derives a significant income from the export of bauxite and other minerals, non-ferrous base metals, alcoholic beverages, and clothing. In order to reduce dependence on sugar, Jamaica has developed free trade zones that offer foreign companies incentives, including low wages and tax exemptions.

As Mauritius discovered in 1981, a new set of problems arises when countries try to diversify. As its textile industry began to expand, it was forced to reduce its textile exports to Britain by one third, under threat from the Multi-Fibre Arrangement (see page 24).

Overproduction

The decline in sugar's value is not in the main due to consumer concern about health; consumption in the UK is not actually falling. The decline in prices has more to do with overproduction, particularly in the EC, and the production of artificial substitutes for sugar.

The EC is now the world's leading producer of sugar. Due to the Common Agricultural Policy, EC farmers were being paid about five times the world market price in 1986. The result has been massive overproduction in the Community, leading to subsidised dumping on the world market, and hence lower world prices. The EC produced 16.3 million tonnes of sugar in 1989, and exports between 4 and 5.4 million tonnes each year, while importing between 1.3 and 1.7 million tonnes; it is now a net exporter. Without subsidies, beet production would be drastically curtailed; so uneconomic is it.

The low world price means that it is just not economic for third world countries to grow sugar; countries dependent on the crop and unable to obtain special deals are in dire straits. Were it not for pricing deals arranged with their major trade partners, the situation would be far worse. However, most of the world's trade is at the world price, and no country can rely on its special agreements in the long term, since they depend on the willingness of importers to pay more than the world price.

An international agreement with a managed quota system and buffer stock would help to stabilise prices. From 1978 to 1984 there was such an agreement, but it was rendered ineffective because the biggest sugar producers, Cuba, the EC, Brazil and Australia could not agree on the share of the world market each should have. But, in the end, such agreements fly in the face of economic reality when too much sugar is produced. In this regard, the EC is the villain of the piece. The absurdity of paying so much, and causing such problems for the third world, in order to produce an unwanted crop, sugar beet, cannot be lost on anyone.

Sugar substitutes

In both the food industry and the retail markets, sugar competes increasingly with artificial sweeteners and, in the industrial market, it also competes with sweeteners made from maize, such as High Fructose Corn Syrup (HFCS) or isoglucose. Isoglucose is used primarily in the production of soft drinks and in food manufacturing. It is cheaper than sugar, and can be made from other grains like rice and wheat, not just maize. This threatens both cane and beet producers, though cane producers will obviously come out worse, since EC and US farmers are protected.

Coca-Cola and **PepsiCo** (in joint ventures with UK companies; *Coca-Cola & Schweppes Beverages* and *Britvic Soft Drinks*) account for half the £3.4 billion UK fizzy drinks market. They also dominate the US scene and became the focus for severe criticism when they changed from using sugar to high glucose corn syrup in 1984. The increased use of this cheap substitute is directly responsible for the severe drop in cane imports to the US. In 1983, 2.6 million tonnes of raw sugar were imported. By 1989, the quantity had fallen to 1.6 million tonnes; 60% of the 1983 level, though quotas were raised at the beginning of 1989 because of lower yields in the domestic crop.

For the Philippines, which has been dependent on the US for anything from 25% to 100% of its sugar exports, the decline in demand from the US has been catastrophic for the economy and in particular for the sugar workers. Following Cuba's revolution in 1959, the US had actually encouraged an increase in sugar production in the Philippines, in order to find a replacement for Cuban sugar.

In terms of poverty, the Philippines is not in the same league as Ethiopia or Bangladesh, yet during the mid 1980s, when the price of sugar fell to its lowest, and the US quota also fell, a devastating famine raged on the fertile island of Negros. Clearly one cannot lay the whole blame on the US; the feudal system of the land ownership in the Philippines played a vital role in fuelling the famine too. But the impact of the market led the plantation owners to stop production (it was cheaper to grow nothing) and the workers were left without jobs, and still had no land to grow food. The Philippines became known as Asia's Ethiopia. So devastating was the effect that the National Federation of Sugar Workers even filed a $2.5 million compensation claim against PepsiCo and Coca-Cola.

While it would be naive to imagine that these soft drinks companies are solely responsible for the subsequent famine that swept the island, they, along with other food and drinks manufacturers played a part, though Coca-Cola believes that the depressed sugar industry can be attributed more to sugar price support policies than corporate economic decisions. Ironically, Coca-Cola is so popular in the Philippines, that the local bottling plant claims to be taking 10% of all the sugar produced on Negros.

In the UK the market for HFCS is controlled in the same way as that for sugar. **Tate & Lyle**, however, is involved in the production of HFCS through its US subsidiary, Staley. **Billingtons** is not involved in the production of any sugar substitutes.

Artificial sweeteners, such as saccharin and aspartame, are used not just in food and drink manufacturing but also in the home. These are particularly popular because they contain no calories and are not as damaging to teeth, though there are other health risks associated with artificial sweeteners. Aspartame, and particularly the Nutrasweet brand, is becoming increasingly common in foods and drinks, since it does not have the unpleasant aftertaste of saccharin.

An old slave trade

Sugar consumption between the 16th and 19th centuries would not have risen so fast had sugar not become much cheaper. Increasing production goes hand in hand with price reduction, due often to the economies of scale. In the case of sugar, a major economy measure, which had been introduced during the 15th century, was slavery. Africans were enslaved and transported to the Caribbean. The ships that brought this human cargo then set sail for Europe laden with sugar and rum, and then back to Africa with goods to swap for slaves. A profitable business indeed.

The structures in place at the time of the slave trade still have an influence on the sugar business. Colonies, once used to provide sugar, still depend on its production, and in most countries the people who do the work are still working in very poor conditions for very poor pay. The wages of sugar workers in Swaziland, for example, are below subsistence and there is no effective trade union. Outgrowers, who work their own plots of land but are obliged under contract to grow and deliver a certain quantity over a certain period to a central sugar mill, have found themselves in a very vulnerable position, often in debt.

We believe companies should favour sources of sugar that offer the best deal to those people who do the growing and harvesting, and particularly to small scale, independent producers. Here **Tate & Lyle**'s very size tells against them, for they cannot be selective if they are to meet their needs. It is unclear what Tate & Lyle's policy is on working conditions, pay and health and safety in its third world based subsidiaries, though it claimed that its associate Booker Tate encouraged Guyana to increase the wages of sugar workers to overcome the labour shortage.

Billingtons is 'extremely concerned that the people making the products we buy have adequate working conditions, and this is one of the reasons for buying our sugars from Mauritius.' All sugar is sold through the Mauritius Sugar Syndicate 'which is under government control to ensure good working conditions, and employment terms for all workers.' Billingtons staff inspect all factories at least once a year.

In Mauritius, wages of sugar workers are, perhaps surprisingly, better than in the newer industries, and comparatively higher than in other sugar producing countries, though hardly ideal. Men's wages are still two-thirds higher than women's. There is an active trade union movement that successfully fought for 16% wage increases across all industries in 1987, after years of declining wages. It is a middle income country (its GNP is $1,490), though income inequality is severe, with the top 10% earning as much as the poorest 80%.

Added value

All companies are in a position to encourage local processing and packaging of sugar; for countries dependent on the crop, this is at least a way to add some value to it before export. **Tate & Lyle** stressed the development role of sugar in the economies of the producing countries; as an agroindustrial (processed) crop, it encourages technical skill development. It is surprising, therefore, that the company has not considered further processing for the UK market in the producing country. The company cites poor quality as an insurmountable problem.

Billingtons, on the other hand, states that it pays an additional £100 premium price per tonne above the EC rate for its sugar; this is due to the additional handling required to produce sugars for direct consumption. It has invested in a packing factory in Mauritius by providing equipment which will allow them to compete with British packing companies. Billingtons has a minority shareholding in the packing factory. Currently, the bulk of Billingtons' sugar is packed for resale in the UK, but the company envisages that the balance will change in time. Billingtons also states that it is keen to develop further value added products in Mauritius, for instance it is involved in developing organic sugars.

The sweetest of the sweet

Two sugar brands do not feature strongly in this book: *Silver Spoon* and *Whitworths*. Both market mainly beet sugar, which is not relevant to the concerns of the Global Consumer. It is more likely to be seen as part of the problem we seek to address. Whitworths does market a small amount of cane sugar from Malawi, though in view of the relatively poor working conditions here, we would not recommend this as a good buy.

An overall summary of the major cane sugar companies reveals, as one would expect, that **Tate & Lyle** is very knowledgeable about the issues that arise from the sugar trade in different countries it purchases from, taking a leading role in the development of the industry, partly through its jointly-owned subsidiary Booker Tate. While Tate & Lyle did not fill in the questionnaire, it did invite New Consumer researchers to meet senior staff at its offices. They proved helpful in answering our questions.

Billingtons' very simple involvement in the sugar business – only one source country; no processing in the UK – and the added value component mean that it represents a good choice for consumers.

In addition to the big sugar companies, **Traidcraft** sells sugar produced and packed in Mauritius where working and living conditions of sugar workers are comparatively better than in the other sugar cane producing countries. Traidcraft also sells sugar from the Philippines, which is expensive because of the tariff imposed on it (it is not covered by the sugar protocol), but its production supports a project on Negros helping sugar workers create alternative work opportunities.

CONSUMER CHOICES

The regulated and oligopolistic nature of the market does, in the short term, mean that consumer power is reduced; choice is limited and the price and level of imports are determined by governments. However, demand can have a long term impact; if demand for cane sugar drops, the quotas are likely to follow suit. If it is maintained or increased, the case of those lobbying for maintaining and improving the third world's access to the EC market is strengthened. In the short term, because of the quota system, an increase in consumer demand for cane sugar would merely mean a transfer of industrial customers to beet sugar; political change is also needed.

It is certainly worth buying sugar processed and packed in the third world where possible; this adds considerably to its value for the producer country. It also means that you can be sure of the country of origin; sugar packed in the UK may well have come from many sources.

- ✔ BEST BUY **Traidcraft**'s sugars. They are not available in supermarkets, though, and are more expensive than other brands.

- ✔ **Billingtons'** Golden Granulated sugar is produced ready for resale in Mauritius, so adding value to the product and supporting jobs on the island. It is available in many shops and others could stock it, if you were to ask.

- ✔ **Tate & Lyle** offers the biggest range and quantity of cane sugar available in the UK. If you want it bright and white then this represents your best buy. Of own brand sugars, the **Co-op**'s is all cane too.

✔ Dark, unrefined sugar is always made from cane.
As well as being a little more nutritious, it tastes
good in baking and puddings. The value to the
country of origin is, however, lower than Golden
Granulated, since the processing required is much
less. Look for locally-packed sugar.

✔ If possible, it is worth avoiding soft drinks
containing artificial sweeteners, isoglucose or High
Fructose Corn Syrup (the most common brand
being Nutrasweet).

Beyond the shopping trip:

Writing to the cane sugar companies can be useful.
Tell them you support the purchase of cane sugar,
and encourage them to put pressure on the EC not
to allow it to be squeezed out when the Single
Market comes into force; tell them that you are
opposed to the introduction of sugar substitutes
such as isoglucose.

An International Sugar Agreement is urgently
needed to stabilise and maintain a fair price for cane
sugar. This will only be a realistic option when the
EC reduces or preferably stops its production of
beet. A removal of subsidies would both reduce the
cost of sugar to EC consumers and increase the
price of sugar on the world market. Writing to MPs,
MEPs and ministers is really the only way to move
towards getting such an agreement back on the
agenda.

Confectionery, Cakes and Biscuits

A key consideration in this chapter is chemical contamination – already a major consumer concern. Like few others, it strikes home with an immediacy that is hard to ignore. Yet this concern only reflects one part of the issue. What of food products that appear untainted on the shelf, but cause problems at the growing stages? Pesticide residues have been found to occur in chocolate; and action has been taken by manufacturers. But damage has already been done to the people growing the cocoa beans. And the environment in the locality of the plantation bears its share of the costs too.

The trade in cocoa raises a number of other important issues: in common with other cash crops, the position of smallholders and plantation workers is cause for concern, and the increasing use of cocoa substitutes poses problems for countries dependent on the crop.

This chapter deals with the confectionery, cakes and biscuits market, since over 50% of the cocoa imported into the UK is bought by the confectionery industry, and most of the rest goes into cake and biscuit manufacture. Very little is consumed as the traditional nightcap. Sugar, the other major third world ingredient in these products, has a chapter of its own.

A sweet obsession

In the UK in 1990 we consumed over three quarters of a

million tonnes of confectionery, worth around £3.7 billion. About 70% (£2.6 billion) of this was accounted for by chocolate confectionery, a proportion that is growing each year and works out at the equivalent of 8.5kg for every adult and child. As with tea and coffee, the confectionery industry in the UK has become highly concentrated in the hands of fewer and larger manufacturing companies.

Cadbury Schweppes plc is the market leader in the UK, with 27% of the market for chocolate confectionery. The company also owns *Trebor* and *Bassetts*, leading sugar confectionery brands. **Mars Inc.**, a privately owned US confectionery and pet food manufacturer, has 24% of the chocolate confectionery market with such brands as *Bounty*, *Galaxy*, *Milky Way* and *Snickers* (as well as the ubiquitous *Mars* bar). and in sugar confectionery the company owns *Lockets*, *Opel Fruits* and *Tunes*. **Nestlé** has a 26% share, (up from only 2% since they took over *Rowntree Mackintosh*). **Nestlé** is the world's leading food manufacturer with heavy involvement in third world countries. Its annual turnover exceeds the combined GNPs of several developing countries. *Terrys* (**United Biscuits**) and Jacob *Suchard* (now part of **Philip Morris**, the giant US food manufacturing and tobacco company) each have a tiny market share, though globally Jacob Suchard is one of the giants. The three top companies that control over 80% of the market have enormous influence over the whole cocoa industry. Nestlé alone takes 10% of the entire world production of cocoa.

Most of the manufacturing companies leave the importing and processing to specialists. Manufacturing companies tend to buy cocoa in its various semi-processed forms, mainly as cocoa butter and cocoa paste. Trading and processing is concentrated in Europe and North America, and is also dominated by a small number of very large companies, such as Sucrés et Denrées and E D & F Mann, who have recently taken over Gill & Duffus, the world's largest cocoa traders.

When it comes to biscuits, we manage to consume 635,000 tonnes of biscuits annually, worth around £1.2 billion. We consume another £1 billion worth of cakes; unwrapped, packaged or frozen. Packaged cakes account for about two thirds of all those purchased, though unwrapped cakes are increasingly popular, due partly to the growth of in-store bakeries. The major cake and biscuit company is the aptly named **United Biscuits**, which accounts for over 50% of the total biscuit market. UB's own branded biscuits include *McVitie's*, *Penguin* and *Crawfords*, and the company supplies own label biscuits to the major supermarkets including **Sainsbury's** and **Gateway**.

Jacob's (part of the French company **BSN**, now the world's second largest biscuit manufacturer) has around 9% of the market (with brands including *Huntley and Palmers*, *Peek Freans* and *Club*. *Fox* (part of **Northern Foods**) has 4%, while *Burton's* (**Associated British Foods**, one of the UK's largest food manufacturers) has 3%. *Cadbury* biscuits (actually a **Hillsdown** brand) and *Rowntree* (**Nestlé**) each have 1% of the market. Cakes, the bulk of which are packaged, are dominated by **Ranks Hovis McDougall**, which takes about a third of sales, with the *Manor (Mr Kipling)* brand and, somewhat confusingly, cakes under the *Cadbury* name. *J Lyons* (**Allied-Lyons**) has 15% and **United Biscuits'** *McVitie's* brand has 4%. Own label cakes have around 36% of the market.

The bean

Around 40 countries exported cocoa in 1988, the major exporters being Côte d'Ivoire, Ghana, Nigeria, Malaysia, Brazil and Cameroon. The UK imported 130,000 tonnes of raw cocoa in 1989, of which around half came from Ghana. Nigeria and Côte d'Ivoire are the UK's two other major suppliers. Between them, these three West African countries accounted for three quarters of our cocoa beans. Brazil is a relatively minor supplier of raw cocoa to the UK.

The geographical spread of cocoa production is changing rapidly, the UK's traditional higher quality West African suppliers now finding themselves under growing competition from South East Asian producers. The newer cocoa exporters, Malaysia and Indonesia in particular, grow cocoa on large estates, unlike the smallholder-based African producers. Malaysia supplied just 57 tonnes to the UK in 1987, but was supplying some 7,900 tonnes by 1989. Such huge growth is very significant, and relates to some of the other changes that have been taking place worldwide in the cocoa industry.

The traditional producers

West African cocoa is grown on small plots of land by peasant farmers, with the help of family labour. The cocoa trees are generally intercropped with food crops, which means that the farmers are usually self-sufficient in food. Cocoa is well suited to smallholder production, and when cocoa prices on the world market are reasonable, Ghanaian farmers can certainly make a comparatively reasonable living from the typical holdings of up to four hectares. Cocoa provides Ghana with 61% of its export earnings, one in four Ghanaians earning a living from it, while the country also exports metals, rough wood, fish and precious stones. Ghana has recently increased the mining of gold and is now re-establishing itself as a major exporter. GNP is low at $390 and there is a severe inequality of income distribution with the richest 10% earning as much as the poorest 80%. Debt servicing will take up 20% of the country's earnings in 1991.

In Ghana, cocoa pods are sold at a fixed price to the state run cocoa marketing board, Cocobod. Cocobod takes responsibility for exporting, as well as for providing producers with technical assistance, inputs such as fertiliser and loans. Cocoa from Ghana is held to be the best in the world, and it usually fetches a premium price.

In Côte d'Ivoire, too, a state run body, the *Caisse de Stabilisation*, controls payment of a guaranteed price to producers but leaves the marketing process to the private sector. Its other exports include coffee, shaped and rough wood, petroleum products, fruit, cotton, vegetable oils and tinned fish. GNP is low ($740) and Côte d'Ivoire has a severe inequality of income distribution, with the richest 10% of the population earning as much as the poorest 80%, while the poorest 40% own just 9% of the wealth. Just under half the 12 million people live in towns and two thirds of the population depends on the cocoa industry for its livelihood. The government has tried to maintain subsidies to cocoa and coffee growers but with an estimated 41% of its earnings going to servicing its debt during 1991, this has been difficult. The IMF introduced a structural adjustment programme in 1989 which involved cutting public expenditure and reducing state involvement in industry. The austerity measures resulted in much violent civil unrest.

A state sponsored board should in theory be able to provide reasonable services to small farmers. This, however, is not the case when the price of cocoa drops, as it did towards the end of 1989, reaching a 14 year low. The reason for this was the huge surplus on the world market; a function, in part, of the emergence of the new producers. There had been an international cocoa agreement that controlled prices through a quota system and buffer stock, but this collapsed in early 1988, because agreements could not be reached on prices and on managing the buffer stock.

Cocoa was fetching $2,412 per tonne in 1983/4 but only half that during 1989/90. The price has since picked up a little, because some of the huge surplus has been sold, and because production has declined in Côte d'Ivoire due to the recent civil unrest, and in Brazil because of bad weather. But the problem of overproduction is now endemic; the curse of cash crops, it seems.

What's your poison?

For unions in Brazil, poor wages have almost become a secondary issue; pesticides have become the key area for action. Banned chemicals like aldrin and 2,4-D are sold openly on the market. Malaysia also has a notorious reputation for the use of pesticides that are often banned in Europe. Ghana by contrast had a policy of testing all new chemicals before they were released for general sale. This stopped recently, when it could no longer afford to carry out tests.

Through the irresponsible ways in which they are exposed to agrochemicals, sickness, even deaths, are common among cocoa workers and their families. Overuse of agrochemicals can be very damaging to the environment and in the long term is uneconomic. But also, the workers who have to use them are very often not provided with adequate training and protective clothing. Instructions on the containers are often ignored because the people using them cannot read.

One of the main problems unions experience is in trying to track down which active ingredients are in the pesticides; they often have great difficulty in getting access to information from the agrochemical companies. Residues from agrochemicals have been found throughout the food chain, even in chocolate. Smallholders (fortunately?) cannot always afford to use agrochemicals.

For the unions representing workers poisoned over many years by the uncontrolled use of such pesticides, a key issue is compensation. The respiratory and circulatory problems associated with the poisoning make hard work impossible, and casualties are sacked after sick leave has run out. With no land of their own, the family has no alternative livelihood, and all too often the children leave school to work in the plantation and support the family, thus perpetuating the cycle of poverty.

Nestlé claims that its enforcement of strict quality standards does encourage growers to use fewer pesticides, though no other manufacturer specifically addresses the issue. To some extent, this is unsurprising, given that most of our cocoa still comes from Africa, where pesticides are currently less of an issue than in Brazil or Malaysia.

Working conditions

As is the case with cash crops the world over, cocoa plantation workers and smallholders are in a vulnerable position. In Malaysia and Indonesia, and to a large extent in Brazil, cocoa is grown under monoculture , on large uniform estates, using waged labour. Malaysia, a relative newcomer to the industry, was looking to diversify out of rubber at the time that the demand for rubber declined sharply. The development of cocoa growing was based on the same structures as rubber and palm oil. Conditions on estates, not just in Malaysia, can be pretty appalling.

Manufacturers should develop policies addressing the problems of plantation workers; they are powerful enough to make a difference. Where governments do not control all aspects of the smallholder system, manufacturers should ensure that contracts with smallholders improve their security through access to credit, technical assistance and other facilities.

None of the manufacturers surveyed are involved directly in the growing of cocoa for export, though some are indirectly involved; **Cadbury Schweppes** has established a cocoa growing project in India, in collaboration with growers and a local university. Jacob Suchard (**Philip Morris**) is involved in the purchase of cocoa in the country of origin, giving it more opportunity to influence the trade. **Nestlé** states that the company gives investment loans or guarantees bank loans to farmers. The majority of companies buy the cocoa on the international market, and none of the others have indicated a policy addressing the issue.

Processing to add value

Primary commodity producing countries needing to diversify their exports and expand their industrial base face enormous problems, and nowhere is this better demonstrated than in the cocoa industry. Cocoa beans are processed into many different forms, depending on end use; a highly complex and very expensive procedure. Over 60% of processing is carried out in the industrialised countries, especially in the Netherlands and Germany; the third world only accounts for 7% of the world's trade in chocolate. Virtually none of the chocolate we buy is made in the third world, so most of the money we spend stays firmly in the UK. In 1990 Nigeria attempted to ban exports of unprocessed cocoa, but this failed because of its lack of processing capacity.

A small number of large, influential companies control the processing industry, from purchasing in the producer countries to the manufacture of consumer goods. The importance of high profile brand names in consuming countries presents a barrier to chocolate manufacturers in producing countries; they simply do not have the resources to launch the sustained big advertising campaigns needed to establish a toe-hold in the market.

The high cost of establishing processing plants means that producer countries can often only afford to enter into joint ventures with transnational companies already involved in the cocoa trade. But a TNC will only enter into an agreement if it complements its existing operations. This is the experience of Ghana, which received no support for its processing industry during the implementation of its economic recovery programme.

The major manufacturers set high specifications for their suppliers to meet. To achieve them requires substantial training and technology – both controlled by the major processors themselves. One result of this is that such processing plants as do exist in the cocoa growing countries are usually owned and controlled by the major transnational processors, much reducing the economic benefit to the host country.

Trade barriers present another problem. In many industries, the higher the degree of processing, the greater the tariff to be paid on entering the UK. This discourages processing in the developing countries. The bulk of cocoa beans entering the EC carry no tariff, while cocoa butter carries 8%, cocoa paste carries 11%, cocoa powder carries 9%. Several countries that are part of the African, Caribbean and Pacific (ACP) group currently pay no tariffs, though it is not yet known what changes will be made when the Single European Market comes into being.

This issue is obscured by the fact that several companies are involved in production in the third world but primarily for local sale. Nestlé, for example, has cocoa/chocolate factories in Brazil, and factories in 39 third world countries in all. Cadbury Schweppes has plants in several. United

Biscuits also has facilities in the third world, tending to prefer working with local companies rather than with establishing wholly owned subsidiaries; a positive move that assists transfer of technology.

Chocolate goes high tech

The chocolate manufacturers are naturally interested in ensuring a regular supply of uniform quality cocoa beans as cheaply as possible. Many, including **Mars**, **Cadbury Schweppes** and **Nestlé**, are involved in research, particularly in Malaysia, into ways of developing high yielding, uniform plants that are resistant to disease. While these developments may be beneficial for third world countries in the long term, they do create problems.

Firstly, the know-how tends to remain in the hands of the major companies; the countries themselves are rarely in a position to control the technology to ensure the maximum benefit. Secondly, since agrochemicals are essential for the success of these high yielding varieties, the majority of small farmers will be unable to enjoy the benefits. Thirdly, the countries that have benefited most from developments in biotechnology (Malaysia predominantly in the case of cocoa) tend to be mainly plantation oriented. Their increased yields have left traditional smallholder-dominated producers like Ghana with severe problems. Some manufacturers are directly involved in this area of concern. This technology is powerful, and potentially beneficial, but cannot be sustainably used without regard for the social consequences.

Few companies indicated whether they were involved in biotechnology, though some initiatives were reported. **Nestlé** has a policy on the application of biotechnology to improve the quality of tropical raw materials, rather than replace them. It was involved in a church-business discussion group on the ethical considerations for the application of genetic engineering. **Mars** has collaborated with the Malaysian government in cloning cocoa plants to develop higher-quality, higher yielding and more disease-resistant plants. These developments in biotechnology research may be of benefit to Malaysia, but some of the UK's traditional smallholder-based suppliers in West Africa (particularly Ghana) are worried about the competition they find themselves facing from the newer plantation based cocoa growers like Malaysia and Indonesia.

Chocolate or not?

The two main cocoa derived ingredients that go into chocolate manufacture are cocoa mass (paste) and cocoa butter. The other main ingredients are sugar, vegetable fats, milk (except in plain chocolate) and other ingredients, such as dried fruit, nuts, and cereals. There has been a general decrease in the share of the cocoa cost component in the manufacturers' selling price. Consumers are buying less chocolate in their chocolates; Nestlé's *Kit Kat* is jointly the most popular bar with *Mars*, for example, and chocolate covered cereal bars are a cheaper and healthy-looking alternative to chocolate.

Manufacturers are also interested in finding cheap alternatives to cocoa and sugar that do not fluctuate wildly in price. Covering all categories of chocolate confectionery, the proportion of the price accounted for by the cocoa fell from a quarter in 1977, to less than 10% in 1988. Alternatives using palm oil and shea butter may benefit countries like Malaysia and Burkina Faso, but are likely to have a detrimental effect on specialist cocoa producers. In the long term, of course, such countries will have to diversify, but the application of biotechnology to the production of cocoa substitutes will make life more difficult rather than less. The evaluation of new technology needs to include social criteria as well as economic and environmental ones.

Currently, all EC members except the UK, Ireland and Denmark, have minimum requirements for cocoa butter content. Much of what passes for chocolate here would not elsewhere, and the phrase 'chocolate flavour coating' is now well known to consumers of confectionery. It is not yet certain how this legislation will be harmonised with the Single European market, but manufacturers in Europe are bound to lobby for the removal of legislation that restricts the use of cocoa butter substitutes.

None of the companies surveyed indicated a response to these issues, though some clearly felt that the issue of Malaysian cocoa replacing traditional sources is still a minor one.

A fair price?

Finally, there is the question of paying a fair and realistic price for cocoa, though manufacturers alone do not bear the responsibility for this. This crucial issue is discussed more fully in the chapter on beverages. As already mentioned in the chapter on tea and coffee, both **Nestlé** and **Allied Lyons** responded directly to this issue, clearly feeling that it is unreasonable to expect them to pay more than the market price for their raw materials.

Mars, while not directly referring to prices, has made a relevant response. Each of its operating units is expected to follow a principle addressing the degree to which trading partners mutually benefit from the exchange. Under this principle, Mars states that 'A deal is never good until it is fair . . . As we negotiate with our suppliers and distributors, we must avoid terms that are detrimental to their business . . . ' Mars in the UK, to whom the questionnaire was sent, did not respond. It is therefore not possible to ascertain to what extent the principle applies to people in the third world who grow and supply the cocoa and sugar.

CONSUMER CHOICES

The lack of direct involvement of the companies surveyed in the growing and sourcing of cocoa does not shield them from responsibility for the social impact of the trade. While they might be one stage removed from the production of cocoa, they can nonetheless make demands of their suppliers that the sourcing of cocoa responds to the social and environmental issues outlined. It is only through the manufacturers that the consumer can influence the trade at all.

None of the companies have made encouraging progress in addressing any of the issues raised here. One or two have taken some initiatives; a similar number have a record of general involvement in the third world that indicates an enlightened approach. **United Biscuits**, for example, is unusual in having a clear and public statement of ethics and operating principles. The company values lasting relationships with suppliers, recognising that it has great power over them, which must not be used 'unscrupulously'. Its statement was produced in 1987, however, and makes no reference to environmental or social issues relating to the third world.

UB responded in some detail to our questionnaire, and in view of the company's ethos, one would expect it to be amongst the first to develop policies addressing the issues that arise from the sourcing of agricultural produce from the third world. However, there is no indication that this has happened.

As reported in the tea and coffee chapter, **Allied-Lyons** gave details of its community involvement in the third world, but no information about initiatives addressing the social implications of its everyday business. **Cadbury Schweppes** 'tries to implement' western health and safety conditions in its factories.

BSN, Ranks Hovis McDougall, Hillsdown, Associated British Foods and Suchard (**Philip Morris**) gave no evidence of policies addressing any of the issues raised, though BSN has a reputation for progressive employment practices in Europe.

Most of us need no encouragement to eat chocolate, so the message here is an attractive one, though there are caveats of some importance. Much of the 'chocolate' we eat is barely worthy of the name, and the declining quality of chocolate confectionery is directly related to the compounding of problems for the traditional cocoa growers. Becoming a chocolate connoisseur, then, is a part of the answer; real chocolate carries benefit for the smallholders of Ghana.

For the countries exporting cocoa, a change in the terms of

trade is the most important issue; only then can they finance their development plans. That means higher prices and the producer countries processing their crops for sale, to add value to them. And it does mean political work, too, to improve the basis upon which third world nations have access to the UK market. Consumer action in these areas can really make a difference.

The nature of the cocoa industry suggests that, as with tea and coffee, there is room for a 'people-friendly' brand; see *Going Further* for details of a proposed Fair Trade Mark.

Traidcraft's cocoa comes from sources that support development, grown in cooperatives and processed in the country of origin. Traidcraft also sells chocolates made in the third world, extending this principle still further.

When it comes to consumer choices on cakes and biscuits, it is less clear cut. It is certainly worth buying cakes and biscuits with as high a cocoa content as possible, but apart from **United Biscuits**, whose general policies are enlightened, there is no other company that can be recommended; none have really addressed the issues presented.

✔ BEST BUY, though only a small range, is the chocolate and cocoa from **Traidcraft**.

✔ **United Biscuits**, while falling far short of any significant policies addressing the social and environmental issues at stake, has at least a record of concern for social issues and an openness about its operation that is encouraging.

✔ Buy chocolate confectionery that has a greater proportion of chocolate in the contents. Ideally go for bars of chocolate, rather than bars that use cheap fillers like cereals.

✔ Look at the cocoa butter content on the wrapper. When buying chocolate assortments as gifts, choose the high quality 'continental' chocolates that use a higher proportion of cocoa butter. European chocolates contain a higher proportion by law.

United Biscuits brands include: Biscuits: *Abbey Crunch, Carr's, Cheddars, Crawford's, Fruit Jaspers, Gold Bar, Hob Nobs, Jaffa Cakes, Krackawheat, McVitie's, Mini Cookies, Penguin, Pennywise, Rover, Simmers, Solar, Sports, Taxi, Tuc, United, Golden Crunch, Victoria, Yo Yo.* Cakes: *Homebake.* Confectionery: *All Gold, Bitz, Callard & Bowser, Carousel, Chocolate Orange, Connoisseurs, Dime, Keelers, Le Box, Logger, Marabou, Moments, Moonlight, Neapolitans, Nutcracker, Nuttals, Pyramint, Smith Kendon, Spartan, Terry's of York, Touch of Class, Velvet, Waifa, York Fruits.*

Beyond the shopping trip:

Write to the confectionery and cakes and biscuits manufacturers and urge them to continue to support the Ghanaian cocoa industry, that is the most beneficial to growers, and to pay fair prices; tell them you are concerned about the use of pesticides because of its effects on your health, through the residues found in chocolate, and more importantly the health of those that work in the cocoa industry, particularly at the production end.

Write to MPs and MEPs and tell them that you would like to see them support EC legislation on the raising of cocoa butter content to the level of the rest of the Community, rather than dropping it down to the lower level currently applied in UK, Ireland and Denmark.

Also tell them that you are worried by the implications that 1992 will have on cocoa producing countries, particularly those trying to market value-added cocoa products.

Fruit and Vegetables

The man from Del Monte, made famous by TV adverts, is seldom seen as a cogent commentator on the international trading scene. Yet with one word he summed up the relationship between small fruit growers and the TNCs that buy their wares. When the Del Monte man says 'yes', growers do indeed jump, though not always with joy. For the Big Man, along with his colleagues at Chiquita, Dole or one of the other powerful trading companies, is not merely the arbiter of quality. He is often the person who decides what is grown on the land; even who can continue to live on the land itself.

Go into any greengrocer or supermarket, and you are faced with a wide variety of fruit, and increasingly vegetables, from all over the world. What issues should we have in mind as we consider buying exotic produce such as papaya, pineapple or passion fruit? What should we think of green beans grown in Kenya?

As with all agricultural crops the issues of wages, working conditions and health and safety are paramount. Plantation based production inevitably creates the situation whereby people are dependent for their livelihood on one employer, who may have an effective monopoly on local employment. As a result they may be subject to wages and conditions well below that needed for a reasonable living. Smallholders, while notionally independent, may be tied into a production system that leaves them shouldering the risks while the traders control the market. The inadequately supervised use of dangerous pesticides is likewise a well documented risk to both the fruit growers and the environment. There are communities in several countries that are 100% dependent on the cultivation of fruit – often one kind of fruit – for the richer markets. Indeed there are some entire countries that are heavily dependent on the export of one fruit for earning valuable foreign exchange.

As consumers, we cannot know the background to every banana or bean. The wholesalers and importers best placed to be aware of these issues are often unknown names well shielded from consumer concern, so responsibility passes to the retailers and canners. They are increasingly setting the terms upon which suppliers operate and should be including these social and environmental concerns in their contracts.

A large amount of our fresh fruit carries no label and so it is difficult for consumers to find out where it comes from and which company was responsible for getting it to the UK. Some fruit however, such as bananas, pineapples and citrus fruit may carry labels on the fruit itself, giving the name of the company and sometimes the country as well. With canned fruit, it is usually easier, since the country where it was canned is given.

FRUIT

The UK market stall

We are eating more fruit than we used to, and a much wider range of varieties not hitherto commonly available in the UK. However, in the main, we eat the traditional varieties; apples and bananas still account for around half of the money we spend on fruit. Banana consumption in particular is on the increase, for it is a convenient 'snack' food, with a healthy image.

During 1989, we imported £186 million worth (over 400,000 tonnes) of bananas, nearly £170 million worth of apples and over £200 million worth of citrus fruit, half of which were oranges. We also imported about £50 million worth of grapes, and £80 million worth of more exotic fruits like pineapple, mango, guava, melon, avocado and papaya.

Some 46% of fresh fruit and 85% of canned fruit is bought from supermarkets; an increasing trend. This has led to an increase in direct distribution, and a decline in the role of primary wholesalers. While many of the major supermarkets now negotiate prices with importers and producers directly, they still use the services of the primary wholesalers to inspect, label and deliver their produce. The better known names importing from the third world are **Geest** (small in global terms but a leading UK importer and wholesaler of fresh produce), **Fyffes** (the Irish importer and distributor of fresh fruit and vegetables), **Chiquita** (one of the world's leading growers and distributors of *Chiquita, Pascual, Chico, Consul* and *Amigo* branded fruits and vegetables, and until 1989 holding a major stake in Fyffes). **Cape**, **Outspan** and **Del Monte** are other well known brands. The trend, however, is for the processors and supermarkets to be an increasingly important influence on the market.

As with so many other food products, there are two companies that dominate the market for canned fruit. **Del Monte Foods International Ltd** (formed in mid 1990 as a result of a management, investor and employee buyout and not to be confused with the Del Monte Tropical Fruit Co., a part of the beleaguered Polly Peck), and *Princes*, a subsidiary of **Mitsubishi Corporation**, part of a large group of Japanese companies with interests in such diverse activities as cars, ships, textiles and foods. These two control a third of the market between them, while *Gerber Pride* (**Gerber**, which principally manufacturers food products for retailers' own label brands) has 4%, as does *Australian Gold*, and *John West* (a subsidiary of **Unilever**, the major manufacturer of beverages, foods, detergents and personal care products) has just 3%. The supermarkets' own label market share is around 33%.

There are two fruits in particular to concentrate on in this chapter: bananas – the most significant third world fresh fruit; and pineapples – the most significant canned fruit.

The global greengrocer

During the mid 1980s, around 40% of all fresh and preserved fruit traded internationally came from developing countries, fresh fruit exports being their fourth most important agricultural export after coffee, sugar and fish. In the UK all our bananas come from the third world, and bananas represent about 25% of all developing country exports of fresh fruits. There are three categories of banana producing country:

The Traditional – the Windward Islands, Jamaica, Belize, Cameroon, Côte d'Ivoire and Somalia;

The European – Guadeloupe and Martinique, the Spanish Canary Islands and Crete;

The Dollar Producers – the Central and South American producers (mainly Honduras, Colombia, Ecuador) and the Philippines.

In 1989 about 60% of our bananas came from traditional suppliers; the Windward Islands alone accounted for nearly half of the total UK market for bananas, though they play a very small part in global production. The remainder of the bananas we consume come from the 'dollar producers' of Central and South America.

Of the three major companies involved in bananas, **Chiquita** is most active at the production stage, though it also sells directly to wholesalers and retail outlets. About one half of the bananas sold by Chiquita are produced by its own subsidiaries, the remainder being purchased under contract from suppliers. In 1989, a third of Chiquita's bananas were sourced in Panama, a quarter from Honduras, and the remainder from Colombia, the Philippines, Ecuador, Costa Rica and Guatemala. No individual supplier supplies any more than 5% of Chiquita's requirements. Chiquita owns about 100,000 acres of land and leases around 45,000 acres, principally in Costa Rica, Panama and Honduras. The majority of the land is used to grow bananas and palm oil, and for 'support activities', which include packing stations, warehousing, irrigation and power plants.

Geest is in a unique position in that it has an arrangement to be the only buyer of Windward Island bananas, and the bulk of its bananas are sourced there.

Fyffes has a very different operation from that of the big American companies, such as Chiquita. While Fyffes sources from all banana exporting countries, its chief sources of supply are Belize, Surinam, Jamaica, the Windward Islands (presumably via Geest), Honduras and Ecuador. By comparison with the banana giants, such as Chiquita, Fyffes operates a 'hands off' policy, restricting its role, by and large, to that of trader, rather than seeking to control all aspects of production.

Of the other major fruits we eat, the bulk does not come from the third world. Some 20% of our oranges come from South Africa (under the Outspan label), 14% from Israel (Jaffa) and 10% from Morocco. Around 20% of our apples come from South Africa and 4% from Chile. Grapes in the main come from EC countries, but around 14% are grown in South Africa and 7% in Chile. We do, however, find an increasing range of third world grown fruits in our shops: blackberries from Chile, grapefruits from Argentina, guavas from Brazil, strawberries from Kenya, mangoes from Thailand and mangosteens from Malaysia to give just a few examples.

By far the greatest proportion of the canned fruit we consume – 80% or so – is imported.

In 1988 we imported some £200 million worth of canned fruit, and Australia and the EC countries dominate as countries of origin, with peaches and mixed fruits being the most popular fruit. In the case of canned pineapple (third most popular) though, it virtually all comes from third world countries; 28% coming from Kenya and a further 25% coming from the Philippines. Malaysia, Thailand, Swaziland, Singapore and South Africa also export canned pineapple to the UK.

'Banana Republics'

Countries like Honduras and the Windward Islands (for whom bananas represent over 36% and 50% of their exports respectively) are dangerously dependent on one crop. The Windward Islands – Dominica, St Lucia, St Vincent and Grenada – have supplied the UK with anything up to 60% of our total banana requirements, over many years. Though comparatively wealthy, with GNPs around $1200, they are unhealthily dependent on one market (the UK) and one crop (bananas). Indeed, bananas have formed the foundation of economic development of these islands for the past 30 years. Ironically, smallholder banana production was introduced with the intention of reducing dependence on sugar cane (and incidentally to reduce the likelihood of 'social tensions' disrupting the independence process).

They are in a still more vulnerable position due to their exclusive arrangement with **Geest**. This arrangement has been both criticised and appreciated; the company is encouraged to invest significant support in a secure source of bananas, but the dependence of the Windward Islands not just on bananas, but also on one company, is more than worrying. The mutual dependence of this relationship contrasts with that of other companies with their suppliers.

Banana marketing, **Chiquita** acknowledges, is highly competitive; unlike Geest with its long standing contract to purchase principally from the Windward Islands, Chiquita will source bananas from wherever the best deal is to be found in terms of price, reliability and quality. While consumers may, in a narrow sense, benefit from this, it is the producers who bear the costs.

WINBAN

Unlike the plantation system of growing bananas typical of 'dollar' producers, Windward Island production is almost exclusively from small and medium scale private holdings. The growers sell their export produce through the individual island banana growers' organisations. These organisations are responsible for purchasing all export quality bananas from individual growers; boxing, delivering and selling to Geest; controlling diseases affecting bananas; and organising and administering extension services.

WINBAN (the Windward Island Banana Growers

Association), was formed to represent growers' interests. It is responsible for negotiating the market and shipping contracts, monitoring contracts, representing growers on the UK Banana Trade Advisory Committee in London, initiating research and providing technical assistance to growers and purchasing inputs needed by growers.

WINBAN has, since the beginning of its existence, been in an invidious position; its critics would say that it is dominated by the fear that Geest will pull out, and that it is more in tune with the needs of Geest than with the farmers it is meant to represent. The relationship between Geest and the Windward Islands is described by critics as being rather paternalistic. There has over the years been a 'cross-fertilisation' of personnel, employees of Geest taking posts at WINBAN and vice versa. According to WINBAN's critics, the services it provides favour the larger farmers.

Geest's current contracts with the Windward Islands are structured so that it receives a more or less fixed fee for the services it provides, while the commission it takes fluctuates in line with the market price of bananas. This means that when prices are high the smallholders do well but when they are low they suffer disproportionately. This contrasts with the usual arrangement in Central America, where bananas are sold on a fixed price basis, regardless of how the retail market fluctuates in the short term.

In spite of these criticisms, banana growers in the Windward Islands do get a better deal and are considered to enjoy a better quality of life than their colleagues working the 'dollar' banana plantations of Central and South America whose poor working conditions and low pay are common to the vast majority of the world's plantation workers.

Dependence on one crop and one company, however, is certainly not a good thing, and there have been attempts to diversify into other crops. This is a risky business though, and cannot be achieved without financial and technical support for smallholders. So in the medium term at least, the Windward Islands are stuck with bananas – a worrying fact, given the fears of 'fortress Europe' in 1992.

Trade and 1992

As ex-colonies, the Windward Islands have a preferential arrangement with the UK. Dollar bananas, though much cheaper to produce, are imported with a 20% tariff, giving the Windward bananas a price advantage. This is in danger of disappearing with the trade liberalisation measures that will be brought in with the Single European Market. This means that the Windward Islands will be at a disadvantage, as the dollar bananas will undercut them by a significant margin.

Geest seems to be planning for 1992 on two fronts. Firstly it intends to expand its distribution in Europe by establishing links with overseas partners; secondly it plans to secure a source of Central American (dollar) bananas. This is bad news for the Windward Islanders; they'll still be dependent on Geest, but the company will be less dependent on them. The company admits, 'The effect of a totally free market is that the price obtaining to Windward Islands fruit would be driven down to a point where many growers would gradually go out of business.'

Geest is fully aware of the threat 1992 poses to itself and to the Windward Islands, and, while hedging its bets, is pressing for preferential access to be maintained. It is also looking to open up new markets for its Windward Island partners. The experience Geest has in importing other exotic fruits and vegetables could be useful in the Windward Islands, assisting the process of diversification, and while the company has been involved in such projects, it declined to give details.

Pesticides

The environmental damage caused by the intensive production of bananas is also cause for concern. Between a quarter and a third of all pesticide imports into Costa Rica are destined for the banana plantations, in order to ensure high volume, low cost production. Besides the damage to the workers' health, and that of the local people (including dermatitis, eye problems and respiratory disorders), local fishing communities are badly affected. The drainage ditches, necessary for plantation production, carry the pesticide run-off to the sea, together with the 25% of airborne chemicals that never reach the fields. Pesticide and soil run-off have destroyed Costa Rica's Caribbean coral reefs; the International Marine Life Alliance reports that the banana plantations are the biggest source of debris in the nearby sea. According to the Pesticides Action Network, however, **Chiquita** has abandoned the use of insecticides on plantations it controls in Panama, Honduras and eastern Costa Rica, due to the worsening pest problems.

Smallholders are not by comparison heavy pesticide users; not only can they not afford them, but the intercropping system means there is less need for them.

The War of the Bananas

A recent initiative by **Fyffes** is likely to prove important as the advent of an additional market strengthens the bargaining position of the banana growers.

In 1990 Fyffes signed a contract with CAGSA, a Honduran growers' cooperative that previously supplied Chiquita. The Fyffes contract offered 50% more for the bananas than Chiquita, a price based on what Fyffes saw as the market rate for the bananas, ready packed and on the boat. Chiquita's price, though much lower, in part reflected the company's additional involvement in the production process.

Outraged that Fyffes was encroaching on its 'territory', Chiquita had a Fyffes shipment seized, and sent in hired men to offload the 52,000 boxes. The conflict has now been resolved by a mutual agreement between the companies, though the Honduran government lost $1.5 million in revenue and taxes. CAGSA is now selling to Fyffes, in accordance with a new contract, under which a premium price is still paid. Technical support is available from Fyffes.

While no doubt motivated by sound commercial considerations, the incident should benefit the banana growers.

Whose land?

The Philippines is a major supplier of both fresh and canned pineapple, 95% of which comes from the southernmost island of Mindanao. The company that has had most involvement has been **Del Monte**, which leases the land on which the pineapples are grown. **Dole**, a subsidiary of the US company Castle and Cooke, has also been heavily involved in the production of pineapple in the region.

Attempting to address the problem that less than a third of the rural population own any land, the Philippine government is in the process of establishing a land reform programme, known as the Comprehensive Agrarian Reform Law (CARL) that began in 1988. Under CARL, one of the many problems that has occurred relates to foreign company leasing and ownership legislation. Foreign companies are not able to own land but can rent or lease up to 1,000 hectares. Del Monte, however, was renting over 16,000 hectares in 1988, of which around 8,600 were being leased from the state owned National Development Corporation.

When so many Filipino politicians (including the family of President Aquino) are among the 10% of people who control 90% of the agricultural resources, it is not surprising that CARL falls short of delivering a fair and meaningful redistribution of land. The government had decided already in 1988 for instance that commercially owned land under the reform programme would be given the option to defer redistribution for 10 years, to give investors time to recover their outlay. Naturally most corporate growers have opted for deferment. This decision has had the effect of excluding 2 million hectares and a quarter of the intended beneficiaries from the reforms.

Some land that has been redistributed to cooperatives is being leased back to companies, though in early 1989, the Department of Agrarian Reform suspended a lease contract which Del Monte had signed with a cooperative representing 8,000 workers on 8,020 hectares of land planted with pineapples. Foreign companies are naturally worried by the chaos and instability in the Philippines, and Del Monte has said it would, if necessary, relocate its pineapple business in Thailand or Indonesia. The companies' other options are to purchase pineapples on a contract basis from outgrowers' schemes. While in theory this might offer greater independence to the workers, experience suggests it may simply shift the burden of risk to smallholders still dependent on the trader for a market and for inputs.

Dole, which also purchases large quantities of pineapples from Mindanao, has arrangements with both corporate growers and smallholders who grow pineapples on a contract basis. Dole has also diversified into prawn farming, with all its environmental implications (see page 88).

Kenya is the other major supplier of canned pineapple to the UK market. Pineapple had been grown traditionally by smallholders for the domestic market since early colonial times. Canning factories were set up by Kenya Canners and other small canning companies, and later with increased involvement of the California Packing Corporation (Calpak). Gradually production came to be dominated by plantations, with smallholders either switching to alternative crops where that was possible, or being taken on as workers in the canning factories. Smallholders have by and large been marginalised, through lack of financial and technical inputs required to produce the quality and uniformity for canning.

Working conditions

Del Monte Tropical Fruit Co. (DMTFC) produces bananas and other fresh fruit and vegetables, including pineapple, for the UK market. Through its leasing of land and processing and distribution of fresh tropical fruit, the company has made a substantial impact on the third world. A church-based campaign in Switzerland which focused on Migros, the major retailer stocking Del Monte pineapples, resulted in the retailer inserting a social clause into its contracts, guaranteeing above average working conditions and social conditions at all Del Monte production locations. Since the break-up of Del Monte, plantations are now run by both DMTFC and Del Monte Foods International (DMFI), each supplying some of the other's demands.

A campaign delegation sent in 1987 decided that the clause was working in the Philippines, and it was then extended to include trade union rights. However, this analysis did not take into account the question of land ownership, which remains a significant social problem in the area. It seems that the campaign may well have influenced other Del Monte sites. In Costa Rica, 5,000 employees are union members and the company provides various welfare facilities. Its Guatemalan workers are also unionised. DMFI maintains that wages and working conditions on all its sites are significantly better than the legal minimum.

In early 1991, Del Monte introduced 'crownless' pine-apples from the Costa Rican operation as an experiment, in **Gateway** supermarkets. These have the leaves removed, and, should they prove popular, they could result in added value and extra work on the plantations as well as yielding tops for replanting.

Plantation workers throughout the world suffer poor working conditions. In Costa Rica a Catholic church organi-sation has highlighted the effects of temporary and migrant labour on workers' families. Some 40% of labour is tempor-ary in nature, on contracts up for renewal every ten weeks. Highlighted more recently is the appalling human rights situation of Colombian banana workers. These workers have been subjected to violent abuses of human rights, with union leaders being assassinated by death squads. This has led to calls, by the unions themselves, for an international boycott of Colombian bananas. Despite a good HDI v GNP rating, Colombia has a severely unequal distribution of income with the richest 10% earning as much as the poorest 80%. Two thirds of the population is landless and 10% of landowners own 80% of the land.

Other tropical fruits

It is also worth considering the less familiar tropical fruits appearing on the market. Although there will be a variety of production systems in use, and the same social and environmental concerns as with all fruit, diversification often represents a good move, especially for countries that are too reliant on one crop. In the Windward Islands, for example, smallholders needing to boost incomes have pushed banana cultivation further up the mountain slopes, giving rise to soil loss. Crops with a better root system to stabilise the soil would be more suitable. Given the variety of countries and crops involved, it is not possible to suggest a best buy; diversification itself is the key benefit.

FRESH VEGETABLES

Only around 20% of the fresh vegetables we import come from developing countries; some 25% of our imported new potatoes come from Egypt; about 9% of the onions come from Chile. Kenya is becoming a major supplier of fresh vegetables, not just to the UK, but to the EC as a whole. Kenya supplies around 18% of all fresh vegetables (apart from potatoes and tomatoes) entering the EC from developing countries. Egypt accounts for 9%. Around two thirds of the green beans imported into the UK in 1989 were from Kenya. As with fruit, a wide variety of other vegetables from the third world is available in smaller quantities; from Venezuelan aubergines to West Indian yams; from Zimbabwean sweetcorn to Panamanian peppers.

For many developing countries that are very dependent on agricultural exports, and particularly those that are dependent on very few crops, vegetable production for export could be a successful way of diversifying, as Kenya is currently demonstrating. For a start, many vegetables are produced annually, and do not require several years of tending immature and unproductive bushes or trees, before any income can be earned from them. Secondly, many vegetables are ideal as smallholder crops, and can be intercropped with crops for domestic consumption or sale.

Intercropping is not only a better system from an ecological perspective, but it also means that the risks are spread – if one crop fails, or prices fall, a smallholder has another crop to fall back on. Certain vegetables, such as peas and beans, are also useful as part of a crop rotation system, increasing the nitrogen content of the soil.

However, as with fruit crops, vegetables have their own related problems, about which consumers should be aware.

Pesticides

For farmers to achieve the yields and quality necessary, they may need to use pesticides at higher levels than for traditional crops. Not only is much of the added value lost in this way, but the environmental costs may be high too. Growing temperate crops such as broccoli in a subtropical environment is difficult, because the lack of a cold season (while allowing year-round production) does not kill off the pests between crops. The problem is made worse by monocrop production – often a feature of such products. Add to this the relatively uncontrolled way in which pesticides are used, and you have a potential disaster; already pesticide poisonings are becoming commonplace in local communities, as the backpack sprayer replaces the machete.

The experience of Kenya

Despite its low GNP of $330, and the severe inequality in income distribution (the richest 10% earning as much as the poorest 80%, while the poorest 40% share just 9% of the country's total income), and despite spending 30% of its export income on debt servicing, Kenya is considered by some to be one of Africa's more successful economies and scores well on the HDI v GNP ranking. Three quarters of the population lives in rural areas and there is enormous pressure on land compared with most African countries. This is partly due to a steep increase in the population (currently 23 million and with the world's highest birth rate), and partly due to the fact that a large area of Kenya is facing encroachment from desert (two thirds of Kenya is designated as arid or semi-arid land unsuitable for arable production).

But perhaps most significant is the accumulation of land by more prosperous farmers and companies. In spite of land reform programmes designed to assist peasant farmers, poverty can often force those with very small plots to sell up in desperation and search for waged employment.

The vast majority of Kenyans work on the land, and most of the smaller farmers are on the marginal less fertile land, the larger holdings monopolising the better land. Marginal land has to be cultivated to enable those who cultivate it to live, but it is unable to take the ecological strain of intensive production, and irreversible problems of soil erosion are at a critical level now.

When not enough can be grown to sustain the family, the male head of the household will probably go to Nairobi to find a job. This leaves the women to head up the household and carry out not only her jobs but also those of the man. She may have to grow a less labour intensive crop for feeding her family as she will not have the time available to devote to both the family's food and the produce she will sell. In some cases the crop she grows for feeding her family will be less nutritious.

For Kenya, the development of vegetable, fruit (and flower) production and export is seen as a way of diversifying out of the traditional export crops, tea and coffee, which after tourism are the two most important income earners. The development of tourism is also seen as a way of diversifying away from dependence on coffee and tea, which are subject to enormous fluctuations in price, over which Kenya has little control. Over 34% of export earnings are derived from coffee alone. Because the terms of trade for commodities like tea and coffee have declined over the years, a country like Kenya, once self-sufficient in food, was by the early 1980s a net importer.

A subsidiary but important issue is that vegetable crops are perishable, and export success depends on the ability of exporters to transport, pack and ship them as quickly and as smoothly as possible. This reduces the opportunities of more marginalised smallholders, and regions that have poor infrastructure.

CONSUMER CHOICES

Fresh fruit

In the case of bananas, **Geest** Windward Islands bananas represent the best value in development terms, because of the production system. Other **Windward Islands** bananas are also a good choice. Fyffes' initiative in breaking into the US dominated Honduran market is also worth noting; the addition of a new outlet and new terms of trade will benefit the growers there. **Fyffes'** Honduran bananas come second, though by and large 'dollar bananas' do not look to be a good option.

On the whole bananas are a good crop as they can be intercropped with food crops, have nutritional value (unlike tea leaves or cocoa pods), are labour intensive, and are suitable for smallholder production as they require very little capital outlay and can be harvested all year round.

In the case of pineapples and other fruit, it has to be said, there are no strong contenders. Given the result of the Swiss campaign, **Del Monte** fresh fruit does look to be a reasonable option, particularly from the Philippines and Costa Rica, though not without reservations.

With both fruit and vegetables, diversification can be a worthwhile option and, despite oft-repeated concerns about the importing of vegetables from around the world, on balance we believe you should buy them. It is worth bearing in mind, however, the social background to the production process, which is much less favourable in Central and South America, for example, than in the Caribbean, Kenya or Côte d'Ivoire.

Marks & Spencer, while not giving any indication of a policy to address the issues arising, appears to have a more direct involvement than one might imagine. One example is a farm in Zimbabwe, which has diversified away from tobacco to grow vegetables for M&S under contract.

Incidentally, Morocco has recently been developing international markets for traditionally-grown organic dates; look out for them in the shops.

There is a subsidiary issue, concerning the impact of the international market upon smallholders in general; that of quality. Quality is important, and consumers have a right to good and consistent quality. However, the high standards of uniformity (as distinct from quality) required can be excessive. It is third world producers that suffer the consequences of these increased standards. They may be unable to meet them because they have limited access to the biotechnological developments that give us such unnatural perfection. And the high levels of chemical inputs that may be necessary to achieve uniform perfection are expensive and damaging to human health and the environment. Retailers should accept good quality produce, not promote uniformity.

South Africa

To boycott or not to boycott . . . not a question addressed in most chapters of this book. The effectiveness of consumer boycotts of the products from particular companies or countries has long been debated. High profile boycotts like the Nestlé boycott over the marketing of infant formula and baby foods in the Third World is one of the best examples of such action against a company. The boycott of all South African goods provides us with an example of a country boycott. The question of boycotts comes up under this section on fruit because South Africa is a major supplier of fruit to the UK market.

This book is designed to provide consumers with information that assists them in encouraging best practice among companies. In the normal course of events, boycotts are inappropriate; one cannot seriously advocate a total boycott of all third world goods to force improvements in corporate and governmental policy.

However, it is a different situation when a group that represents workers in the third world has specifically called for a boycott. On a single issue like apartheid for instance, a boycott called for by the victims of apartheid themselves should be respected. Democratic non-racial organisations are saying that, yes, they will suffer, but are suffering anyhow, and are prepared to do so to bring a quicker end to apartheid. They should be listened to.

South Africa is a unique case; it is difficult to see Cape and Outspan fresh fruit, and canned fruit with South Africa (sometimes coded 'RSA') named as country of origin, as representing good value. The severe income and land ownership inequalities (the top 10% earning as much as the poorest 80% and 90% of the land owned by just 17% of the people) have led to a poor HDI v GNP ranking of −14 and are most pronounced in the farming sector. South African farm workers, according to the government in 1987, earned an average of £215 a year, and have no legal protection in respect of wages, working conditions, health and safety or holidays; employment legislation specifically excludes farm workers.

Avoiding the products of such a system is a good idea until such time that consumers are advised otherwise by democratic non-racial organisations. There are signs of movement in this area as we go to press; it is important that consumers keep abreast of the situation.

Of the supermarkets surveyed, only the **Co-op** has taken the decision not to stock South African produce. Asda, Gateway, Safeway, and Sainsbury's have decided to continue to do so, while Tesco has apparently removed such products from its shelves in Brixton and Bristol.

Canned fruit

When it comes to canned fruits, the name on the can is the most important element, and a wide range of companies is involved in this business. Neither **Gerber**, who market under the *Gerber Pride* name, as well as under many retailers' own brands, *Princes*, part of the giant **Mitsubishi** group, nor **Del Monte** Foods International completed our questionnaire. While Gerber and Del Monte did supply information, there is no indication that any of these companies have developed specific policies addressing the issues raised here. Del Monte's pineapples come in the main from its own plantation and canning plant in Kenya, the rest coming from Del Monte Tropical Fruit's canning plant in the Philippines. Del Monte pineapple would seem good value, bearing in mind the Swiss campaign, though recent land reform developments have not been responded to. Del Monte's 'deciduous fruits' (peaches, pears and apricots) come from South Africa.

Unilever, whose *John West* brand also markets canned fruit, did respond in some detail, though most information relates to its operations overseas, rather than its sourcing of products; John West's products are canned by subcontractors in several third world countries, though this is not part of a policy to add value in the third world.

The largest share of canned fruit is supplied by supermarkets under their own labels. There is no indication that **Asda**, **Gateway**, **Safeway**, **Sainsbury's**, **Tesco** or **Waitrose** have developed policies addressing the issues raised, though Tesco's tough stand on pesticides may be of indirect benefit to producers.

The one supermarket that has made some moves towards addressing these issues is the **Co-op**, a clear leader in adopting social policies on a broad front. The CWS is a major importer of canned foods; 'for commercial as well as ethical reasons, there is an increasing trend towards the import of finished products.' Examples given include pineapple from Botswana. This is a worthwhile initiative; it would be good to see it applied to other products.

Of the 'alternative' sources, it is worth bearing **Traidcraft** in mind. Its range of foods is small, but it does market canned fruits and dried fruits, which will represent the best value for consumers able to buy them. **Equal Exchange**, too, are worth a look; they stock dried fruits and may begin stocking canned fruit.

✔ Check for labels on all fruit, especially bananas and pineapples. If there are no labels, check the boxes, otherwise make a point of asking; consumers should know the country of origin.

✔ Try a greater variety of tropical fruit, if you can afford to. Avocados, mangoes, star fruit, papaya, lychees and passion fruit are just some that are being sold in major supermarkets. Go for the Caribbean or African.

✔ Try exotic vegetables you have not eaten before. If there are Asian, African and Caribbean retailers in your locality, they are worth a visit; they can give advice on cooking them too. Much of the produce will have been imported from a variety of developing countries.

✔ Do not confuse quality with uniformity. Some of the best vegetables have blemishes and come in different sizes; buy organic vegetables and fruit from the third world, if you can find any.

✔ Buy bananas with the **Geest** label. Failing that, buy **Fyffes** Honduran bananas.

✔ For other fresh fruit and vegetables, the **Del Monte** brand at least comes from some researched sources, and **Geest** brand produce from the Windward Islands represents a good option.

✔ BEST BUY canned fruit from **Traidcraft** where possible. Otherwise go for the **Co-op**'s own brand produce. **Del Monte** canned pineapple looks a better bet than others.

✔ Respect the Anti Apartheid Movement's call for a boycott of South African fruit and other products.

Beyond the shopping trip:

Keep up to date with changes in South Africa. Consult the Anti Apartheid Movement and the End Loans to South Africa campaign, for up to date information.

Write to your supermarket; ask them to take action to include social as well as environmental criteria in their purchasing of fresh and canned fruit and vegetables.

Fruit Juice

'Made from concentrated juice from more than one country'. Concentrated it certainly is, but the description suits not just the product itself, but also the structure of the industry! Around 75% of the orange juice we consume can be traced back to Brazil, and half to just two Brazilian companies, though it will usually have been imported via Germany and the Netherlands.

We consume approaching a billion litres of fruit juice in the UK each year – an amount that would fill 2,000 average-sized swimming pools and costs us around £1 billion. Growth in consumption has been significant, as 'healthy eating' awareness has grown. However, fruit juice covers a number of categories, some more healthy than others. 'Pure fruit juice' has to contain 100% pure juice at the same strength and consistency as when originally squeezed, but there are also 'fruit drinks', which should contain more than 50% juice. Other drinks are slightly less concentrated, including carbonated fruit drinks. In volume, pure fruit juice accounts for 70% of sales (of which 70% is orange and 16% apple), fruit drinks account for 23%, carbonated juices, 4%.

In the pure juice category, retailers' own brands dominate with 65% of the market. Of the branded ones, **Del Monte Foods International**, the canned fruit and juice manufacturer, has 10% of the market. *Sunpride*, a brand produced by **Gerber Foods International** (the canned and frozen foods manufacturer), *Princes* (**Mitsubishi**), *Just Juice* and *De L'Ora* (both manufactured by **Ranks Hovis McDougall**, the major cakes, bread and biscuit company) and *St Ivel Real* (**Unigate**) share 14% of the market between them. The fruit drinks category is more concentrated, with **Nestlé** (the leading food, beverage and confectionery company) taking 28% of the market with its *Libby's C* brand, followed by *Five Alive* (**Coca-Cola**) on 21%. **Del Monte** *Island Blend* has 10%, while own label brands account for 21% of sales.

Most fruit juice sold in the UK is imported in concentrated form, to minimise transport costs, and is then diluted to the appropriate strength in the UK. An EC tariff on juice imported from outside the EC (19% on orange juice) exists, and there is likely to be an increase in promotion of EC sourced juices, especially apple and grape juice, as the single market takes hold.

Brazil has accounted for 90% of the world trade in orange juice since frost damaged the US crop in 1989. There has been a big growth in the industry, particularly in the São Paolo area. It is now the world's largest citrus growing area as sugar cane and coffee, which were severely affected by a combination of frost followed by drought, give way to oranges.

There are around 22,000 farmers in this region, mainly small scale, who sell their oranges to one of six processors. The two largest, which between them supply two thirds of orange juice exports, are the Brazilian owned family firms Cutrale and Citrosuco Paulista. Despite providing the bulk of the oranges, the groves of São Paulo are about half as productive as those in other parts of the world, due mainly to the fact that producer prices have been very low, and growers have had to cut costs. This has increased soil erosion, and the incidence of weeds, pests and diseases. In 1988, prices soared when drought affected 15–20% of the crop.

Problems and answers

In many respects, the same issues arise as for the fruit business in general. Working conditions and health and safety on plantations and the contracts that characterise the links between traders and smallholders are of concern. Land ownership is an important issue; driving people off land for the sake of producing fruit for foreign markets is entirely unjustifiable. The unsafe use of pesticides is also an issue.

Another major area of concern is dependence on one crop. While Brazil itself is not dependent for a large proportion of its income on just one commodity the way so many other countries are, there are many small producers in this part of Brazil who are very vulnerable as they have no control over the prices they will receive for their crop. Many diversified out of sugar cane and coffee, but, as with all attempts at diversification, there are enormous risks involved, and the smaller the producer, the greater the risks.

There is certainly room for a system that guarantees growers a minimum price or some other security; in common with growers the world over, dependent on a single commodity, they bear considerable risks from factors they have little power to influence. The existence of such a small number of big processors, upon which the growers are dependent, also puts them at a disadvantage. Companies should be concerned about the relationship between their suppliers and the growers they buy from.

Apartheid is also an issue here. Many fruit juices are blended from concentrates from several countries of origin, including South Africa. Consumers should know which countries. It is likely to be difficult for the companies to label informatively, as they will be taking concentrate from a variety of sources over a period of time, depending on price and availability. Nevertheless, consumers should know which of a range of countries the juice they are buying is likely to come from.

The companies directly involved in these issues often do not deal directly with consumers, and this gives the manufacturers and retailers the responsibility for applying pressure for change on the consumers' behalf. They are increasingly setting the terms upon which suppliers operate and should be including these concerns in their contracts.

Nestlé, though replying to our questionnaire, gave no indication of policies relevant to the sourcing of fruit juice. **Gerber** declined to respond to our questionnaire, but volunteered the information that the company is to launch a range of organic fruit juices from Israel. **Mitsubishi** and **Ranks Hovis McDougall** did not respond, and there is no indication of any policy addressing the issues raised here.

Of all the companies surveyed, **Del Monte Foods International** (DMFI) is the closest to the production process, running pineapple plantations in Kenya, though since Del Monte was broken up, the fresh fruit business, Del Monte Tropical Fruit Co., runs the Philippines pineapple plantation that also supplies DMFI. As mentioned in the chapter on fruit, these operations were the subject of a campaign and investigation by a Swiss church based group which found that the working conditions were relatively favourable. However, this analysis did not look at the question of land ownership, which remains a significant social problem in the area, with many people made landless to make room for plantation agriculture.

Supermarket own brand juices are very significant in the market, so it is worth looking at their overall response to third world issues. The huge range of products they sell makes it unlikely that any could develop policies specific to juices. Of the major supermarkets surveyed, only the **Co-op** had any policies addressing social issues in the third world. That's not to say, of course, that Co-op brand products themselves are necessarily a best buy, but it is worth 'voting' for a company that is showing a comparatively high degree of concern.

CONSUMER CHOICES

As long as consumers are unable to find out from which country their fruit juice is sourced, their choice is limited. It should be possible for companies to give source information, particularly when policy decisions to exclude some countries (such as South Africa) have been taken. As Brazil is so dominant in the orange juice market, choice of country is effectively limited here, but this is not the case for other fruits; Israel, Morocco, Kenya, Argentina, the Philippines and

Peru are all significant exporters of fruit juice to the EC.

Buying drinks containing a higher proportion of fruit (juices and drinks, as opposed to squashes and fizzies), especially those containing tropical fruits, is likely to have a beneficial impact on developing countries. Such a change, while not guaranteeing a fairer trade, does open up the market for the other producers. Taken together with encouraging companies to respond to other development concerns, this can lead to real benefits in much the same way as the purchase of 'minority' fruits. It does, however, have cost implications, since squashes are much cheaper, and not every consumer has this choice.

With so few of the companies involved having developed policies to address the issues outlined here, this is one product in which consumer choice does not revolve around the selection of a brand; none stand out particularly well. Having said that, Del Monte is at least involved at the production end and has shown itself to be open to consumer concern in the past; here at least is the chance of progress.

✔ Go for soft drinks containing more real fruit, especially orange, pineapple and other tropical fruits.

✔ Favour **Co-op** brand fruit juices or **Del Monte** (especially pineapple); not perfect, but marginally better value than others, it would seem.

Beyond the shopping trip:

Write to your usual supermarket; ask them to look into the issue of working conditions and land ownership in their sourcing of fruit juice.

Write to the fruit juice companies; ask them to do the same in their purchasing of fruit juice.

Oils, Soaps and Detergents

Palm oil, coconut oil and groundnut oil represent major export crops for a number of third world countries. Tropical oils are unusual in that they are found as ingredients in two very different product groups: in foods, such as margarine and cooking oil, and in soaps and detergents. They are also in direct competition with oils from two other sources: from other vegetables, such as soya and rape seed, and from the petrochemical industry.

The key issues to consider in this chapter are the precarious market for tropical oils and the different production systems involved, with their differing impact on the environment and on working conditions.

Tropical oils have been used for cooking in the third world for centuries, but only became important in world trade during the industrial revolution. When people began to take washing more seriously, demand for soap created the need for the raw material. In the early 19th century, West Africa, the original producer of palm oil, was exporting a few thousand tonnes each year. By the early 20th century, this had risen to nearly 90,000 tonnes.

Coconut oil, also used in food products, was developed as a raw material for soap during the last century. Also at this time oil began to be extracted from the kernel of the oil palm fruit. Palm kernel oil and coconut oil are both better suited to soap making than the original palm oil. The increasing use of tropical oils, however, was not entirely due to the newly found Victorian obsession with personal hygiene; the invention of margarine in the intervening period also boosted demand.

By the First World War, nearly a quarter of a million tonnes of palm kernels were being exported every year from the British colonies of West Africa. Despite this, there was great competition for the supply of oils. This led Sir William Lever to apply for concessions to develop plantations in Sierra Leone, Gold Coast (Ghana) and Nigeria. The applications in Ghana and Nigeria were turned down by the colonial governors on the grounds that the Crown made no claim to be able to dispose of land belonging to the native people, a sentiment sadly lacking in modern business negotiations.

Lever then turned his attention south to the Congo basin (now Zaire), where he gained large concessions, and his business came to dominate the world trade in oils. **Unilever** still bases a large proportion of its business on oil, with interests at every level from plant breeding and plantation ownership to chemical manufacture and consumer goods marketing.

The UK market

Oils and fats in the UK have had a mixed press over the past few years, mainly focusing on health issues. The traditional fats, such as lard and butter, are declining in sales as many people now avoid eating saturated fats. This trend has also hit palm oil and coconut oil since they too are high in saturated fats. The less harmful fats (those high in mono- or poly-unsaturates) are taking over the market, with rapeseed oil, sunflower oil and olive oil all becoming increasingly popular.

The market leader in edible fats is **Unilever**, producing such household names as *Stork* and *Flora*, though **Mitsubishi** (Princes) is important too with its *Trex* brand. **CPC** (the US food manufacturer of *Mazola* corn oil and some of the best known names in spreads and condiments in the UK market) and the supermarkets' own brands are also significant. The bulk of this market, however, does not use third world oils.

The area in which palm and coconut oil still hold their own is soaps and detergents (most soaps being based on a mixture of animal fats and tropical oils), although they still have to compete with petrochemicals. Soaps and detergents continue to be growth areas – the average UK citizen, we are told, now takes four or five baths a week. **Unilever** is a leading manufacturer here, too, with *Sqezy*, *Sunlight*, *Shield*, *Lux*, and *Lifebuoy*. The two leading US manufacturers, **Procter & Gamble** (the manufacturer of *Fairy* and *Camay* whose TV adverts were the original soap opera) and **Colgate-Palmolive** are the major competitors. **Paterson Zochonis**, though not a well known name, is behind some well known brands – *Imperial Leather*, *Morning Fresh*, *Cussons*. **Body Shop**, while much smaller, is nevertheless moving its way to the top rank of personal care products companies. The major reason for its inclusion here is its unusual trading practices, including awareness-raising on behalf of the rainforest and its people.

Oil and the third world

The Philippines is the world's leading exporter of coconut oil, and provides some 75% of the EC's needs. Coconut oil is, in fact, the country's major recorded export. It is estimated that a third of the population of the Philippines depends on the coconut for a living; some 3.5 million workers and their families.

The coconut palm is the recycler's dream plant. Its fruit yields oil, food, drink, copra for animal feed, coir for rope and matting while the shell is used for household implements and handicrafts. The leaves provide roofing material for village homes and the wood is used in construction. Nothing is wasted. Much of the coconut crop is grown at village level; any family with a small plot can gain the benefit from one or two trees. However, much of the income from the oil goes to the processors at present. The government coconut agency is planning village-level processing to ensure that a higher proportion of the income finds its way into the local economy.

Palm oil, in contrast to its early history, now comes largely from South East Asia. Malaysia is the major producer; nearly all of its production is destined for export, making vegetable oils its third largest source of earnings. Indonesia is rapidly expanding its exports too, and has overtaken the African producers. Of these, Nigeria is the biggest exporter of kernels and kernel oil (though it earns 95% of its income from exports of crude petroleum), while Côte d'Ivoire leads in palm oil. Supplies of the various palm oil products to the EC are also dominated by Malaysia and Indonesia, with Papua New Guinea accounting for a smaller share.

Soya oil, which is now the leading vegetable oil in world trade, is mainly produced in the US, and 80% of world trade is in the bean itself; most processing takes place in the importing country. Brazil and Argentina are significant exporters of soya beans and oil (about a third of world trade). By contrast palm and coconut oil tend to be extracted near the source, the extra value added benefiting the producer country. The EC imports over £300 million worth of oil seed cake for animal feed each year from palm, coconut and groundnut producers, but a much larger quantity of soya cake from Latin America.

The EC is also a major importer of groundnut oil, mainly from China and Senegal, though the trade is less significant than the other oils.

Production and growing methods

The different production systems used for coconut and palm oil raise important issues. Oil palms were introduced into South East Asia in the early part of this century as a plantation crop. Within 20 years, the plantations could produce more than the traditional growers in Africa. In Indonesia, oil palms were originally established in estates and smallholder schemes, primarily in Sumatra. More recently, the palms have been planted on forest land previously cleared for agriculture, where the trees can give better yields than the annual crops. Arguably, they are also more likely to stabilise the soil, though a return to secondary forest, where possible, could be a better long term option.

In Malaysia, planting of oil palms has been taking place on rubber or coconut plantations, as the country has sought to diversify and take advantage of the high oil prices. Later developments have included the widespread use of forest land to produce the crop, too. In some cases, this has been declared 'idle land' – by implication, a good use of resources – but in fact much of it was merely land left fallow by local farmers. The slash and burn system they use may make little sense when observed over a short time, but over 100 years shows itself to be sustainable for low populations. State sponsored settlement schemes in West Malaysia have also contributed to the rise in production of palm oil. These schemes allotted small areas to individual families or created communally managed plantations.

From 55,000 hectares of oil palm in 1960, Malaysia could boast a million hectares by 1980. The environmental costs of this expansion, measured in terms of forest destruction and effluent from oil extraction, have become major causes of concern, though oil palm does at least retain the soil and drainage characteristics of secondary forest. The impact on rural labour has, in some ways, been favourable, since the high labour demand has led to increases in income and a shift towards more secure monthly wages rather than piece rates. These protect the workers against the short term changes in production or world price that make piece rates so insecure. The work is also better paid, being heavy, and the need for labour is greater. Indonesian migrant labour, mostly illegal, is filling the labour shortage. However, the impact on forest communities has been negative, driving them further into the primary forest.

The African producers have a mix of production methods. The plantations introduced at the turn of the century have not completely replaced the original system of village-level groves of trees in the forest. As late as 1950, half the palm oil in the world market came from African groves, but wars and disturbances in West Africa put paid to the trade. Côte d'Ivoire, however, is still a significant exporter, using a system of plantations and village level plantings after the traditional model. But most African production is now devoted to local consumption. Similarly, Senegal's exports of groundnuts have fallen drastically, due partly to competition from soya, but mainly to the growing domestic market and to falling yields caused by the continuous monocropping characteristic of annual cash crops. China's exports of groundnut oil are also declining.

The Philippines, already suffering badly from the decline in sugar exports due in part to the production of sugar substitutes, now suffers competition from Indonesian and Malaysian oils. Since the coconut industry is especially important to poor rural communities, development concern focuses on the need to maintain it. Oil palm, compared to coconut, is more of a plantation crop, though small scale schemes do exist.

Sourcing policies

Such is the progress made in oil technology by companies like **Unilever**, that oils from almost any source can now be used interchangeably as raw material. This frees manufacturers from dependence on one crop or supplier, but clearly has implications for the producing countries, who are rarely as free from dependence as are the manufacturers. Increasingly, for example, palm oil is eating into the market for coconut oil.

A key issue that arises is the ability of manufacturers to switch the raw material they use in response to market pressures. The rise of palm oil has been at the expense of coconut in the past, and now the rise of soya and rape seed is affecting palm oil producers, as supply begins to exceed demand. In the long term, producing nations need to diversify away from dependence on oil, but this is not a simple matter, requiring financial inputs and the ability to predict future markets. Malaysia, for example, moved into palm oil in order to reduce its dependence on rubber.

Accepting that there is little that food producers can do to maintain the market for palm or coconut oil, the responsibility falls upon the manufacturers of soap and other oil products. Policies regarding the future use of tropical oils are vital in this respect. Within a market shifting towards palm oil and palm kernel oil, it is essential to continue to source coconut oil from the Philippines, especially since the benefit to poor communities is likely to be greater. It is also important to maintain a market for vegetable-based oils in the face of petrochemical sources, for social reasons as well as for the environmental reasons more commonly cited.

Companies should ensure that working and living conditions on the plantations that they manage or source from are consistent with the International Labour Organisation's Recommendations and Conventions on standards for the employment of rural people. They should also encourage and support the development of processing industries in third world countries that increase the potential for adding value and creating employment.

Unilever controls over 72,000 hectares of plantations in 12 developing countries, oil palm production accounting for just over half. The company's plantations are likely to be amongst the best employers in the countries in which it operates. Zaire and Malaysia between them account for the bulk of its palm oil. Unilever's use of tropical oils is increasing, though currently they account for about 30% in the European market (in oil-producing countries 100%).

Procter & Gamble, which has operations in some 30 third world countries, has a published paper on good corporate citizenship in a host country which is well thought out, covering issues such as the employment of local people in management positions and community involvement. A major objective is, 'To be sensitive and responsive to the social and economic conditions in the host country.' However, the company buys all its raw materials indirectly, from various sources at various times, and does not include specific social clauses in its contracts with suppliers of these materials. The company uses raw materials from both vegetable and petrochemical sources in the manufacture of its products. It selects on the basis of technical performance, quality, environmental quality, availability and price.

Colgate-Palmolive has a published Code of Conduct, referring to its 'civic responsibility to support health, education and welfare of the community.' The company emphasises the provision of training and employment, and opportunities for advancement for indigenous staff to all levels. Company practice is to recognise independent unions if the majority of the employees at that plant so elect. Colgate-Palmolive sells its products in over 160 countries, manufacturing in 30 countries in the third world. It applies the same health and safety standards in every factory, keeping records locally. Though company policy is to avoid political issues, it has lobbied for free unions in South Africa, and was among the first to recognise black unions.

Regarding the sourcing of raw material, in particular coconut and palm kernel oil, the company does not generally purchase directly from smallholders nor does it own or manage plantations. The company uses materials and ingredients from natural sources 'whenever possible' and has a coconut processing facility in the Philippines. Its policy on purchasing of materials is, 'to ensure, as far as possible, that purchases of materials, ingredients or services are made at arm's length from established, referenced suppliers of good repute.' This would seem to indicate that the company does not see any responsibility for monitoring the policies and practices of its suppliers.

As part of **The Body Shop**'s environmental policy, it uses only renewable ingredients in its products; a measure which coincides with the need to maintain a market for tropical oils. The company plans to use brazil nut, copaiba and babassu oils, all sourced from the rainforest, in a new range of products. It is not known, however, what proportion of the vegetable oils used as a base for soaps and other preparations are of tropical origin, nor where they are sourced. The Body Shop is actively pursuing the sourcing of other ingredients in the third world; locally bought and at 'fair' prices. It is not clear, however, how such prices compare to world prices generally, nor to what extent materials are processed locally to add value.

Paterson Zochonis did not respond to the questionnaire, and its annual report pays scant attention to the sourcing of its raw materials in the third world; surprising, given its heavy involvement in Africa. The company has historical roots in West Africa; indeed its turnover in Nigeria is greater than that in the UK. It also has subsidiaries in Indonesia, Thailand and Kenya. The company states that it has a policy of encouraging nationals into the management and direction of its foreign subsidiaries 'on merit', and supports educational programmes in West Africa. It has a research facility in West Africa, though its role is not known. There is no indication of policies or initiatives addressing the social impact of its trade with the third world.

Biotechnology

The recent advances in cloning more productive and more easily managed varieties of oil palm that have catapulted Malaysia to the top of the league have also resulted in a declining need for labour. Though this has been masked by increasing production in Malaysia and Indonesia, the net loss of work worldwide is probably considerable, falling primarily on African producers.

Unilever is carrying out research into oil palm cloning in Malaysia and Zaire. Unilever believes that the improved varieties benefit local farmers, giving them better returns and employment opportunities. Contracts to supply the company ensure prices often better than on the open market. There seems however to be no policy to monitor the impact of these developments on non-participating farmers.

CONSUMER CHOICES

Of the companies surveyed, only **Body Shop** had any policy relevant to the raw material source for soap and detergent products. A range of detergents using coconut oil as the base is available nationally from **Ecover**.

- ✔ BEST BUY products are **Ecover** detergents and **Body Shop** personal care products.

- ✔ Buy soaps and detergents that are derived from vegetable oil (especially coconut oil) rather than petrochemical based products. Many of the supermarkets' own brand ranges of 'green' detergents are labelled as using vegetable oils. The Co-op's green fabric softener is coconut oil based.

Beyond the shopping trip:

Write to the major soap and detergent manufacturers; ask them to develop sourcing policies reflecting the social and environmental benefits of tropical oils.

Tobacco

Advertising hoardings up and down the country proclaim the message; you, too, can aspire to the glamorous, successful, romantic and adventurous lifestyle of the elite. For a few small coins, you can be transported to another world of affluence and beautiful people. An exaggeration? Certainly not if you travel to almost any country in the third world, and study the cigarette adverts that abound. Prior to tough controlling legislation, the same values were implicit in many cigarette adverts in the UK, too.

There can be few products on sale where the sometimes subtle, and occasionally crass, claims of the advertisers so badly fit the reality on offer. Tobacco is unique in another way, too; it is *the* world crop par excellence. Grown in temperate as well as tropical climes, it is valuable for third world and rich countries alike. It is also sold by the same handful of transnational corporations in almost every part of the globe. As a cash crop, much the same issues arise here as for products such as coffee or sugar: working conditions and wages, pesticides and plantations, smallholders and dependence.

Whose brand on the packet?

In the UK, we puff our way through some 100 billion cigarettes every year – more than five a day for each adult and child. Around half the tobacco coming into the EC comes from the third world, Brazil being the major supplier. Zimbabwe also accounts for a large share, followed by South

Korea. Because the UK imports most of its tobacco via the EC, the same countries are major suppliers to the UK market, though South Africa and India are also significant sources. The bulk of 'non third world' tobacco comes from the USA.

The top companies are **American Brands Inc** (whose UK subsidiary **Gallaher**, takes 45% of the UK cigarette market) with *Benson and Hedges* and *Silk Cut* and also owns *Old Holborn, Condor* and *Hamlet*; **Hanson plc** (whose subsidiary **Imperial Tobacco** manufactures *John Player Special, Embassy, Regal* and *Superkings* as well as *Golden Virginia, St Bruno* and *Castella*); **Rothmans** (*Dunhill* and *Peter Stuyvesant*) and **Philip Morris**, the world's largest international cigarette manufacturer with the world's leading brand, *Marlboro*. Between them, they share 80% of the cigarette market. Together with **British American Tobacco** (BAT), which does not sell cigarettes in the UK, they also dominate world trade and are involved in every stage from growing to marketing.

Untapped markets in the third world

Of particular concern is the fact that, as smoking declines in the rich countries by about 1% a year, the tobacco giants turn their gaze upon the untapped markets of the third world; worldwide, smoking is increasing by between 1% and 2% each year. By a dreadful irony, it was in part the US Food for Peace programme that began the trend. Tobacco farmers are a powerful lobby in the States, and after the war the government sanctioned the use of aid money to encourage third world governments to buy US tobacco. The programme was designed to develop a taste for the mild Virginia tobacco grown in the US.

But smoking was not new to those countries, and state monopolies still produce most of the third world's cigarettes; China is the largest producer and consumer, with 300 million smokers. But the big four tobacco companies are targeting third world women and young people in particular to boost consumption of their own brands, and of cigarettes in general.

While companies protest that advertising only seeks to

increase market share, the disproportionate amount spent on adverts aimed at women, who smoke far fewer cigarettes than men, indicates a desire to create new markets, not to redistribute shares within existing ones.

The lower health requirements in many third world countries, coupled with minimal or non-existent advertising controls in some, mean that the impact of the tobacco industry is far greater than in the rich countries. Thailand, in an attempt to restrict imports of cigarettes, imposed a levy on them. A complaint by the US led to GATT, the General Agreement on Tariffs and Trade, ruling against this as an unfair discrimination. It was pointed out that Thailand could discourage smoking more fairly by restricting advertising instead.

Cigarettes manufactured by the tobacco TNCs are far more expensive than the local brands. Despite this, the trend is clearly towards the foreign brands with their more glamorous image: a poor use of scarce household resources and a consequence of high pressure advertising. Tobacco companies must recognise the need for more responsible advertising practices.

Tobacco and the farmer

Looked at dispassionately, tobacco isn't a bad choice for the farmers of the third world; it is often grown on small farms rather than plantations, where labourers are in a very dependent and precarious state. In South Korea, for example, over 90% of the tobacco is grown by smallholders. The income is good, due in part to the help offered by tobacco companies to small farmers; loans, fertiliser and other chemicals are typically available at cost. As one farmer put it, only marijuana could earn him as much!

And tobacco need not compete for land with badly needed food crops; in Indonesia, for example, the crop is rotated with rice and other crops. Zimbabwe has produced food surpluses in the face of growing tobacco production. In fact, very little of the land there is under tobacco; less than 1% of the commercially-farmed land. Despite a programme to redistribute land to black farmers, around 6,000 white farmers still own half the land and serious inequalities of income persist – the top 10% earning as much as the poorest 60%. Its GNP at $580 is fairly low, though Zimbabwe has the strongest economy of the SADCC countries (those nations of Southern Africa cooperating to reduce their dependence on South Africa).

Patterns of land ownership vary from country to country, Brazil being the obvious counterbalance to South Korea; with 60% of the land owned by just 2% of the farmers and 75% of agricultural workers landless, there is little room for smallholders. Land ownership is also a significant issue in India and, of course, South Africa, where the unequal division of land is institutionalised.

Plantation workers are among the most vulnerable employees. They are often taken on as temporary labour, without the rights of permanent workers. Often working in isolated places, they have little political power and few other job opportunities. They may depend on the plantation owner for housing, food, education, medical care . . . in short, for their lives. Unions can help to protect their interests, but few have been able to break into the system.

Smallholders are in some senses in a stronger position, being able at least to grow food, and make their own decisions about what crops to grow. But in practice they can often be controlled by the government or by traders who set the rules of the game. Dependence on one marketing channel or on one source of inputs such as loans or agricultural chemicals, can leave smallholders as weak as plantation workers, but also shouldering the risk of crop failure.

The tobacco giants have a responsibility to see that the growing of tobacco yields fair returns for the people who grow the crop, whether they be smallholders or plantation workers. The top companies account for the vast bulk of tobacco traded on the international market and have extraordinary power and wealth at their disposal. The tax revenues they create also give them great influence with governments.

None of the companies in the survey appear to have specific policies addressing the social and environmental impact; **Rothmans** (whose cigarettes are manufactured in many countries including India, Pakistan, Egypt and Zaire, and are available in 160 countries); *Imperial* (**Hanson**) and **Philip Morris** did not respond to the questionnaire. **Philip Morris** has a corporate accountability statement, but this makes no reference to the social impact of its sourcing policies in the third world. Only **Gallaher** responded, stating that it does not own or manage plantations, outgrowers schemes or processing plants in third world countries. It imports the tobacco leaf which is purchased through dealers and runs an office in Zimbabwe, staffed entirely by nationals, supervising the purchasing of tobacco leaf throughout Africa. It sources tobacco from a large number of countries in Latin America, the Caribbean and Asia as well. On the issues of working conditions and smallholder security, **Gallaher** gave no relevant information, save that the company 'only deals with reputable local and international dealers', effectively avoiding the issue. It does however provide technical advice and consultation to farmers and growing organisations.

In response to concern about the use of dangerous chemicals in the production of the tobacco, **Gallaher** believes that governments throughout the world closely monitor the use of pesticides on agricultural crops, including tobacco – not a widely held view. 'Tobacco growers', says the company, 'use only licensed pesticides in accordance with their government guidelines.' Whether this is an article of faith, or based on any research, is not clear.

No smokes without fire

The smoke produced by the worldwide burning of 30 billion cigarettes a day may have a significant effect on global warming! But it is the production process itself that is of more concern. Tobacco is produced in several varieties, the main export varieties being flue-cured Virginia and burley, which produce cigarettes to the Western taste.

Fire and flue curing require fuel, usually wood, while some other types can be cured in the sun. It has been estimated that one hectare of woodland is required to cure one hectare of tobacco; two or three hectares to produce a tonne. The UK's third world imports of tobacco must burn up nearly 200,000 hectares of woodland each year; a very significant cause of forest loss in tobacco growing areas. The responsibility that the tobacco giants have is to ensure the sustainable curing of tobacco: the growing of trees, at a sustainable level, the development of alternatives and the development of more efficient processes (80% of the heat is wasted).

In response to this, **British American Tobacco**, for example, has encouraged small farmers to plant trees to compensate, but few are willing or able to sacrifice tobacco land to trees. It is unlikely that replanting schemes anywhere have begun to meet the need for firewood. Indeed the World Bank estimates the cost of replanting the wood used would amount to £15 billion. For local people, dependent on wood for household fuel, the search for wood becomes more desperate each year. The impact on the forest itself, of course, is disastrous as tobacco contributes yet another turn of the screw.

Gallaher, however, claims that over 90% of its tobacco is Virginia flue-cured, mostly using coal, oil or gas (though half the world's tobacco is flue cured using wood). **Rothmans** claims to have an International Environment Policy Steering Group, though gave no information about its work. It did forward a copy of *Tobacco Forum*, an industry newsletter, which highlighted the problem of deforestation and initiatives taken locally to address it.

A serious case of addiction

Tobacco is unusual in that the major focus for public concern is not the source of the crop, but its marketing, both in the rich countries and the third world. The health controversy has raged for decades now, and the vested interests of governments in both consumer and producer nations have been plain to see. That there is still a controversy is itself stunning, as even the industry – by its funding of research –

has in effect accepted that there are health risks inherent in smoking. The fudging of health issues and advertising legislation has been astounding as governments attempt to have their cake and eat it.

The UK government has, for example, accepted since the '50s that there are health risks, but since then has admitted that it cannot forgo the tax income, now some £6 billion a year. The Zimbabwean government, to take an example from the producer end, is happy to ally itself to calls to stop smoking. But equally, it sees nothing inconsistent in its encouragement of farmers to produce the crop from which the country earns nearly 25% of its export income. Malawi is even more dependent on tobacco; almost 50% of its export income derives from the trade.

Much has been written about the ability of the tobacco industry to buy off criticism from government and media alike – the latter too dependent on the advertising revenue to bite the hand that feeds it. The industry spends approximately £1.5 billion a year encouraging tobacco consumption worldwide, and sponsors sports and other events to boost its image with a health conscious public. Gallaher states, 'Tobacco is one of the best sources of cash income for many thousands of farmers in a range of under-developed countries'. In terms of economic significance, it picks out Zimbabwe and Malawi in particular. The company also referred to the UN Food and Agriculture Organisation's paper, The Economic Significance of Tobacco, which emphasised the economic benefits of the crop to both farmers and countries. Interestingly, however, the UK government announced in 1991 that it would no longer fund development projects involving the tobacco sector.

CONSUMER CHOICES

The tobacco market is a peculiar one. As with many commodities, the product is auctioned in bulk, blended and sold on again. So consumers don't have the luxury of choosing cigarettes from Indonesia or Zimbabwe, for example. And the situation is further complicated – the brands we are familiar with are often made by different manufacturers in different countries.

So, to a greater extent than is usual, we are dependent on the tobacco companies for information about our product choices. Unless, that is, we decide to take the step of denying them a market altogether . . . To smoke or not to smoke is still a controversial question, and arguments about individual liberty abound on both sides. But it has to be said that it is difficult to see tobacco as a sustainable industry – environmentally, or in terms of human health, despite its short term advantages for the grower.

One way of at least addressing the value-added element is to buy tobacco products manufactured in the country of origin; cigars principally. Processing raw material is a good way to encourage employment and to earn a lot more money from the crop. While the countries of the third world produce nearly half the world's traded tobacco, they market less than 10% of the tobacco products.

Tobacco companies are diversifying away from tobacco, while still deriving much of their profit from the business; one clear option for consumers is to assist the process of diversification by not buying tobacco. Some may argue that in doing so, we might push the manufacturers to concentrate their marketing efforts more on third world consumers. That may be a concern, but it is counsel of despair; it is happening anyway, and the more pressure on companies and countries to diversify the better. As they broaden their own product range, the tobacco giants should also respond to the need of their suppliers in the third world for new products and markets.

Overall, it is clear that there is no 'best buy' from among the tobacco companies; there is so little to distinguish between them in their response to the issues.

✔ If possible, don't buy tobacco products. Spend your money on other third world products that are less damaging.

✔ If you are a cigar smoker, consider buying cigars manufactured in the tobacco producing country – Cuba for instance.

Beyond the shopping trip:

If you are a smoker, write to the manufacturer of your brand and mention that you are concerned to learn that it does not appear to have developed any policies addressing the social and environmental impact of the trade on the third world.

Clothing

Of all the products we buy from the third world, it is undoubtedly clothing that has developed the reputation for poor working conditions. The sweatshops of Bangkok have attained the status of mythology. Many consumers have begun to feel that perhaps their only response is to avoid third world clothes altogether.

The answer is not simply to Buy British, however. The clothing industry is the most important manufacturing industry for the third world; at nearly $23 billion a year, exports of clothing are second only to oil for the third world. The UK based its industrialisation on the textile and clothing industry, and many third world countries are doing the same. The technology is cheap, even in today's high tech environment, and manual labour can compete with the machine. The industry is a valuable source of income and potential source of liberation for women.

The garment industry is just the kind of development to encourage; as an industry it is relatively benign environmentally and it is often a first step to reducing dependence on the very cash crops so frequently blamed for environmental abuse. Its low tech nature, the relatively low level of investment required, and the small scale upon which it can operate effectively means that development even at the village level is possible (though village industries often find export very difficult). Third world clothes are part of the answer, not part of the problem.

Another factor to bear in mind is that the UK rag trade is not all it is dressed up to be. The same balance of power exists here as elsewhere. Small factories subcontracting from larger ones have poor wages and working conditions. And, right at the bottom, an increasing army of homeworkers make garments for £1 an hour or even less.

Homeworkers are the ultimate 'flexible workforce' for the new cost-conscious '90s; hired and fired at will, they meet all their own overheads and can be paid by piece rather than by the hour. Since they work alone, and often come from ethnic minorities who feel vulnerable, they don't make a fuss. To keep things simple, they don't even have to be registered, so inconveniences like National Insurance and health and safety inspectorates are neatly sidestepped.

While in some industries, such as electronics, the manufacturers hold the initiative, this is not so in the case of clothing. In electronics, manufacturers make what they think will sell and retailers buy the goods that suit their market. In clothing, the retailers produce the designs and hawk the patterns round the manufacturers to find the best deal.

This may seem an abstruse point, but is the key to the whole business. The balance of power is firmly in the hands of the retailer, which is good news for the consumer, but not for the producer. Without the technology, the designs, the understanding of the market or the access to consumers themselves, manufacturers in the third world are dependent on retailers or their agents for everything. The only thing they have to offer is labour; orders will go to those who can produce most cheaply and quickly to the required standard.

While retailers are not directly responsible for the many problems we see in the industry, they do set the terms that put pressure on manufacturers. And, because the bulk of the clothes that we buy are effectively retailers' brands, they are our primary link; consumers' relationship with retailers is the only effective way to express their responsibility to the producer.

So, when you check through the rails of garments next time you need a shirt, a dress or a pair of trousers, what do you watch out for?

The story behind the label

In searching for the answer, we must look behind the labels on our clothes, not only to the third world factories where many of them are made, but to the policies and practices of the high street retailers.

Most of us buy our clothes – over £300 worth each year for every child and adult in the UK – from the big retailers. The bulk of the £17 billion clothing market is divided up between **Marks & Spencer** (which takes about 16%), the **Burton Group** (*Top Shop, Dorothy Perkins, Principles, Harvey Nichols, Evans* and *Debenhams*), **C&A, Storehouse** (*Blazer, Richards, Mothercare* and *BhS*), **Next, Littlewoods** and **Sears** (*Adams, Fosters, Hornes, Miss Selfridge, Wallis, Warehouse* and *Your Price*).

Most of these firms sell primarily 'own brand' clothes or 'exclusive' labels (which really amount to the same thing). The label may have a country of origin, but clothes are made on a global production line: thread from one country, buttons from another; design in the UK, assembly in Dhaka; zips attached in Cyprus, labels stitched in Battersea.

Countries in the global factory

To get things in perspective, only around 36% of our clothes are imported. Of that approximately half come from a number of third world countries, most of the rest coming from EC countries. Hong Kong accounts for 20% of imported garments, South Korea 6% and India 4%. Between them Taiwan, Thailand, Cyprus, Singapore, China, Pakistan, Indonesia, Mauritius, Malaysia, Philippines, Macao, Sri Lanka and Bangladesh account for 17%. The third world as a whole accounts for half the world trade in garments, earning just over 5% of its income from the industry.

Thailand, while being the country most widely associated with poor working conditions, has a surprisingly favourable HDI v GNP rating of +23, though income distribution is severely unequal; the top 10% earning as much as the poorest 80%. Rural poverty is serious, driving many people from the poor North East into Bangkok in search of any kind of work.

The most remarkable clothing exporter, in many ways, is Hong Kong, which has come to be synonymous with the clothing industry in recent years. Wages here are the highest in Asia, apart from Japan, and this is due in no small measure to the impact of the garment industry on the economy. Hong Kong derives 33% of its export earnings from clothing. Other major exports include toys and sports goods, telecommunications equipment, watches and clocks, office machines and domestic electrical equipment – altogether accounting for 62% of export earnings – indicating a diversified economy. With a GNP of $8,070 Hong Kong is on a par with most European countries. Income distribution is average for third world countries that supply the UK, with the poorest 40% of the 5.7 million population sharing 16% of the income. It has an export-oriented economy with little government control, low taxes and virtually full employment. The development of the clothing industry in the third world has been hampered since 1974 by the Multifibre Arrangement (MFA – see page 24). During this time, jobs have been lost in the UK and imports have continued to flow in from other developed countries. It looks as though the days of the MFA are numbered in the push for global free trade, but this may well leave the poorest countries worse off, unable to compete with the newly industrialising countries such as Hong Kong and South Korea.

So, what is the real cost of the shirt on your back? It is clear that a large part of the cost is borne by the people who made it, in terms of low wages and poor working conditions. Part of it is borne by the country in which it was made, in terms of low export prices. But then the benefits of the trade are real, too; the job may well be better than any alternatives. And, as in the case of Bangladesh and Mauritius, the garment industry may provide possibly the only alternative to continued reliance on the export of agricultural produce.

The focus of consumer concern is on what can realistically be done to improve the benefits and reduce the costs borne by garment workers. More specifically, the focus will be on what the UK retailers, the most powerful players in the deal, can do to push for the urgently needed improvements.

Long hours, low pay

Wages in the garment industry are amongst the lowest in manufacturing (a situation common to all countries, including the UK). We've all come across stories of garments costing £20 of which only £3 goes to the third world factory that made it; such mark-ups are by no means out of the ordinary.

For countries with little economic power, wages are often the only bargaining counter they have. They have little to offer in terms of skills and technology; which accrue from development itself. In most cases companies that export garments to the rich countries and those owned by foreign multinationals offer better wages and conditions than local companies. That is part of the answer, not the problem. Part of the 'transfer of technology' argument is that foreign firms encourage better labour standards that rub off onto local firms.

A common problem is that overtime is too long, enforced or unpaid. All three are illegal in most countries, but cases are reported from many countries such as Thailand, the Philippines and Bangladesh. The basic problem, apart from unreasonable delivery schedules imposed by buyers, is that the workers are simply unable to enforce their rights.

For Bangladesh, the clothing industry represents the first faltering step away from dependence on jute. Bangladesh has always been in a vulnerable position and, even with the growth in the clothing industry, 84% of its export earnings are derived from a very small number of products. Along with clothing, Bangladesh exports textile products (both cotton and non-cotton), fish, jute, leather, tea and some petroleum products. The clothing industry got underway in 1978, and by 1986 it had grown so rapidly that clothing became the most important export, earning 21% of the country's income. The industry now employs some 300,000 people. Much of the capital, however, comes from other

Asian countries 'suffering' from higher wages, and most of the initiative still lies overseas. Even the 'Made in Bangladesh' labels are manufactured in Taiwan or South Korea, since the machinery needed to produce them is expensive.

Though Bangladesh really acts as an offshore factory for foreign companies, the industry is crucial, especially to women. For many, their jobs are the first experience of life outside the home, and the income, though meagre, the first influence they have gained over family budgets. To set against this, many women are illiterate – and in no position to argue – or too dependent on the factory owner to risk the sack. Workers without a contract of employment, mass sackings, the presence of 'yellow' unions (see page 233) and workers being abused are all reported widely.

This is not surprising, given the massive population combined with tremendous pressure on land – some 87% of its 110 million people live in rural areas, making it one of the world's most densely populated countries. With 10% of the population owning 50% of the land, and with much of the land annually being under water, there is a large landless rural population that relies on unpredictable seasonal employment. Bangladesh is also one of the poorest countries trading with the UK to any great extent. It carries a massive debt burden, with a predicted quarter of its income to be swallowed up in debt service repayments during 1991. Its GNP is just $160 and income distribution is seriously unequal, with the richest 10% of the population earning as much as the poorest 60%.

Bangladesh continues to be a highly vulnerable country as two events during the first half of 1991 showed. One way a poor and populous country has of raising income is to export its labour. Bangladesh relies heavily on the income sent back from those working in the Gulf states, many of whom worked in Kuwait and had to leave during the Gulf War. Kuwait is now reluctant to invite foreign workers back. The second event that shook Bangladesh was the devastating cyclone and tidal wave in April that as well as taking a huge toll in human life and livestock destroyed some of the new industries. Many foreign companies will think twice before investing in Bangladesh again.

Yellow unions are a common feature of manufacturing industries in South Korea as well. Years of union repression in South Korea have left a workforce still comparatively unorganised and even now, unions can only represent workers at one factory. However, a popular movement for free unions is gathering pace, despite the restrictions that are still in place. South Korea's clothing industry employs a quarter of a million people, and provides the most important export, earning nearly $5 billion in 1986 – 15% of the country's income. The workers are mostly women and, though conditions have improved dramatically over the years, working hours are very long – 12 hour shifts are still common.

The Philippines has some of the lowest industrial wages in South East Asia, and its very relaxed legislation on foreign companies' operations (its debt burden is one of the highest in Asia) has led to much of the export business being officially carried out at FTZs such as the Bataan Export Processing Zone (BEPZ). Many foreign firms have subsidiaries here. There are active unions at BEPZ and while conditions could undoubtedly be improved, they are comparatively good in the context of the Philippines garment industry as a whole.

However, these firms subcontract work to other factories outside the zone, where wages can be very low. Subcontracting is used as a threat to stifle union action at bigger plants; there is always the option to close down and subcontract more work. There are also commonly-used methods of circumventing employment legislation; workers are frequently laid off every eleven months and rehired. That way they only qualify for temporary wage rates, while those employed for a year are entitled to additional benefits.

According to a UN study, one European owned factory in the Philippines insists that new workers, even skilled machinists, sign on for a six month 'apprenticeship' scheme on low wages and without union rights. Workers were frequently laid off at the end of this period.

A dispute between the workers and management of

IGMC, a BEPZ subsidiary of the UK company William Baird plc, gained some attention here in 1990. The company claimed to be unable to meet the cost of a statutory 25% rise in the minimum wage and closed the factory. Workers picketing the plant claimed that the production was subcontracted to factories outside the zone. Baird brands, including *Dannimac, Telemac, Windsmoor* and *Centaur* were subject to boycott calls. Baird also makes own brand clothes, including *Canda*, for high street retailers.

Health and safety is also a big issue in the garment industry. Many women are injured by poorly guarded machinery, and compensation is often non-existent. The following example is typical. One worker in the Colombo Free Trade Zone in Sri Lanka suffered damage to her eye when a needle broke. The management tried to pressurise her into signing a statement that it was a birth defect; when she refused, she was offered $2 compensation. A union campaign resulted in this being raised to $156. More common are lung problems caused by cotton dust and stress-related injuries, both of which are rarely compensated for.

In response to existing consumer demand, many retailers already inspect the sites of production, to check that the quality is adequate, targets are being met, that the machines are good enough for the job. Consumers can also demand that retailers monitor standards in the quality of employment; wages and working conditions.

Littlewoods, with 117 retail outlets and several home shopping operations which were put up for sale in 1991 (*Janet Frazer, Brian Mills, Burlington, Peter Craig, John Moores Home Shopping* and *Littlewoods*), is the most innovative in its policy on sourcing, and was the first to establish a code of practice which included reference to social issues for those doing business with the company. The code states that merchandise must be produced in conformity with a section of the UN Charter governing economic and social cooperation with specific reference to workers' rights and working conditions, and with local laws covering workers' rights, minimum wage and working conditions in the country of manufacture. It also covers respect for, and observance of, human rights and fundamental freedoms for all.

In the past the company has terminated contractual arrangements with suppliers of garments on ethical grounds, but the company would not elaborate on this. Nor does it say how it intends to monitor suppliers' adherence to this policy. This is likely to be difficult in the absence of specific criteria, given the charter's very general wording. It will be interesting to see how well this enlightened policy works in practice.

C&A is unique among the companies in the survey in that it is owned privately by a Dutch family – the Brennink-meyers. While it did not complete the questionnaire, the company did send an informative letter. It has around 530 retail outlets in Europe and, as each national company is separately owned by members of the family, it is not technically a multinational, though it shares many of the same characteristics. Since each company is a private un-limited company, the directors have no liability protection and hence no legal obligation to divulge the information that limited companies are required to. C&A prefers to source in the UK, but accepts that orders placed in the third world benefit long term development. It will consider ordering from any country, with the current exception of South Africa, as long as suppliers can meet quality/reliability criteria and 'honour all relevant codes of practice'. Should these requirements be knowingly ignored, C&A 'will have no hesitation in terminating business relationships.' A letter relating to this has been sent to all UK suppliers. It is unclear what the company means by 'relevant codes of practice', since none have been adopted by the clothing trade, and examples of cases were not provided.

In common with many companies, C&A tends to place orders with larger manufacturers who in its estimation are more likely to offer better conditions of employment and are more likely to comply fully with legal requirements. Its buyers visit factories wherever possible 'so that they are able to judge conditions for themselves.' However, it is unclear whether or how subcontractors are monitored for compliance. C&A recognises that the visits are no guarantee of 'freedom from exploitation', but believes that the system of visits is both necessary and helpful in reducing incidents of exploitation.

C&A is adopting a number of initiatives intended to address the problems of exploitation more directly, including the development of a training and awareness programme for all buyers, and a revision of the standard order form to incorporate legally binding terms and conditions applied to these issues.

The company did not supply New Consumer with any detail of these initiatives, nor any indication about the degree to which they have been established. These appear to be positive departures, if applied, and we await results with interest.

Next, as well as retailing clothing and home furnishings, has interests in financial services and property. Its *Grattan* mail order operation was sold in 1991. Next has no manufacturing facilities of its own in third world countries, but gives buyers and designers 'complete discretion as to the countries from which they source products.' It purchases significant, though unspecified, quantities of completed garments, footwear and accessories particularly from the Pacific Basin and Mauritius, Taiwan, Hong Kong, South Korea, Thailand, India and Jamaica, and has recently looked into the possibility of purchasing from Madagascar.

While Next is not directly involved in manufacture, it does see it as necessary to train and assist in terms of quality control and design in the manufacturing process. The company believes that the extent to which it works with its manufacturers has been instrumental in raising standards. 'The individual workers have been engaged in making better quality products and have attained higher technical standards. This is reflected in improved wages and working conditions.' There is certainly a case to be made for this, but no figures are given, or, it seems, collected by the company. A policy on working conditions should be possible in view of the company's long term links, though the company does not see the necessity of keeping information on health and safety standards of suppliers.

Great Universal Stores (GUS) is the market leader in home shopping in the UK, with catalogues produced under 20 different names, including *Marshall Ward, Great Universal, John England, Choice, Kit, John Noble, Fashion Extra, Family Album, Trafford* and *John Myers*. The company also produces clothing under the *Burberry* label. It does not have subsidiaries in the third world, but has two in South Africa, selling furniture through 340 retail outlets. It was among a number of clothing companies mentioned in a *World in Action* programme in 1984 that looked at the involvement of British companies in the exploitative garment manufacturing industry in Bangkok. GUS denied direct involvement as it purchased through agents, and indicated that it had since changed its agents, and stopped purchasing from Thailand until it was 'satisfied with the position'. It is unclear what steps if any the company has taken to ensure that working conditions are satisfactory in the factories where its garments are made.

Other clothing retailers **Marks & Spencer, Storehouse, John Lewis, Sears, Burton Group**, and **House of Fraser** gave no indication of any policies on the sourcing of garments from third world suppliers.

Long term involvement

Poor countries tread a wobbly tightrope between low wages/low development and high wages/high development; as their low wage advantage evaporates, they hope to find a new mix of comparative advantage – in terms of skills, technology or location – to stay in business. The argument about whether wages are kept down by government policy to too great an extent is important, and a question to which we will return. But the issue for companies is the other side of the equation.

One way countries' comparative advantage can be measured is by the activity of companies that buy from the third world. As one country loses its advantage, buyers flock to another. The garment industry characteristically follows low wages around the globe, as Hong Kong has found. So one issue for retailers is, how rapidly do they change their source of supply?

This question reveals a lot about the nature of the relationship between supplier and buyer. As discussed earlier, manufacturers are dependent upon buyers for designs, new techniques and market information as well as for access to distant markets; a long term relationship provides much better scope for development of skills and techniques. In the long run, this could well be of benefit to the retailer in terms of a better product, but it is certainly beneficial to the manufacturer.

Retailers are in a position of great power, since they have access to much information not available to their suppliers. This means they have a responsibility for the security of their suppliers, through long term relationships in which skills and knowledge are transferred – to the benefit of both. Retailers hope to instil loyalty on the part of their customers; they should adopt the same standards themselves towards suppliers.

Next's apparent policy to develop long term relationships with suppliers is a good one, but little attempt has been made to verify the supposed improvements. None of the other companies surveyed indicated policies addressing the issue of relocations, though M&S in its dealings with UK suppliers at least has a reputation for long term involvement and very rigorous standards.

Subcontracting

At first sight, this may seem a bad idea; sending work down the chain further separates the supplier from the end customer, making information flow even more restricted. At each stage, too, a cut is taken, resulting in much lower wages at the bottom of the pile. It is commonly used as a means of shackling the unions; if management consider passing production to another factory, the threat of less work clarifies the unions' options wonderfully.

And yet subcontracting remains one of the chief means by which local firms can break in to international markets. What buyer from Big UK Clothes plc is going to tout patterns around the backstreets to find Acme Local Garments Ltd? Far simpler to go straight to Big Thai Garment Inc. and get the contract agreed straight away. Information flow to local manufacturers about what Western markets want, in terms of quality standards and assembly techniques, may be slower than it should be, but without subcontracting, it wouldn't happen at all.

The key issue, of course, is to ensure that subcontracting isn't used as a means of holding down wages or preventing union formation.

Unions

Part of the answer globally is to ensure the right of workers to organise to improve their working conditions. There is a free market notion that wages and conditions will come into balance, given free trade. But legislation by government or direct action by employers to prevent the development of free independent unions is a clear hindrance to this process. There are widespread cases of union organising being prevented by the sacking of activists, by the assault or even killing of union leaders by hired thugs or by the closing of the factory and reopening under a different name, with a non-unionised workforce.

This sort of restraint holds wages artificially low in many countries – it tightens the screw of competition several turns. The improvements in conditions demonstrated by foreign-owned firms will only rub off when independent unions exist to encourage the adoption of common standards.

Legislation

Another, simpler, issue is that of minimum wage legislation. A global minimum wage is an impossible dream at the moment, and damaging to the very countries needing a better deal. Some countries have taken the risk of passing laws stipulating the lowest acceptable standards. It is a risk, because they could price themselves out of the world market, but in fact legislation is rarely enforced. Minimum wages are also pitifully low sometimes; in the Philippines, for example, they are barely enough to support the wage earner. A family dependent on one income would simply starve.

But minimum wages do at least provide a yardstick against which to measure company performance and provide a focus for wage negotiations, and all retailers should ensure that they are met by all their suppliers. We need to work towards raising the general 'market level' of wages; that can help the wage bargaining situation in all poor countries.

Fabrics

The advent of artificial fibres has certainly affected the cotton producers, as well as traditional weavers, whose looms are designed for use with cotton. Artificial fibres are increasingly popular with consumers in the third world, because they last well and are cheap.

We can expect various shades of 'green' cotton to come on to the market in the next few years and they are worth looking out for. Currently, however, the focus seems to be on post-harvest treatment, such as bleaching, and its effects on consumers and their environment, rather than the much more serious issue of pesticides abuse. **Next**, for example, is beginning to explore the issue of green cotton, but currently has only unbleached cotton available (see page 208).

CONSUMER CHOICES

The clothing industry is a good one to encourage as it facilitates those countries trying to develop economically without destroying the environment. Buy third world for preference – it employs women in the main, is economically useful and environmentally relatively benign.

Different countries offer very different prospects for the

clothing worker; not surprisingly, conditions are generally worst in the poorest countries. But that is to be expected, and it is futile to boycott Bangladesh merely because of its poverty. However, we can identify countries that seem to be achieving more with what they have available, and, in this respect, **Thailand**, perhaps surprisingly, comes out well, as do **China** and **Sri Lanka** with favourable HDI or GNP ratings, for example. **Singapore** compares unfavourably, with wages lagging well behind its national income. **Bangladesh** is better than average, and being so poor and so dependent on its clothing industry, rates as a good buy.

As for the retailers, the response was, it has to be said, poor. **Traidcraft**, in the context of a recent campaign to raise awareness of these issues, developed a Code of Practice for clothing retailers, which received a similar response. The industry is complacent to the point of smugness; a typical response is of the kind; 'We buy clothes at the top end of the market from reputable suppliers where such problems don't exist.' It suggests that apart from the isolated cases reported above, garment retailers in general make no attempt to check on conditions at suppliers' factories.

In response to the Traidcraft campaign, **Storehouse** indicated only that it would 'be happy to discuss the situation with the manufacturer concerned' if a specific case was brought to their attention, but since it does not reveal its sources of supply, that is not a very helpful response. **Storehouse** subsidiary BhS has a similar policy of 'mutual trust and harmony' with its suppliers. The **Burton Group** maintains that it avoids suppliers with poor labour practices, though cannot guarantee that all manufacturers were acceptable. It believes that the whole issue should be addressed to the manufacturers themselves.

It is clear, and it has been demonstrated in the past, that clothes are produced for sale in reputable high street stores under the most appalling conditions. While we can't impute guilt by association to all manufacturers, it is important that steps are taken to root out such practices.

With the exception of **Littlewoods**, and possibly of **C&A**, there is little to choose between the major chains, but there are a number of small retailers specialising in offering development-friendly clothes. The two with national coverage are **Traidcraft** and **Oxfam Trading**, both of whom sell via small shops and mail order. They have a limited range but use traditional handcraft skills.

✔ BEST BUY from **Traidcraft** and **Oxfam Trading** where possible.

✔ No high street store is without criticism, but buy from **Littlewoods** (*Brian Mills, Burlington, Janet Fraser, John Moores, Littlewoods, Index, Peter Craig*) in preference to other stores. **C&A** may be an alternative.

✔ Buy clothes made in **Bangladesh, Thailand, China** and **Sri Lanka** for preference.

✔ Buy clothes made from **natural** fibres, such as cotton or wool, preferably pesticide-free, if it becomes available.

Beyond the shopping trip:

Write to your usual retailer; mention that you are using this book to help you plan your shopping with a sustainable world in mind and ask them to reconsider their policies.

Write to **Littlewoods** and **C&A**, congratulating them on their initiative, and ask them how effective they find their policies are at addressing the issues and what evaluation they have done.

Write to retailers asking them to produce clothes made from pesticide-free cotton.

Textiles

Textiles, like clothing, are ideally suited to the development needs of poor countries, and indeed, the poorest communities within them. In a country such as India, where a great deal of our textiles are produced, three levels of industrialisation exist – virtually side by side – reflecting the different levels of development within the different communities.

The traditional practice of weaving on simple, portable looms made by the weavers themselves is still common. Productivity is low and so the cost of the cloth is high, but the method is appropriate to the poorest communities without electricity and without access to the capital which would enable them to buy equipment or large amounts of yarn. In such communities, the yarn may even be spun by hand, creating large numbers of jobs, though poorly paid.

A more common means of village-based production is hand-powered shuttle looms, still locally-made, but much more productive. These provide employment at village level, and allow cloth to be sold to the towns, or even exported. Each loom provides work for as many as five people, including those who wind the bobbins and help to set up the warp threads on the loom.

A further step on the road to industrialisation is the creation of textile factories, using large power looms and large workforces. Here productivity is much higher and wages correspondingly so. But the number of jobs available is lower, too; this is part of the all too familiar process of higher technology displacing manual labour.

As in the clothing industry, textiles for export are produced in any situation from small workshop to large factory. The variety of issues that arise from the trade reflects these various production systems: low wages, lack of worker representation, health and safety and child labour are all concerns relevant to the textile industry.

The major players

UK consumers spend some £1.5 billion each year on textiles and soft furnishings, and a slightly larger amount on floor coverings. The market is characterised by a very high level of imports; in some sectors, as much as 80% may come from other countries. The UK imports over £500 million worth of textile products from the third world each year (about 14% of imports overall). Three quarters of the UK's third world imports come from India (over £100 million worth), Pakistan, Hong Kong, China, South Korea, Taiwan and Indonesia. Many of these are imports used in the production of 'made in the UK' clothing.

Specialist shops such as *Habitat* (**Storehouse**), *Accord* and *Brentfords* (**Lonrho**), **Laura Ashley**, **Mackays**, and **Liberty** are the major stockists of textiles. The multiple department and variety stores, such as **Marks & Spencer**, **Littlewoods**, **John Lewis** and *BhS* (**Storehouse**) account for much of the remaining sales.

There are also two main manufacturers producing their own lines as well as making 'own brand' textiles for the retailers. **Coats Viyella**, now Europe's largest textile manufacturer, produces *Dorma*, *Vantona* and *Horrockses*, among others. At the time of writing, Coats Viyella had just taken over the other major textile company, Tootal. **Courtaulds Textiles** (the second largest manufacturer after Coats Viyella, and recently demerged from Courtaulds plc) makes, for example, *Christy's* and *Ashton's*, and manufactures own label garments for Marks & Spencer, BhS, Mothercare and Littlewoods. (M&S accounted for 25% of Courtaulds Textiles' turnover in 1989.)

The fabric of the third world

Textiles are almost as important a source of income for the third world as clothing. Altogether, the third world accounts for some £16 billion worth of cotton, textiles and related products and accounts for between a quarter and half of world trade in various textile products; a situation viewed with some alarm by manufacturers in the richer countries.

The Multifibre Arrangement (MFA), introduced in 1974 to limit clothing imports from the third world, also covered textile products, but imports have been held back for much longer due to the MFA's rather persistent predecessor, the Short Term Arrangement. Together they have succeeded in severely limiting the beneficial effects of the textiles industry on the development process of producer nations.

The textile industry has much in common with the clothing industry and, indeed, the two are closely associated. In countries such as Mauritius, the clothing industry came first, to diversify away from traditional industries that were yielding poor and unpredictable returns. Using at first imported cloth, the industry subsequently became 'vertically integrated' by the development of a textile facility. In other countries, such as India, the textile industry has grown from its indigenous village roots and the clothing industry has developed as a way of further processing the textile products, using their comparatively cheap labour. The issues of low wages, lack of worker representation and health and safety issues are as relevant here as in clothing.

India is a massively complex, highly fragile and volatile grouping of very diverse nations, religions and castes, with three quarters of its 820 million population living in half a million villages. There is a huge rural landless population and poverty is fuelled by a rigid caste system. With a GNP of just $300 India is one of the poorest of the third world countries supplying the UK with goods, but despite a serious inequality of income (the richest 10% earning as much as the poorest 60%), its HDI v GNP rating is good. Debt servicing eats up 25% of export income.

Pakistan has a similar GNP, but its heavy military

expenditure and political instability, together with the repression of unions, combine to limit social progress. Literacy, health care and life expectancy are relatively poor. In both these countries, a village-based textile industry is both socially and economically important.

Dark, satanic mills?

The bulk of textile imports (and, indeed, the fabrics used in the clothes we buy) are made in factories using large scale mechanised spinning machines and looms. The factories are typically noisy and dusty, due to the speed and concentration of the cotton processing machines. This gives rise to significant health problems; lung diseases are frequently reported.

The speed of the processes involved in the factory operations is also a major cause of concern because it gives rise to accidents. Pressure of work often means that people adjust or tend the machines while they are in operation and the loss of limbs is not uncommon (or properly compensated for in many cases). The very repetitive movements sustained over long working hours cause injury, too. One UK-owned factory in Brazil, for example, has normal working hours of 46¾ hours a week.

As is the case with other areas of industrial production, one of the key issues is the ability of the workforce to associate and to press collectively for better wages and conditions. Advances in technology should go hand in hand with better working conditions, but in countries where the position of unions is weak, because of controlling legislation or high unemployment, it does not always follow.

The large industrial weaving mills in the north of India, for example, are very much a product of the industrial revolution, with the dust, noise and potential for industrial injury that are often part of the package. However, since they have a large and stable workforce, they are also highly unionised. This has resulted in comparatively good wages and significant improvements in working conditions over the years.

Coats Viyella has a number of manufacturing facilities in 23 third world countries, mainly involved in thread, hand-knittings, and craft material manufacture. It states that health and safety information is handled locally in each country; the company does not keep records of labour turnover, nor has it any policy regarding unionisation. In its 1989 annual report, Coats Viyella stated that in its thread division, a number of projects are being developed in Eastern Europe, though it made no statement concerning the effect that might have on the company's sourcing in the third world. Coats Viyella has expanded recently in the third world, acquiring a leading sewing thread manufacturer in Morocco and enlarging its interests in Malaysia, India, Chile and Colombia. Considering the size of Coats Viyella, and the extent of its involvement in the third world, the lack of initiative indicated in working conditions and other social issues is unfortunate.

Neither **Courtaulds Textiles** nor **Lonrho**, the other two major textile companies, filled in the questionnaire (though Courtaulds did provide information for a previous publication), and there is little indication in their written material that either company has any policy or initiative addressing the social and environmental impact of their sourcing or operations in third world countries. In Lonrho's case especially this is particularly unfortunate given its very extensive involvement in so many third world countries. Courtaulds is undertaking a large campaign to address the problem of repetitive strain injury, though this does not seem to apply outside Europe.

For the retailers, it is once again a matter of checking their sources. Their role is to raise these issues with suppliers and apply pressure for improvements in working conditions, especially in the small scale suppliers of hand loom cloth and carpets.

In response to a recent campaign on working conditions in the clothing industry initiated by **Traidcraft**, **House of Fraser** stated that the buyers of oriental carpets supplied to the company visited production sites wherever possible to ensure that child labour is not used. There is, however, no other indication of policies addressing the social issues arising from the sourcing of the company's products in the third world.

Of the other retailers of textiles – **John Lewis, Marks & Spencer, Storehouse** (BhS and Habitat) and **Littlewoods**, only Littlewoods (as reported in the chapter on clothing) has set up a code of practice for its suppliers.

Although 'oriental' carpets form but a small proportion of the textile products to be found in our shops, there can be few stories that have shocked consumers more than that concerning the carpet children of India. During the 1980s, a horrifying picture began to emerge of the conditions under which carpets were being hand woven for export. Children, sold into slavery, were working for long hours in cramped workshops. Some were even tied to their looms and had to sleep in the workshop. Others, caught trying to escape, were beaten. The cramped and dimly-lit conditions were distorting growing bodies.

But, disturbing as this story was, it only scratched the surface. Child labour is very common in many poor countries; parents, unable to earn enough to support their family, are forced to make impossible choices for their children. Continuing education is often ruled out on cost grounds, anyway, and economically useful work within the family is often the only alternative. The most common form of child work is helping with the harvest or tending livestock. But, for the poorest, the promise of a well paid job away from home appears heaven sent.

Such work may indeed be a good option, with training provided and decent wages. But in the main, children working away from their families are merely a cheap and relatively compliant source of labour, in some cases replacing adults and compounding the very poverty that gives rise to child labour. Child slavery is the disturbing tip of the child labour iceberg, which in total must involve a huge proportion of children in the third world.

The hand loom v the power loom

In India the government has for many years assisted hand-loom weavers in setting up cooperatives to protect their interests. Individual weavers are very dependent on traders both for their raw material and for their income and a cooperative can shift the balance of power considerably in their favour. Large 'apex' cooperatives, each nominally controlled by a number of weavers' co-ops, can further assist with the production of yarn and the marketing of the finished cloth.

However, technology has now bridged the gap between the village-level hand loom and the large scale textile factory. Small scale power looms have made their appearance in villages and are now becoming the major producers. They are highly profitable, since labour costs in the villages are low, and power loom workers are not members of the weavers' co-ops. Some evidence suggests that power loom workers are actually paid less than hand-loom workers. At the same time, each power loom puts several hand-looms out of action.

It is a difficult situation, because clearly the role of hand-looms is diminishing, and without subsidies they could not compete. Alternative employment has to be created, since far fewer workers will be able to find jobs in the power loom sector. Faced with this dilemma, some agencies working with village co-ops are turning towards the formation of power loom cooperatives as part of the answer; at least power looms can retain some employment in the villages. The situation is paralleled in the UK, where employment in the textile industry has been in decline for some years.

As with other products, the impact of technology is closely tied in with companies' policies on long term involvement, technology transfer and local processing of raw material.

Coats Viyella sees its long standing involvement as being a key benefit to third world countries; third world subsidiaries are treated 'in the same way as other subsidiaries and associate companies'. Its policy is 'to promote and recruit on individual ability and achievement'; many nationals hold senior positions, and some third world nationals are now in senior positions in non third world countries, though no figures are available. The company continues to invest in modern technology and states that local employees are trained in its use, but there is no suggestion that such technology passes into local control and no information is given as to whether any of the technology introduced has affected the levels of employment at the factories.

Neither **Lonrho** nor **Courtaulds Textiles** indicated any policy relevant to this area.

Green cotton

There has been growing consumer concern about the bleaching of cotton; **Next** were the first national chain to market clothes made from 'green' cotton. The use of unbleached cotton avoids the harmful effects of chlorine-based bleaches and, in particular, the formation of dioxins. This is a positive step; companies are responding to consumer concern, but few clothes or textile products are yet affected, and the most destructive part of the production process is not addressed.

Cotton is one of the most environmentally damaging crops to grow, requiring very high levels of insecticide application to combat the many pests that regard it as food. Central America provides an unmatched example of the problem. The countries of the region have been assured plentiful supplies of pesticides from the USA, particularly those known collectively as the 'Dirty Dozen' (including Aldrin and 2,4,5-T). Despite the ban on these in developed nations, exports have continued.

Normally, as pest populations increase so do predators and, given a complex environment, a broad balance can be achieved. However, in modern monocultures, in which only one crop is grown over large areas year after year, the balance is destroyed. Pests can multiply very rapidly when food is so easily available and populations reach epidemic proportions before the predators begin to have an impact. They in turn suffer a population explosion and the pest population crashes, causing a disaster for the predator.

The farmers observe regular outbreaks of pests which wipe out the crops, and seek to control these with pesticides. Heavy and continuous use of pesticides can be as addictive as a drug; predators disappear, through the combined effect of the loss of pests and the pesticide, leaving chemicals as the only form of control. The spread of pests resistant to common pesticides is the next turn of the screw. Costs rise and crop yields fall over several years as this effect takes hold.

The effects on humans are a particular cause for concern. Farmers may be driven into debt by the increasing reliance on pesticides, but it is the field workers who are most at risk. Safety precautions are not observed, safety instructions are frequently in a foreign language, or the operator is illiterate and lacks training. The sale of dangerous pesticides is frequently uncontrolled; the chemicals being sold privately in small quantities and in different packaging, so the instructions are missing. Protective gear is frequently unavailable, ineffective, or unwearable in the heat and humidity.

In Central America in particular, one of the most worrying aspects is the large scale aerial spraying of dangerous chemicals. Spray drift renders large areas of land unsuitable for growing food, due to the persistent nature of some of the pesticides, as well as the loss of natural predators. The amount of land devoted to cotton in Guatemala increased by a staggering 2000% between 1956 and 1980. It has one of the highest levels of pesticide use – up to 40 applications a year – and there were 1000 *reported* poisonings annually during the 1980s. There is also the suspicion, on the part of peasant organisations, that these spraying operations are a deliberate attempt to drive squatters off the land.

The answer, though it takes a good deal of research and effort, is Integrated Pest Management (IPM). It recognises that, with current economic and trading constraints at least, organic farming is not an option for many individual farmers, but that many other methods of pest control can be used, leaving chemicals as a last resort. In Nicaragua IPM has been attempted to control the boll weevil, a major cotton pest. All farmers in one area cut the cotton stems after harvest and plough them in on the same dates, so the pests have little chance to find alternative accommodation. Small areas in each field are left untouched so the homeless weevils make their way there and can then be sprayed effectively. The results so far show yields up by 15% while pesticide use is down by a third.

It is hoped that, though it is no simple matter, green cotton will begin to address these rather more pressing issues. Textile manufacturers and retailers should be pushing for the availability of cotton grown without the excessive use of pesticides.

CONSUMER CHOICES

The textile industry is less concentrated than the clothing business, so it is more difficult to pinpoint where the major power lies. The major textile manufacturers have overseas operations, and can therefore have some influence on working conditions in the textile mills and in any smaller scale factories to which they may subcontract. They also have a more direct link with the source of the cotton and can keep an eye on the issues of health and safety, the formation of independent unions, and the environment.

Textiles is an important area of trade for the developing countries, and there is every reason to continue to support it. In particular, since the bulk of our cotton comes from the third world, the producer countries such as Pakistan and Egypt should increasingly be able to add value to it through processing. The textiles industry offers one of the best hopes for the producing nations to develop an industrial base.

For India and Pakistan, hand-loom cotton represents a means of retaining employment in the villages, based as it is on the traditional weaving industry. In terms of jobs generated per pound spent, this industry is good value for money, so hand-loom cotton makes a good buy. Alternative trading organisations, such as **Traidcraft**, **Oxfam Trading** and many local 'third world shops', offer genuine hand-loom cotton fabrics, household textiles and garments made by community based groups and cooperatives; look out for them.

When considering oriental carpets, remember the issue of child labour, though it is common in other sectors too. The Anti Slavery Society is working with UK importers to develop a labelling scheme to identify carpets made without child labour; a good initiative to look out for, should it bear fruit.

✔ BEST BUY, wherever practically possible, from 'alternative' suppliers such as **Traidcraft** and **Oxfam Trading**.

✔ Buy third world textiles and hand-loom cotton ˙ where it is available; it is a vital industry.

✔ Of the major retailers, choose **Littlewoods**, whose Code of Practice is a welcome recognition of responsibility.

Beyond the shopping trip:

Write to manufacturers, tell them you have seen their company mentioned in this book, ask them what policies they are working on which address the issues outlined in this chapter.

Write to Littlewoods and congratulate them on their code of practice and ask them how effective it is proving to be. Ask them how they are monitoring the success of the policy.

Write to the other retailers of textiles and ask them if they are considering a similar code of practice.

Footwear

The issues that arise from the footwear trade are not dissimilar to those of the clothing industry – several countries depend heavily on the business, and as part of the process of industrialisation it is primarily a trade of low wage countries. As wages improve, there is likely to be a gradual shift away from footwear into higher technology industries.

Once again the major areas for concern are the wages, working conditions and health and safety of the workers. Evidence suggests that the export trade offers better conditions than the average for the footwear industry as a whole. This is because exporting firms are larger, so tend to be more unionised and are more accountable to whatever labour standards hold in any country (though these in themselves are cause for concern in many cases).

Another issue involves the part played by fashion in footwear design and marketing. The recent trend towards the highly expensive sport shoe – surely one of the defining clothing items of the fashion and fitness fixated '80s – is of concern when looked at in the context of the lifestyles of the people making it. The bulk of the price consumers pay goes towards the development and marketing of the latest shoe, not its manufacture.

Walking the streets

In the UK we spend nearly £3.5 billion a year on shoes, half of which is spent at one of the big retailers. **Sears** (British Shoe Corporation) is the biggest by far, taking nearly a quarter of all sales through its chains of shoe shops such as *Dolcis*, *Saxone*, *Manfield*, *Cable & Co.*, *Shoe City* and *Freeman Hardy & Willis*. The next biggest is **C&J Clark**, retailing shoes under the names *Clarks*, *Lord & Farmer*, *Ravel* and *K Shoes*. Including **Marks & Spencer**, **Storehouse**, *Barratts* **(Stylo)**, **Olivers/** *Timpson*, **Stead and Simpson** and *Lennards*, the top retailers take half the market.

In the sports shoe market, the older firms – **Adidas**, and its rival, **Puma** – have been losing out to the more fashionable **Nike** and **Reebok** from the US and **Hi-Tec** from the UK. More recently, the almost entirely fashion oriented **LA Gear** has made an entry. Nike have now achieved about 17% of the world market for sports shoes, leaving Adidas with a little less, followed by Reebok. LA Gear and Puma trail with less than 5%. The latest UK figures suggest Reebok, Nike and Hi-Tec now take 45% of the market here, a market, however, that is changing fast.

The biggest retailers are also manufacturers – many brands are really own brands or surrogate brands – though Sears actually imports most of its range from subcontractors and sources some of its footwear and shoe components in Brazil and the Far East. About a third of the UK's imports – which are growing every year – come from the third world (Italy is a big supplier of the rest) but a good proportion of the shoes we buy from within the EC will come originally from the third world, too; the German firms Adidas and Puma both source much of their range in Asia.

The global market

The major third world countries we buy from are Taiwan, South Korea and Brazil, who each supply us with over £60 million worth, and depend on the shoe trade to a surprising extent. It accounts for over 7% of Taiwan's export earnings and, at over $2.6 billion, footwear is its second biggest export after clothing. Taiwan's industry accounts for a massive 40% of the third world's footwear exports, and almost 17% of the entire world trade! Adidas, Clarks, Reebok, Puma, Nike and Hi-Tec all source in Taiwan. In the case of Brazil, footwear is the biggest manufactured export after motor vehicles. Other significant countries we buy from are India, Thailand, Hong Kong and Indonesia.

The bulk of our shoes are branded by the big retailers and manufacturers, and made in the third world to specific contracts and designs from the EC or the US. This means that the third world manufacturers are effectively subcontractors, having little room to manoeuvre and little to offer but the ability to produce quickly and cheaply to the required standard. While we import all kinds of shoes (and parts for shoes assembled here), the big growth area is sports shoes; over half our imported sports shoes come directly from the third world, in addition to those coming via Europe.

One of the reasons for the high level of third world imports is that shoe making is still very much a manual job. Whilst there are mechanical processes involved in the production of rubber and plastic soles, for example, the assembly operation still has to be guided by hand. The addition of laces and fashionable accessories is a job for humans too. Low labour costs give the third world countries an advantage.

Computer technology has eroded this advantage in the clothing industry, but is more difficult in shoe manufacture since the nature of the materials (such as leather) is less uniform and the assembly work more complex.

Like the clothing industry, footwear represents a good first step on the road to industrial development. It allows poor countries to use their advantages to break into world trade and, in theory at least, the income and improved skills allow them to move into higher paid, less labour intensive work. In view of the importance of the footwear industry to the third world (at $6.5 billion, it ranks only behind clothing and electrical and telecommunications equipment as a manufactured export), it is surprising how little is written about it. However, it is possible to piece together a picture of the business. It seems rather familiar.

Working conditions

In 1989 we imported some £60 million worth of leather shoes from Brazil (from whom we also buy tobacco, wood, electrical goods, preserved fruit and orange juice). As is all too often the situation in Brazil, working conditions are poor, since the military governments of the '80s indulged in a policy of union repression. When it comes to inequalities of wealth, Brazil is exceptionally bad, even in third world terms. The richest 10% of the population earn as much as the poorest 80%, while the poorest 40% earn just 7% of the total income. Three quarters of Brazil's 144 million people live in towns and with a GNP of $2,020 it is one of the wealthiest of the third world countries supplying the UK with goods.

Brazil is endowed with plentiful natural resources, has a growing and diversified economy – the top six exports, including coffee, account for just 36% of export earnings – and is a leading producer and exporter of several commodities. Despite this, large numbers of Brazilians live in grinding poverty – there is a high level of infant mortality, widespread malnutrition and low levels of literacy and health care. There are sharp regional differences too, the north eastern part of Brazil being the poorest. The drought of 1990 has led to real threats of starvation.

Inflation has hit Brazil badly, and during 1990 the government took action to curb it by liberalising imports, privatising state industries, freezing wages and prices, and at one stage froze individual and business withdrawals from banks and investment accounts.

There are particular concerns, voiced by organisations such as the Anti-Slavery Society, about the high level of child exploitation in Brazil's footwear industry – although in the majority of cases this is an economic necessity for poor families; without the income of children, many families would go under altogether.

A major problem specific to shoe making is the nature of the glues used to stick the uppers and shoe together. These are dangerous and, since adequate ventilation is a low priority and working hours long, exposure of children and adults is too high. Also, accidents occur due to the pressure of high speed work. They include the loss of fingers or hands in the cutting machinery and hand injuries caused by stitching machines. While some accidents are inevitable, the rate at which they occur is a cause for concern, as is the compensation paid, when it is paid at all.

There are homeworkers in the footwear industry too, working on shoe assembly for lower wages than the factory workers. In recent years, there has been union activity among both factory workers and homeworkers, though the leaders face harassment and violence. The most active unions, however, are in the rural areas.

The footwear industry in the Philippines consists of some 2000 firms, most of which are very small (fewer than 20 workers) and are engaged in the production of leather shoes, mainly for the local market.

In contrast with these small factories, shoes made using plastic or artificial rubber tend to be made at larger sites. The capital needed for the equipment to produce the compounds and mould the soles, for example, is too large for small family firms. The Philippines' export business to the UK is mainly in sports shoes; for example, one locally owned firm (one of the largest companies in the Philippines) has devoted entire factories to the production of sports shoes for **Adidas**.

The Philippines is still a poor country (its GNP is $590), despite its aspirations to become another Asian Tiger, and its high HDI v GNP rating belies severe inequalities in the country, the income distribution being similar to that in Brazil.

By comparison with other sectors of industry, working conditions in footwear are generally not bad. The existence of unions often ensures provision for sick leave, maternity leave and collective bargaining rights. However, 'yellow' unions abound, their leaders effectively in the pockets of the management, and workers do not join for fear that the union will benefit only the employers (or the union leaders). Workers often complain that, having been set production targets, these are raised each time they are met. Not only does this contribute to stress-related illness, but it denies the workers the promised bonuses. Forced overtime, especially for workers who fail to meet production targets, is reported too.

Wages and relocation

The official minimum wage in the Philippines is so low that several members of a family must work in order to earn the amount recommended as a minimum family income. Wages in the footwear industry are generally well below this, and below the general labouring rates officially notified to the International Labour Organisation.

By contrast, the industry in Taiwan has been 'suffering' from high wages in recent years – a cost of economic development. As with other sectors of industry in Taiwan, firms have been closing down to relocate in cheaper countries such as China. Late in 1989, two factories in one of the Taiwanese Free Trade Zones closed down, leaving the workers without their due pay, compensation or insurance that should have been paid.

To recoup the wages owed and raise awareness of their plight, the workers (mainly women) removed all the remaining shoes from the factories and started selling them on the streets. This example illustrates a few of the difficulties faced by workers in Taiwan and South Korea as the countries develop economically.

With their history of antagonism towards unions, low wages, support for home based industries and the inducements offered to foreign firms to set up, these nations have rapidly expanded production during the last few decades. However, rising living standards and an increasingly vocal population have led to problems; wages are now well above other Asian countries, unions are beginning to form, and the advantages the countries relied on are diminishing – caught between the protectionist North and the cheap labour South.

Can these nations maintain their position, through increased use of modern technology, or will the growth stop? Relocation is a major problem in this area and firms that relocate secretly, taking the inducements offered in the '70s and '80s and disappearing without paying compensation, are the worst.

A long term relationship with a few suppliers can in the long run be beneficial to both retailer and supplier, resulting in better quality products for one and increasing skills and technology transfer for the other. However, companies cannot be expected to ignore the advantages that cheaper labour offers. A large part of the responsibility for controlling relocation lies with the governments of the third world like Brazil and the Philippines that run their economies rather like businesses.

The companies' role

The basic area in which the major firms do bear some responsibility is over general working conditions. In view of the relationship between the major brand holders and the third world companies that actually make their products for them, it is reasonable to expect them to take working conditions into account when they choose a subcontractor.

If the only things they are concerned about are the quality, the price and the delivery, then it is inevitable, given the weak position of the subcontractors and their workers, that competition will produce the kind of poor conditions already mentioned. We should expect companies to be aware of the working conditions – the existence of free unions; the figures for accidents at work; the wages and so forth. If they are not, nobody else is in a position to ensure that conditions are acceptable by any standards.

None of the companies responded to our questionnaire, and there is no indication that they have begun to take on board the social issues arising from their trade with the third world.

Adidas did send published material and comments. The company, set up by Adi Dassler in 1948, remained as a German family firm until 1990, when it was sold to a French company, Bernard Tapie Finance. Adidas sells and licenses its brand name products (including *Le Coq Sportif*) in 160 countries. Intense competition from other manufacturers has forced Adidas to cut in-house production in favour of cheaper, mainly Asian suppliers. The company states that it transfers production processes developed in Europe to its factories in Asia, which meet all legal requirements for working conditions.

By 1990, the proportion of footwear produced in Germany was reduced to around 17%. Adidas has subsidiaries in Brazil, Mexico, Morocco, Colombia, Hong Kong and South Africa, and licenses production in a number of other countries including Malaysia, Indonesia, China, Chile and Argentina. It has recently increased its production facilities in North Africa. Bernard Tapie is a socialist member of parliament; it is too early to say whether his principles will influence the company's sourcing policies.

C&J Clark is a privately owned company, set up by a Quaker family in 1825, and has gained a reputation as the sensible face of footwear. It is a major international manufacturer with 32 factories and 1500 directly owned retail outlets worldwide. It has a sizeable market in North America and Australia. Clarks has two subsidiaries in South Africa, both of which it states are non-trading.

As a Quaker company, it developed a reputation for local benevolence, providing housing for its workers for instance in the town in which it was originally established. In respect of responsibilities to suppliers in the third world however, Clark's appears not to have a policy. Shoe components are sourced in Thailand and Taiwan, with India growing rapidly as a source of shoe uppers, emphasising the global nature of its production line.

Though a relative newcomer, **Hi-Tec** is now the UK market leader in sports footwear. The bulk of Hi-Tec's shoes are made in the Far East, primarily Taiwan and South Korea. Plans to move into China had to be shelved after the Tiananmen Square massacre, but it is not clear for how long.

Nike has grown so rapidly that it has overtaken older brands such as Adidas to become the world's market leader. This American company prides itself on its diverse production base, sourcing its shoes in South Korea, Thailand, Indonesia, China, Mexico, Malaysia and Argentina, as well as Italy and the USA – from around 50 factories. It also rates as important its 'on-site production specialists' who oversee the manufacturing process. This concern to keep an eye on things is potentially a good move, since it gives the company access to the kind of information needed to develop policy on the social issues arising from the third world sourcing of footwear. However, while the annual report mentions the need for the company to maintain long term relationships with retail customers, there is no equivalent sentiment regarding the suppliers.

Puma still operates in the same German town as Adidas, though it is owned now by Aritmos of Sweden. Like Adidas, Puma has shifted the production of its sports footwear increasingly to the third world, in order to compete with the newer entrants to the market. Puma has only a small share of the world market, though it has a significant share in the UK market. Puma's shoes are made in South Korea, Taiwan and increasingly in the Philippines and Indonesia, where labour costs are substantially lower. The company has also opened a joint venture in Guandong Province of China.

The US company, **Reebok**, which brought the old 'pump' into the '90s with the £130 inflatable sports shoe *The Pump*, is treading the thin line between fashion and serious sport. It has begun to rival Adidas in the world market, though is not as big as its US rival, Nike. Reebok until recently subcontracted 80% of its shoes to manufacturers in South Korea, though is diversifying to give a bigger share to Taiwan and China. The company itself does very little manufacturing; its role is in marketing and design. Rapidly changing fashion and sourcing decisions have clear implications for the manufacturers.

Though not a familiar name with shoppers, **Sears** has over 4000 retail outlets throughout Europe and the USA, primarily in footwear and clothing. (The US company, Sears, is no relation.) In the UK it has over 2000 outlets and also owns the Millets and Olympus leisure chains. Though the company markets its own brands of footwear and clothing to a large extent, the manufacturing is all done by subcontractors, including many in developing countries. Sears sources footwear and shoe components from Brazil and the Far East and clothing from many developing countries, though it is reported as trying to source nearer to home.

CONSUMER CHOICES

One of the key issues is the general lack of awareness of companies that are very much in the consumer market. They are all, but particularly the sports shoe companies, part of a fashion industry and subject to changing consumer demand. As such, consumers are already influencing their sourcing decisions, but not very positively. A major role for consumer pressure is to put the issues explored here onto the companies' agenda.

In view of the companies' overall lack of response to the issues, we cannot recommend a best buy. It is clear that all the companies approached need to be much more aware of their role in influencing working conditions in suppliers' factories.

Since there is grave concern about the footwear industry and the general position of workers in Brazil, for example, consumers may well conclude that their money is better spent in South Korea or Taiwan. Brazil's HDI v GNP rating is very low; its wealth is very poorly distributed, and income clearly does not 'trickle down' to where it is needed.

While buying UK manufactured shoes may seem like a reasonable alternative, it is hardly the answer. The UK industry uses shoe components from the third world; like the clothing industry, it is a global production line. For the third world, to manufacture a complete shoe is more valuable than merely to make the bits.

✔ Consider the value of high fashion, high technology footwear, both to you and to the third world communities that supply the labour. There are often better ways to spend the money.

✔ On the basis of development value for money, it is difficult to see Brazilian shoes as a good deal; better to go for the Asian suppliers.

Beyond the shopping trip:

Write to footwear manufacturers; ask them what they can do to ensure good working conditions in the third world factories that supply them.

Write particularly to Nike, suggesting that they give their on site production specialists the job of monitoring and reporting on working conditions.

A letter to the Brazilian Embassy expressing concern about the continuing – and some would say increasing – disparities of wealth might increase the government's awareness of international concern.

Electronics

Electronics is one of the more difficult areas for consumers; on the one hand, it is an important industry for several third world countries, a second step up from clothing in the ladder of economic development. Conditions are often quite poor for the people who work in the industry, most of whom are women, although it does provide a job which is often preferable to alternatives where they exist at all.

On the other hand, it is an industry based on over-consumption. Built into electronics goods of all kinds is the 'need' to upgrade as soon as the next generation with new knobs and flashing lights has been launched. In the UK we now spend over three times as much on household electronics goods as we did in the mid-'70s. If the inventiveness and effort that went into CDs or microwaves was devoted instead to the real needs of the world, the argument runs, where might we be?

Technological advances in electronics goods do little to benefit the people who make them. Indeed many advances reduce the need for labour and put third world countries out of the running as manufacturing bases. The major purposes of such advances are to reduce costs or to encourage product replacement in a saturated market; this at least ensures a growing demand for the product, and hence continued employment.

The UK market

In the UK we import items such as televisions, videos, audio systems and other domestic electronics goods from a large number of countries. The most important in the third world are South Korea, Singapore, Hong Kong, Thailand, Malaysia, Brazil and the Philippines.

Altogether, the third world accounts for around 20% of the household electronics available in our shops – that is over £800 million in retail sales a year. Taking the EC as a whole, over half of imported radios are from the third world, along with a quarter of the TVs and just over a tenth of audio equipment. In general terms however, the EC imports a little less than one half of its consumer electronics goods, the rest being supplied by factories within the Community.

The UK market is dominated by familiar names; *Ferguson* (**Thomson**) is brand leader in televisions and in videos, with **Philips**, **Hitachi**, **Toshiba**, *Panasonic* and *JVC* (**Matsushita**), **Sony** and **Amstrad** all having significant shares. The audio market is led by **Philips** in the music centre business, followed by **Sony**, **Sanyo**, **Sharp** and **Matsushita** with the component business split between **Matsushita** (*Panasonic*, *JVC* and *Technics*), **Toshiba**, **Sharp**, **Sanyo**, **Sony** (and the related **Aiwa**), **Pioneer** and **Hitachi**.

In addition to these companies, the major retailers also market 'own brand' products. For the purposes of this book, retailers with own brand products are treated as manufacturers, since they bear the same responsibilities as any manufacturer subcontracting the job elsewhere. About a quarter of the total market is accounted for by retailers' brands, of which **Dixons**' (including *Curry's*) *Matsui*, *Logik* and *Saisho* are the most commonly available. The Dixons Group now has over 900 shops.

All these companies are involved in the international production system, with manufacturing plants in the third world. Very few brands, however, are owned by third world companies, the main exceptions to this being some South Korean companies, such as **Samsung**, that manufacture internationally, including in the UK.

Global electronics

For many countries of the third world, the electronics industry is indeed a step into the world of high tech manufacturing. **Sharp** has three factories in Malaysia that between them contribute 1.4% of the country's total GNP. **Philips** is emerging as one of China's largest foreign investors, planning to put US$ 200 million into nine manufacturing and assembly joint ventures by 1992.

To the third world nations exporting electronics goods, the industry is vital; for the last 20 years, domestic electrical equipment has been the fastest growing export from the third world as a whole, from a mere $35 million in 1970 to over $2 billion in 1986, accounting for 20% of world trade in these products. Hong Kong now earns over $600 million from its exports of domestic electrical equipment, a little more than Taiwan. South Korea earns over $400 million and Singapore $200 million. Malaysia and the Philippines are more recent entrants into the market, taking advantage of the lower labour costs they can offer.

As a high technology industry, electronics requires enormous capital investment. Research and development done in Japan, Europe and the US gives these countries a lead in the production of electronics equipment. The bulk of the market is also in the richer countries. While much of the industry grows in the Free Trade Zones (FTZs) that third world countries have developed to attract the necessary investment, the industry itself is sometimes treated as a FTZ in its own right. In Malaysia, for example, as a 'pioneer industry' it has many of the perks one associates with the Zones, no matter where the factory is sited.

Most of the component parts you find in your TV or video are manufactured in the industrialised countries but assembled in the low wage countries. Such labour intensive work is more profitably done where labour is cheapest, and so Japanese, European and US manufacturers began in the early 1960s to shift production to the newly industrialising countries (NICs) of South Korea, Taiwan, Hong Kong and Singapore whose policies of export-led growth have encouraged TNC investment. South Korea, one of the world's most dynamic countries, is considered by many as a model for other countries struggling to industrialise. It has developed its own indigenous industry in just three decades, with much encouragement from the government. Exports of consumer electronics grew by a startling 50% a year during the 1970s and it is now seeking to acquire its own research and development facilities. South Korea's population is largely urbanised, with only 31% living in rural areas. A radical land reform programme, together with successful industrial growth, has created a comparatively good distribution of income, the richest 10% earning as much as the poorest 40%. There is good access to health, education and clean water, despite low government spending, though there is a pronounced urban bias.

As the industry grew during the 1970s and '80s, a number of changes began to take place. Firstly, imports from Japanese companies began to eat into the market share of European companies, so European governments placed restrictions on imports to protect the home industries. This in turn led Japanese firms to open assembly plants in the EC countries to avoid such restrictions. (At the same time, of course, European companies are moving manufacturing to the third world, to save costs!)

The success of the NICs' export industries had the effect of pushing up wages, though more due to a shortage of labour than to effective union organisation. The growth in production in those countries began to falter as companies shifted production to a second rank of countries – Malaysia, the Philippines and China – where labour costs were lower. South Korea's growth rate for instance, which was 20% a year during the mid 1980s, declined to just 6% in 1989. Consumer electronics exports – the backbone of the industry, actually fell. This is not due solely to increased wage costs, but to severe global competition, adverse exchange rates and the protectionist policies of the major importing countries. The NICs are having to concentrate on moving up the technology ladder in order to compete.

However, other companies, taking a longer term view,

invest in low wage countries, not just to take advantage of lower costs. As labour costs rise, they stay put, to make inroads into the growing local market for their products.

South Korean firms have followed the Japanese companies in the face of heavily disguised protectionism and have opened factories within the European Community. **Samsung** has a factory in the UK producing video recorders and microwave ovens. Since imported Korean videos, televisions and CDs are cheaper than equivalent EC made machines, the Korean manufacturers were accused of dumping: selling below 'real costs' in order to carve out a market share. Duties of up to 33% have been levied on such imports, costing EC consumers nearly £280 million a year on these products alone, according to National Consumer Council estimates. It is also clear that in many cases, it is too easy to assert that 'dumping' has occurred, when in fact the price merely reflects a genuine lower cost of production.

This is one of many examples we find throughout the book, where attempts by third world countries to develop markets for the products of their fledgling industries are thwarted by the protectionist policies of the rich nations and economic blocs.

A number of electronics companies have also moved into Mexico, taking advantage of the low wage, non-unionised factories on the northern border close to the US market. **Matsushita, Sony, Hitachi**, and many other foreign companies have established these operations, known as *maquiladoras*. They are exempt from Mexican legislation on control and ownership (foreign companies can have 100% control) and are also exempt from the usual requirements in Mexico, to source a proportion of components locally. While wages in the *maquiladoras* are generally higher than the average in Mexico, they are still amongst the lowest in the world.

The net effect of all these factors is that we now have companies from the industrialised countries, who shifted production to the NICs, shifting in turn to poorer countries, to be joined by South Korean companies performing the same trick. And we have Japanese and South Korean companies setting up shop in Europe in order to cope with the fear of an emerging Fortress Europe. Truly a global production line!

How do we as global consumers keep up to date with the issues arising from this industry in which the global situation is changing rapidly – a reflection on the rapidly changing technologies employed? There are a number of universal themes and issues arising from the trade that give cause for concern among consumers.

Up the union! (as long as it keeps quiet)

Trade unionism is the one issue that is central to the electronics industry in the third world, and an important factor in discriminating between companies. With low pay, poor health and safety records, long working hours and generally harsh conditions, one would expect to find a high degree of labour organisation in factories owned by TNCs.

But even where a TNC is willing to allow independent unions, local conditions in the host country may render union formation quite ineffective. TNCs do have the power to seek to improve conditions by pushing to the limits and making representations to host governments to legislate for the development of independent unions. Some companies have recognised, from their experience in developed countries, that the existence of genuine union representation can, in the long term, be a stabilising factor, while others refuse to recognise unions even when officially registered with the government.

Hitachi for instance, despite a comparatively good record on labour relations in the UK, told its workers in Malaysia in 1988 that they would receive bonuses if they sent petitions to the labour minister opposing a proposal to allow the electronics industry to unionise.

NICs have been able to build up their industry by offering their unique mixture of qualities, amongst which low wages and a compliant labour force are the most significant. The electronics industry is seen as being so crucial to development that it has to be 'protected' against the 'unreasonable demands' of unions, especially in its formative years.

For example, Malaysia specifically prevented union organisation in the electronics industry, despite the existence of independent unionisation in the related electrical industry. Later, the initial phase of protection of the 'pioneer industry' was stretched from three years to an indefinite period; a change not unrelated to the tendency for electronics TNCs to relocate to cheaper countries; Malaysia was becoming priced out of the market.

This can give rise to an unholy alliance between the government and TNCs that would be laughable if it were not so destructive of human life and potential. The name of any union in Malaysia (and several other countries) has to be registered and has to include the name of the factory. In order to prevent union formation, companies can and do change the name while the registrar of unions takes time to register the name. Registering a new name requires all the rigmarole of a secret ballot, which further holds up the proceedings while the company plans its next move. An example of a related problem is given by **Philips**. In 1988, its Hong Kong subsidiary changed its name to include reference to new operations in China, with the result that, under Hong Kong law, the 'new' company did not have to honour long service severance pay arrangements. However, after long negotiations, the length of service in the old company was recognised.

By 1988, Malaysia had lifted a ban on unionisation in the electronics industry, though only in-house unions were permitted, and unions still only represent about 10% of the total Malaysian workforce. This was due in large measure to international union solidarity, with US trade unions putting pressure on the US government to threaten sanctions against the industry unless such freedoms were accorded. While no doubt unhealthy protectionist feelings in the US contributed to such action, it is nonetheless an example of international action to improve the lot of third world workers. Ironically American electronics companies with subsidiaries in Malaysia influenced the Malaysian government's decision to renege on the lifting of the ban on unions after only three weeks.

In-house unions are a widespread feature of the global electronics industry. South Korea, after a history of union repression, has instituted a system of in-house unions. The law demands that unions may only represent the workers at one plant, and only one union is allowed at each place of work, making industry-wide organising impossible. Disputes are dealt with by committees representing employer, workers and government, but the government in reality nominates all the representatives. Strikes have to be approved by the government. National unions, such as exist, are not allowed to intervene as 'outsiders' in disputes between management and labour. While companies, and TNCs in particular, can control investment between plants and even countries, unions can only operate at the single plant level, making them effectively powerless. In Singapore, the trade union movement is headed by a government minister!

Matsushita has no policy on unionisation at its subsidiaries, but states that it always adopts each country's customs. It also inspects the factories of subcontractors to ensure labour standards are equivalent to its own. The level of unionisation in different operations varies according to host country, and even from plant to plant within a country. Whereas in Japan all workers are unionised, in Singapore, in 1988, only 3 of the 7 plants had any level of unionisation. In Indonesia, 100% of the 3000-strong workforce were unionised during that period, while in Colombia none were.

Similarly **Sony** has no policy on independent unions but states that it does not inhibit free union organisation within its operations. The company was unable to comment on the labour standards of subcontractors.

Toshiba states that the company is 'scrupulous in its observation of local laws, including those supporting freedom of association [and] unionisation'.

Hitachi says little about its employment policies and practices and did not offer any information on its policy on trade unions. In June 1990, an industrial dispute took place at the Hitachi television plant in Malaysia. The company, supported by a government ruling to accept only in-house unions in the electronics sector, rejected the formation of a national union. Staff went on strike, to secure the reinstatement of eight colleagues who had been dismissed. The strike resulted in the majority of workers returning to work (after having to apologise for the strike) but without any changes to their terms of employment and without membership of a national union.

Casio, Thomson, Sharp and **Dixons** have given us no indication that they have policies on unionisation or on monitoring working conditions in their factories or those of their suppliers.

While some companies (**Sony** for instance) do not appear to inhibit the formation of unions, we have no evidence that any of the companies in the survey positively promote them. To abide by local laws (**Toshiba** and **Matsushita**) could be considered a good policy if local laws favoured the development of independent unions. This is clearly not the case in the countries where these companies have many of their third world subsidiaries.

In-house unions are also open to domination by management. Since only one union is allowed in each plant, it is expedient sometimes for the management to get in first and start one up for the workers. Alternatively, the leadership of an existing union can be offered inducements and privileges to cooperate with management. Either way, such a union is neither representative of the workforce, nor working for their benefit. Such unions are known as 'yellow' unions and are endemic in Brazil, the Philippines and South Korea in particular.

If anything can be said in favour of in-house unions, it is that from the women's perspective, they can be less hierarchical than cross-industry unions, and may offer women a greater opportunity to become actively involved.

In January 1990, the Council of Korean Trade Unions, Chunnohyop, later known as the Korea Trade Union Congress, was established and then banned. Its president and 500 activists were imprisoned. The government is keen to protect the industry and will go to enormous and frequently violent lengths to squash industrial disputes, even to the extent of providing police to break up demonstrations and meetings. The recent riots, part of the pro-democracy movement, may indicate a long term shift in the balance of power. Management is also able to prevent union formation by simply transferring production away from South Korea to Malaysia and closing the factory down, without necessarily compensating workers.

In South Korea, the official union body, the FKTU, is too closely identified with the government and its repressive legislation against unions for most workers to wish their union to join, but the law requires it, before recognition will be granted.

Samsung was the last of the conglomerates to succumb to pressure for unionisation, preferring to rely on above average wages and an open door policy on complaints from staff. Even the FKTU claimed in 1988 that workers trying to organise unions were being sacked or transferred, and that yellow unions were being started by the management. It is not known whether any independent unions are organised at Samsung's electrical factories.

In the Philippines, two rival bodies exist: Kilusang Mayo Uno (KMU) is regarded as politically radical, and its leaders are attacked, imprisoned or killed by government backed paramilitary groups, while the Trade Union Congress of the Philippines (TUCP) is seen as a tool of government.

In the interests of balance, it should be pointed out that the formation of unions is not necessarily a panacea; for one thing, in the global market, a country can be 'priced out' if wages rise. That's not to say wages shouldn't rise, but in the absence of controls on relocation of TNCs, it is a genuine dilemma for governments.

Danger, women at work

In South Korea, around 80% of employees in the electronics industry are young women – not an untypical proportion in other countries either. Much of the work they do involves labour intensive, tedious and repetitive tasks such as the assembly of chip-based circuits, which requires superhuman powers of concentration, good eyesight and manual dexterity. One of the big cultural shifts has been the increasing work opportunities for women provided by the growing industries of electronics and clothing.

In Thailand, for example, the industrial workforce as a whole changed from being 43% female to 52% between 1970 and 1976, due to the growth of electronics and clothing within the economy. The conventional wisdom is that young Asian women are 'naturally endowed' for the work: patient, compliant, hard working, dextrous and with small hands. But there are other considerations at least as important.

In South Korea, a typical worker is on duty for over 50 hours in an average week. While in some factories hours have become shorter recently, they are still far longer than typical factory hours in the UK. This to a large extent accounts for the high productivity levels achieved. Sometimes workers stay all night to finish urgent orders. In the all out push for greater productivity, corners are cut, too. South Korea has an unenviable record for industrial accidents; its factories are widely held to be the most dangerous in the world.

In the absence of union representation, there are a range of health hazards associated with assembly work in the electronics industry. Solvents, such as trichloroethane used to clean up the components, can be carcinogenic and can also cause severe headaches; workers are frequently expected to operate without masks for protection, or given dust masks totally ineffective against fumes. Eyestrain is very common among people working for hours each day soldering hair-fine wires to the chips. In one study in Malaysia, 44% of the workers complained of this problem.

This fine detailed work requires 20/20 vision, of course, which leads to one of the major problems for workers in the industry. The management requires a young workforce, with a high labour turnover in order to minimise the costs of health problems. This is why the vast majority of electronics workers are 16 to 24 years old and female; part of a coherent strategy of cost minimisation on the part of the manufacturing companies.

None of the electronics companies surveyed for this book stated that they had policies to ensure that health and safety standards were in force. **Matsushita**'s reply was fairly typical of the hands-off approach: 'We always comply with local government health and safety regulations.' **Sony** states that standards also conform to the standard of factories in the home country (Japan). **Toshiba** states that local health and safety requirements are normally exceeded and the company provides health care and welfare facilities.

Complying with local laws is fine if local laws are effective. All too often they are not. We have not been given any indication of *how* these companies monitor safety and health in their own factories or those of their suppliers.

Cultural factors, in many countries, create the tendency for young women to be expected to be less demanding than their older or male counterparts. An explicit strategy is evident to encourage workers to see their employers as father figures, to reinforce obedience and loyalty. The employment of young women also holds wages down; the reasoning being that they are only earning pocket money. In fact, young women are frequently the major wage earners for their families, sending as much as half their wages back to their homes in poor rural areas. Another reason why young women are employed is that they leave to have children – and, with a high labour turnover, there is less opportunity for them to organise. It does appear, however, that, compared to local firms, TNCs, while still using a high proportion of female labour, do maintain lower wage differentials between men and women.

In South Korea, wages rose by 60% between 1986 and 1990, which appears very good until one takes into account the very long hours worked, the fact that wage figures, unlike previously, now include meals and transport; and that inflation over that period was very high. In spite of the increase, wages here are lower than in Taiwan and Singapore. Wages in the electronics industry tend to be a little higher than in equivalent light industries. Wages also tend to be a little higher in the TNCs than small local companies, but TNCs do subcontract parts of the production process out to local companies, thus reducing wage costs. Singapore is a wealthy country – its GNP just 20% lower than the UK's – yet wages are low at around a quarter of those in the UK, and income inequality is serious with the top 10% earning as much as the poorest 60%. This results in a poor HDI v GNP ranking of –14, despite good literacy and health figures. Taiwan is also comparatively wealthy, with a GNP in the region of $5000, though wages have stayed low as companies have relocated to low wage countries. In both countries, workers from the Philippines and Thailand move in to take low paid jobs.

Samsung is said to have 'compromised' on wages and working conditions (suggesting improvements in both), but is also moving into lower wage countries such as Thailand.

The use of short term contracts is common, too. This is another way of keeping turnover high, minimising costs and militating against effective worker organisation. In most operations, workers achieve peak productivity in a few months, so high turnover of labour carries few disadvantages for the companies. In Hong Kong, for example, young women from rural areas in China are given two year contracts, after which they return to their villages.

Footloose and fancy free

While the importing of labour is one side of a coin, the other is relocation. While Chinese workers are employed in Hong Kong and Indonesians in Malaysia (where casual wages are far higher), factories are closing down in higher cost countries and relocating to cheaper ones. For example while **Philips** is currently carrying out an extensive restructuring programme, which will involve the loss of around 20% of its worldwide workforce, it is also moving into the new free enterprise 'special economic zones' of China. **Samsung** is moving into Thailand and other low wage countries.

What can we really expect from manufacturers in this situation? Is it unreasonable to expect companies to ignore the existence of countries offering cheap labour? Indeed the best chance a country has to industrialise may be through

TNC investment. It is through the influence of industries such as electronics that wages can improve. The technology involved can have important spin-offs for other local industries, especially when production is subcontracted out.

But the problem occurs when the more footloose companies take advantage of tax and other incentives to move in, and move out as soon as a better offer is made; cheap labour becomes a commodity and wages are held down globally.

Since the main selling point is labour, the processes subcontracted will normally be manual, low technology jobs. As wages rise, the technology 'rises' to minimise costs – a form of development. But the concern frequently is that, instead of developing within a developing economy, TNCs can merely relocate to the next cheap country, leaving nothing home grown to carry on the job. In Hong Kong, for example, small firms dependent on subcontracting from TNCs are laying off workers as the TNCs 'restructure', i.e. relocate to China.

In an expanding industry like electronics, where demand is growing, especially in the NICs, TNCs such as **Toshiba** are finding benefit in staying close to the market they serve; the domestic market is theirs to develop. It is reasonable to expect TNCs to form long-term partnerships with local firms, joint ventures with the sharing of technology, rather than wholly-owned subsidiaries or merely subcontracting. Some companies have made more positive steps than others in this direction.

Neither **Sony** nor **Matsushita** closed any plants between 1987 and 1990, in fact these companies each established 11 new plants in Malaysia, Thailand, Singapore, India and the Philippines during those three years. **Sony**'s policy is to avoid relocation, establishing a continuing business near the markets it serves. As labour costs rise, it transfers production technology consistent with 'local infrastructure and skills'. The company does not, however, deny that it seeks out low cost countries in which to produce.

On the other hand **Amstrad** states in its 1989/90 annual report that it has closed its Hong Kong factory and trading company. It is moving away from the Far East as part of a

UK and European manufacturing and component sourcing policy. Sixty per cent of its materials and products are now procured from the EC. The company transferred audio production from Taiwan to Malaysia and China, though Amstrad have since pulled out of the audio equipment market altogether; no indication is given of concern over the cost of the pull-out to those subcontractors affected.

It is unclear from communication we have had with **Casio**, **Thomson** and **Sharp** whether they have specific policies relating to relocation.

Technology transfer

The establishment of joint ventures between local firms and TNCs is an important step to ensure that they are less footloose and allow some transfer of technology and skills to local industry.

Developing countries are justifiably concerned that they do not get access to the technology relevant to their needs, and some governments, such as Malaysia's, require undertakings on technology transfer or requirements for the use of local components in order that local firms can absorb some of the technology involved. But in a buyers' market, countries selling labour cannot afford to haggle too much. Even in South Korea, around a quarter of the value of a video is due to Japanese components.

Some of the companies appear to have more established policies than others on training of local people and transfer of technology – notably **Hitachi**, **Sony**, **Sharp** and **Matsushita**.

Hitachi states that it believes strongly in sharing technology advances. It has more than 80,000 industrial rights and patents, all of which are available for licensing. It includes local people in its Research and Development work, encouraging them in advancing technical skills. However, it seems that the only R&D facilities outside Japan are based in the US and Europe. The company sponsors technical trainees from third world countries to visit Japan. Over 30 years, 1300 technicians from 30 countries have undergone training.

Hitachi has a training programme, under which employees from outside Japan visit Japan for individually tailored courses, and the company sponsors educational programmes and assists Asian graduate students to study at some of Japan's universities.

Sony states that it hires 'local nationals at various levels, providing engineering and management training to the same standard in all its local operations, and using local parts in production provided these meet relevant quality control standards.' While this policy is pursued in third world locations, it is not as advanced as in industrialised countries. Sony runs the Sony Business Manufacturing School, that teaches local managers methods in production management.

Sony also operates a policy known as 'Upstream Integration Concept', which involves setting up local sales and marketing in a country, then establishing local production facilities followed by localised research and development, depending on the engineering skills and infrastructure available in the country concerned. Local researchers and engineers are provided with training in Japan, varying in length from three months to three years, depending on the nature of the technology being transferred. All external training is followed by on-the-job training.

Toshiba cites technology transfer as a means of stimulating economic development. It has entered into agreements with 35 partners in third world countries including India, China, Taiwan, Malaysia and South Korea. Toshiba has 722 joint ventures in Asia; in most it is not the majority shareholder. The technology for these all originates at Toshiba.

Engineers in **Matsushita**'s subsidiaries worldwide take training courses in Japan. It is not clear how many engineers are from the third world, however. The company states that its subsidiaries manufacture complete products for sale, rather than just assembly work or component manufacture. The main South Korean-owned electronics companies have acquired technology from Matsushita.

Philips is willing to share technology with subsidiaries, providing the knowledge can be protected. It is not clear whether this also applies to the many joint ventures the company is involved in. **Thomson** is involved in a project with a Chinese firm to develop a colour TV for the local market which involves some transfer of technology to the local firm; potentially a useful venture.

Sharp's annual report mentions the strategy of transferring technology and manufacturing locally to the market in order to fulfil its 'social obligations'. Sharp's new Thai factory manufactures finished products and 'enables local procurement of parts', a strategy to reduce costs, but with benefit to the local economy, too. The company, it is reported, works with local suppliers helping them to achieve the quality needed.

Amstrad, **Casio** and **Dixons** did not indicate any policies on technology transfer.

CONSUMER CHOICES

There seems no reason to avoid the third world as a source of electronics goods; there is significant potential benefit in the trade. Some countries clearly offer better wages and conditions than others, but this is largely a function of the poverty of the country. Only in the cases of Brazil and Singapore can wages be shown to be damagingly low compared to what could be achieved. One pound spent in either country achieves less in development terms than one spent in some of the other producing countries.

Finding out what the companies' policies are is not easy; knowledge is inevitably partial, and we have to look for clues to help us to evaluate performance. A company's policy (or lack of one) on training of local staff, involvement of local people in management and the transfer of technology is also crucial.

Some companies, notably **Matsushita**, **Sony** and **Hitachi**, have been more willing than the other electronics companies to cooperate with New Consumer's research. It is therefore difficult to make comparisons across the ten companies surveyed, as those that did provide us with material naturally wanted to be seen in the best light, while it is possible that companies that did not cooperate have developed enlightened policies. **Toshiba** is a case in point; the results of previous research indicate that its wider record on social responsibility, personnel, relations with suppliers and support of local legislation on freedom of association and unionisation compares well with other companies.

Likewise **Casio** did not cooperate with the research, but its 1990 annual report reveals an awareness of its role in wider economic and social issues.

What is clear, however, is that none have made progress on several of the issues raised, particularly on unionisation and the central recording of working conditions, both areas in which a great deal of progress can and should be made.

Dixons provided the most depressing response: 'Almost by definition the economies of third world countries are not yet sufficiently advanced as to constitute a source of supply of the type of product which we sell.' When pressed on the sourcing of products from the Far East, Dixons stated 'we consider sources of supply of merchandise which we sell to be confidential . . .' In its role as retailer of own brand electronics goods, however, it clearly takes on the role of manufacturer in its relationship with subcontractors and should develop equivalent policies.

Thomson, **Sharp**, **Philips** and **Amstrad** similarly indicated no policies addressing the issues raised.

On the basis of the information we have, there is no brand that we could label as a 'best buy'. However, it is fair to pick out a few companies as representing the best of what is currently available; not without their faults, but none the less aware of many of the issues and clearly responding to a degree not matched by the others.

✔ Before you buy, consider the 'lifestyle' questions: are you being led into the consumer spiral of ever-increasing consumption? What else could you use the money for that might represent better value?

✔ If you are intending to buy electronics products
look first at **Matsushita** (*Technics, Panasonic, JVC*),
Sony, Hitachi and possibly **Toshiba** and **Casio**.

Beyond the shopping trip:

The issue of effective independent unionisation and
the working conditions in factories is an important
one. Letters to companies, and to the trade attachés
at the embassies of South Korea and Malaysia in
particular would not go amiss.

Holidays

Shivering in front of that brightly-lit travel agent's window on a wet winter evening, you could be forgiven for thinking that Indonesia is a paradise. Sun, sand, exotic food and culture. But travel agents, like estate agents, are in the business of selling dreams – and between the dream and the reality falls the shadow of the credibility gap.

These dreams are not just peddled in Balham or Bootle. The governments and people of host countries in the third world have dreams too, and it is their fulfilment (or otherwise) that this chapter addresses. Tourism offers great benefits both to the third world countries and to Western tourists, but it also creates great problems. Can we have one without the other? Is third world tourism on balance a Good Thing, or do we resign ourselves to reading romantic travel books as we sit on the promenade at Clacton?

The UK market

Tourism is big business and it's growing. Between us we spend nearly £9 billion a year abroad and over £4 billion on air travel. Most foreign holiday trips are packages (nearly 14 million a year), and the bulk are to Spain, France and Greece. The trend is towards less frequented locations, as popular destinations become 'spoiled' by the tourist trade, although this was affected during 1991 by falling levels of disposable income and reluctance to travel during the Gulf War.

The holiday business is divided up between the tour operators, who develop and manage the holidays, and the travel agents, who merely retail them. However, the distinction is not hard and fast, as several companies handle both sides of the business, some even owning the hotels and airlines too.

Kuoni, the UK subsidiary of the Swiss Reisebüro Kuoni AG, is the best-known company for 'exotic' holidays. It runs tours to Egypt, Kenya, the Seychelles, Indonesia, Hong Kong, India, Malaysia, Nepal, the Maldives, China, Singapore, Sri Lanka, Thailand, Mexico, Brazil and various Caribbean islands. But **Thomson** has recently overtaken it as the long haul market leader. Part of the Canadian leisure, travel and newspaper group Thomson Corporation, Thompson is the leading tour operator overall, with *Horizon, Wings, Skytours, HCI, OSL* and of course *Thomson Holidays*. The company also owns *Britannia Airways* and the travel agent *Lunn Poly* with 505 outlets in 1989. During 1990, Thomson was expecting to sell 170,000 exotic holidays, 20,000 more than Kuoni. In 1990–91 it was offering holidays in Egypt, India, Kenya, Tanzania, the Maldives, Mauritius, the Seychelles, Sri Lanka, several Caribbean islands, China, Hong Kong, Indonesia, Malaysia, Singapore and Thailand.

British Airways, better known as the world's largest international airline, runs *Speedbird, Poundstretcher* and *British Airways Holidays*. It sold *Redwing* in 1989 and *Four Corners* to Thomas Cook in 1990.

One casualty of the recent downturn in the market was **International Leisure Group**, which went into liquidation as our research was being completed. It is unclear what will happen to its operations which include *Intasun, Global, Club 18–30*, and the ill-fated *Air Europe*. While ILG sold holidays to 11 third world countries, the company stated in its returned questionnaire that these countries accounted for only a small proportion of its business.

Airtours, mainly acting as a travel agent, has recently started offering tours of its own. The company claims to have increased its share of the operator market to 6.5%, making it the third largest operator in the UK. **Thomas Cook** is the second largest travel agent with 12% of the market (though the largest in business travel) and also operates its own scheduled long haul tours. It derives a quarter of its business from long haul holidays. **Pickfords Travel Group** (part of NFC plc) includes *Tradewinds*, the long haul holiday company, and is the third largest travel agent with 9% of the holiday market in 1988. **W H Smith Travel** has 150 outlets offering holidays through all the major operators, though it is likely to pull out of the market, selling its business to **A T Mays**. This is another leading company, with 300 outlets at the end of 1989, though a minor player in the long haul market.

Of the companies surveyed, **A T Mays**, **Pickfords**, **Thomas Cook**, **Thomson**, **W H Smith** and **Kuoni** did not respond to questions about their third world holiday business. **ILG**, **Airtours** and travel agent **Hogg Robinson** all responded to the travel agent questionnaire, while **British Airways** declined. **Airtours'** response was rather sparse, in part because the company has very little involvement with the third world. Airtours runs holidays in Mexico and Kenya, establishing contracts with local agents and hotels to provide the necessary services.

The dreams

By 1988, the third world was earning some $55 billion a year from tourism; some countries, such as Thailand, have based their economic strategy on it. Tourism is now Thailand's main 'export'; it receives some five million tourists a year, from the USA, Europe and Japan in the main. Kenya is in a similar position, using its safari parks to attract a new generation of hunters, armed with cameras instead of guns. Malaysia has seen its number of visitors almost double in just one year, reaching over eight million in the first half of 1990 alone.

Tourism is often seen as the precursor to other forms of economic development: once tourists have put the place on the map, they are more prepared to come back on business. Using the same logic that persuades countries to compete to make huge losses hosting the Olympic Games and other big events, governments believe in the value of a high international profile. Many of the developments that are needed for tourism have useful knock-on effects when it comes to attracting business too. Hotels are needed for conferences or to house travelling executives; golf courses are now an indispensable part of the trade arsenal.

There are also, of course, direct economic benefits. Tourists are wanted primarily for their money, and one of the first duties of a socially responsible holiday maker is to spend as much as possible! The average visitor to Thailand spends over $150; in Singapore, the average is nearly $400, while Malaysia bemoans its lot at just $20 (it seems tourists in Malaysia go over the border to Singapore to shop). Some of the industries based on this financial input are informal, such as handicrafts, and the benefits can reach relatively poor people quite quickly.

Since the best tourist destinations are often off the beaten track, the industry extends some hope of economic development to poor regions with few other natural assets or communication channels to the centres of power. So tourism can help to prevent population drift to overcrowded cities, keeping communities together and culture alive, though sometimes only as exhibits in a living museum.

Tourism seems on the face of it to be an ideal industry to finance development. It needs little in the way of high technology so can be set up more cheaply than major manufacturing industry. Third world countries have many assets to attract the tourist: sun, cheap prices, different and exotic cultures. For small island states, in particular, tourism offers a way to use one of the few assets they have – a coastline. And, as was once pointed out by a famous prostitute, 'you've got it, you sell it; you've still got it'. Tourists may take the odd souvenir home, but the beaches and mountains they came for are still there.

The cold light of morning

If tourism offers at least the hope of economic development, how well does it perform in practice? The answer, predictably enough, is, 'it all depends'. It depends on what sort of industry is encouraged; how well the host government can plan for and control it, how the operators choose to run their business and what the tourists do on their holidays.

For most people, holidays in the third world consist of travelling by air, staying in smart hotels, shopping in colourful and cheap bazaars, toasting on a beach, visiting cultural sites or shows in air conditioned coaches, eating exotic food and taking lots of photographs. Perhaps that is what most people are looking for; more importantly, it is what most people are *offered* by the large tour operators. Mass tourism by definition needs to handle people in large groups, with obvious consequences for the kind of travel, accommodation and entertainment on offer.

The hotel syndrome

The travel business is increasingly computerised. Travel agents, to perform the service required of them, are linked into worldwide networks. These give them immediate access to flight schedules and availability; we'd all have to wait days for a reservation to come through if not. But the network also gives access to hotel bookings, car rental, train connections and even flower services. For the tourist planning a holiday independent of the package operators, this is a valuable aid.

But it also means that there is a tendency for both independent and package tourists to be routed to hotels owned by transnational companies and other foreign firms, rather than to locally-owned establishments. The trend is exacerbated by the fact that the costs of packages are held down by limiting the range of hotels, resorts and means of travel. Added to which there is a growing integration of the business with airlines, for example, owning or part-owning tour operators or hotel chains. The hotels (and especially the resorts) specialise in meeting the needs of the foreign visitor.

Particularly in small countries, much of the material used to equip the hotels has to be imported, to meet the standards expected. Likewise, much of the food may come from abroad, in order that the necessary variety is on offer.

Coupled with the foreign ownership of hotels, this means that much of the money spent by the tourist goes straight back home.

Estimates vary, but according to the *Economist* magazine, between 40% and 50% of hotel profits leak out of the host country in one way or another. Estimates in the Caribbean put the figure as high as 77%, due presumably to the Islands' dependence on US imports. In considering the extent to which tourism is economically beneficial to third world countries, we must take this into account.

The situation is made worse by growing competition amongst both operators and host countries. **Thomson** expects to be cutting prices to its third world destinations; 'The chances of a tour operator finding a hotel in the Mediterranean that is prepared to cut its prices have long since gone. In the Far East, Africa and even America, mass tourism is only now beginning to take off, and with the strength of a company of our size behind them our representatives have been able to force down prices substantially.' Sri Lankan holidays were expected to be 30% cheaper in 1991, Kenya and Thailand from 5% to 10%. Third world countries are clearly prepared to go to tremendous lengths in a bid to attract tourism.

While tourism undoubtedly creates jobs in the construction industry in the short term and in the service industries in the longer run, these jobs are frequently amongst the lowest paid in the country. The hotel and catering trades are notoriously badly paid, and few if any local people can find management jobs. Most are menial: gardening, baggage carrying or room cleaning jobs, offering little in the way of income or security. Many are by their very nature seasonal.

Hogg Robinson 'expects those providing products and services' to provide good working conditions, since it does so itself. Its policy on unions is to 'work in harmony' with its suppliers; 'where this involves unionisation, we work to that policy.' What this means is not clear. **ILG** said its operations were too small to justify employing indigenous staff except as representatives. (The company employed local people in Europe, where its operations were larger.)

Conflicts of interest

Investing in the tourist industry, while it may help local business, often causes tensions between the requirements of the local and national economy, with local people finding their resources highjacked by the tourist trade. Alternatively, investing in hotels, telephones, road and rail lines in one particularly attractive area may play havoc with national planning, contradicting the longer term needs of the wider economy. Tourism can be a quick fix but it may militate against longer term challenges and it is a notoriously fickle business, especially at the romantic end. Once a location becomes popular, it loses some of its appeal; high-cost, low impact adventure tourism develops into low cost, high impact mass tourism . . . and then where? Trekking holidays in northern Thailand now bring twice as many tourists to see the hill tribes near Chiang Mai as the entire population of the area. Sri Lanka has lost its tourists to the Maldives – due in good part to the recent communal violence, of course; nothing spoils a good holiday like terrorism.

There are other pressures too. In many tourist areas, water is in short supply. It is not uncommon for local people and local businesses to go short because of the excessive use of showers and swimming pools in hotels. The Bangkok Bank observed in a recent report that tourism also puts a great strain on sewerage and electricity systems. The demands of a Western lifestyle are difficult to sustain in a poor country. But tourist hotels must maintain a façade which belies the conditions in the country as a whole; that is the essence of a good holiday, we are told.

Operators and agents should where possible use or recommend locally owned hotels and resorts and locally owned transport, to maximise the return to the local community. In addition, operators should involve local community representatives in planning decisions, and develop monitoring procedures to assess and respond to the social, economic and environmental impact of holiday operations.

The only company in our survey to state it used locally-owned facilities wherever possible was ILG.

Environmental costs

Environmental damage is another factor to weigh in the balance. It extends from the simple erosion of paths in popular hill trekking areas, to the unplanned, even illegal building of resorts on fragile coastal ecosystems. The effect on agricultural and fishing communities respectively are seldom measured; fishermen and farmers become waiters and washerwomen. Even the Bangkok Bank (hardly a radical institution) identified in its report on tourism the illegal building of resorts in National Parks as a significant problem.

Hogg Robinson has assisted the *Observer* Travel Watch campaign and 'has made it known where possible of any potential negative impact of tourism anywhere', though the company has not provided examples. Previous correspondence with **Thomson** has suggested that the company is intending to develop policies addressing environmental issues, though there is no indication that this has happened yet. Carlson Travel, **A T Mays'** US parent company, has recently begun offering 'natural and environmental tours' worldwide, though no indication is given as to whether these aim to protect the environment, or merely observe it.

A meeting of cultures?

This is another kind of dream that tourism offers and which is an important element in the attraction of long haul holidays. But mass tourism cannot really offer a meeting of cultures; the isolation engendered by the accommodation and transport organised by the tour operators ensures that the only sort of culture involved is the 'for sale' kind.

More importantly, genuine local culture cannot cope with mass tourism. The cultural façade needed to attract tourists is maintained in many ways; since tourists must see everything during their two week stay, events are staged at a convenient place every week and culture is bought rather than celebrated. As a Maryknoll Sister once said, 'Human contact has become human contract'.

The huge economic mismatch between tourist and host

can result in more than just the sale of culture; an entire community is created to service the needs, desires and preconceptions of visitors, with fishermen for instance becoming boat tour operators. The community loses (or changes) its identity. The relationship between tourists *en masse* and the local population inevitably comes to be seen as that of master and servant rather than as guest and host. Locals are seen, and even see themselves, defined in relation to the outsider, with whom all the initiative lies and from whom all life flows. An entire class of people move in to exploit the wealth of the tourist. Beggars are the most obvious group; found where the easy money is, not where poverty grips the tightest. Controlled by local mafiosi, probably earning more than the rural poor and exploiting the guilt feelings of tourists, beggars create an image of third world countries that is hard to shift.

Responding to this image problem, which is bad for business, third world governments wage clean up campaigns: not just moving beggars away from the tourist areas, but demolishing shanty towns with little or nothing in the way of alternative accommodation. This sweeping of poverty under the carpet is sometimes called development, but is at best cosmetic and at worst pushes poor communities further into poverty. One particularly striking irony has been pointed out by Survival International. During 'Visit Malaysia Year' 1990, government promotional posters depicted 'colourful native people' in traditional dress, while the indigenous people of Sarawak were being imprisoned for blockading the logging companies.

Many people argue that the resort approach to tourism at least has the benefit of limiting the damage to one area. The alternative, to spread the impact as thinly as possible, could lead to greater cultural damage, especially in small or less populated countries.

Even tour operators who lead small scale visits to local communities, with the intention of fostering a genuine meeting of cultures, are aware of the damage that can be caused. Repeated visits not only subtly effect undesirable change; they can also change power relationships and lead to conflict within host communities. Drugs and prostitution are on the increase even in the villages of the hill tribes in northern Thailand as the service industry takes the place of increasingly impoverished agriculture. **Kuoni**, however, in its promotional Thailand video asserts that the tribal villages are unspoiled by tourism.

A stunning parable of the potential for mass tourism to prostitute a culture is the sex tourism of Thailand. Mass tourism took off in South East Asia when the servicemen of the US fleets descended on the Rest and Recuperation bases set up during the Vietnam war. Their impact on host nations was graphically reflected in the pale faces and round eyes of the next generation of children. Olongapo in the Philippines is a city based on prostitution, night clubs and drugs, all to serve the US navy. Thailand's claim to uniqueness as a holiday resort is sex; according to a study by the International Labour Organisation, one massage parlour in Bangkok is especially famous. It offers only massage! Following the coup in early 1991, Thailand's new government pledged to clean up the sex industry, saying 'sex tourists are no longer welcome'. They should 'go back home and exploit their own women and children'. Thailand is now looking at alternative ways to employ the women affected.

Companies should distance themselves from sex tourism, ensuring that publicity brochures and advertisements do not encourage negative or exploitative images of local people. In view of the responsibility tourists have to travel sensitively and creatively, companies should work towards more informative briefings of travellers, focusing on social and cultural issues as well as historical perspectives.

Kuoni offers a video service to people before selecting holidays. 'These are not just promotional films but very interesting documentaries on Kuoni holiday destinations.' As far as we know, this is the only mainstream tour operator to offer such a service to customers. One Kuoni video advocates taking photos from the window of the minibus, a habit that emphasises the 'zoo visit' aspect of tourism. Generally it is more honest to take pictures openly – where possible seeking permission from the subject. The video provides a generally good briefing about what to expect, a little about local culture and suggestions to get out and sample local foods. No information is given about social issues and specifically those arising from the tourist trade. Nor is there much information and advice given about minimising the potential negative impact of tourism in the company's brochures, though what there is tends to be a little more informative than most.

About India, Kuoni says 'A country rich in culture and heritage and sadly misunderstood in the minds of so many due to the problems facing the country today.' A general piece of advice: '. . . don't expect things like they are at home. The food and climate are different, a smile and some tolerance for another way of life may work wonders and a generally positive attitude and a word with our representative or the hotel manager may be more useful than a copy of the Trade Descriptions Act.'

In **Thomson**'s promotional brochures, the photos and text usually present the countries concerned in a light that emphasises rich cultural heritage; but there is virtually no advice given on how to conduct oneself sensitively.

Referring to Thai nightlife a **Thomson** brochure claims, 'the notorious nightlife, while always there in the more developed resort, is unlikely to intrude on your holiday.' However, it goes on to recommend that one samples 'neon-lit nightlife – in notorious Patpong, or elsewhere in the numerous bars, discotheques and clubs.' Of Pattaya it says 'An excellent value resort which whilst it undoubtedly does cater for the "single male" in its nightlife is also very relaxed and a friendly place with lovely beaches which everyone can enjoy.'

References to the responsibilities of tourists, in the **ILG** literature supplied to New Consumer, while scant in terms of sensitivity to local culture and customs, are better than in most other examples. In a section on Thailand, we are told: 'A strong Buddhist influence means respectful dress is required in the many holy places. Don't pose for photos in front of Buddha. Showing emotion openly (e.g. anger) is frowned upon and gets you nowhere. Agree taxi fares before you start your journey.' Virtually no historical background is given in their literature, though one unfortunate description is given: 'Ancient influences are all around, but as the Conquistadors were the first European holiday makers there is a strong Spanish influence.' According to ILG, guidance was also available to tourists while at the resorts. References to sex tourism in Thailand are fairly neutral, indicating that it is easy to avoid.

An **Airtours** brochure advertising holidays to Mexico and the Caribbean makes no mention of how tourists can take account of local customs in their behaviour, though it does mention the strong cultural heritage of the countries concerned.

Hogg Robinson produces an annual guide called 'Recommended Resort and Hotel Guide', in which it highlights favourable and unfavourable aspects of tourism in certain places. It seems to be the only travel agent that does so and this is a potentially useful initiative. The guide is available for consulting at some of the company's outlets, and provides profiles of several countries, including a few in the third world – Thailand, Jamaica, St Lucia and Tunisia. As well as the usual things tourists need to know, the profiles give a brief historical and cultural background and describe economic structure.

Regarding sex tourism in Thailand, **Hogg Robinson** does not seek to 'ombudsman', though it states that it can be avoided. Of Bangkok it says: 'Outside the "Go-Go Bars" are barkers inviting passers-by in . . . The area is quite small and most of it is locked away following strict laws. In fact it was a depressing nightlife rather than an exciting one . . . If you are likely to be offended as to the explicit nature of some of what's being offered, it is best to avoid these areas.'

Of Pattaya it says: 'Lots to see and stare at. Most of the bars in Pattaya are "pick-up" bars . . . Most hotels in Pattaya allow gentlemen to return with female visitors!' Pattaya is 'for those who will not be surprised to find a commercialised resort with a saucy and raunchy nightlife.'

Companies compared

Although the greatest influences on the third world tourist trade are probably government policies, an industry sensitive to the problems of inappropriate tourism can do much to mitigate the local effects and to maximise the benefit to the host community.

Hogg Robinson's involvement in the Travel Watch campaign is a good sign. Other than that, the company says that it encourages tourism to all countries where it is considered safe to travel, including those in the third world. Overall, the company's awareness that tourists need to know something about the country they are visiting is hopeful, though the information does not address many of the important issues and is not readily available.

A T Mays' new US parent company, Carlson Travel, 'believes that world travel, locally operated by local inhabitants, offers the best prospect for world peace through mutual understanding', though how it intends to foster this is unclear.

The survey question on company initiatives to minimise the negative social and environmental impact of tourism received a formula answer from ILG: 'Only respected high quality resorts and accommodation facilities are used.' No attempt is made to define 'respected', nor those who respect them. No reference is made to efforts to monitor the social impact of its operations.

It is not clear whether **Kuoni** has developed any policies addressing the environmental and social impact of its holidays on the host communities, though the individualised travel arrangements generally leave more room for initiative on the part of the tourists themselves.

Airtours, Pickfords, British Airways, Thomas Cook, Thomson, W H Smith and **A T Mays** gave no indication of any policies specifically addressing the social and environmental impact of tourism.

Where does all this leave the consumer? The overall question, 'Is tourism good or bad?' is unanswerable; the benefits and costs are often imponderable. But there are guidelines that can be followed by individual tourists which will help to maximise the benefits and minimise the costs.

CONSUMER CHOICES

In choosing and taking a holiday you have more consumer power than is apparent in almost any other section of this book.

Whatever kind of trip you choose, planning and preparation are vital; only if you know something of the country and culture you are visiting can you hope to ensure maximum benefit to you, and your hosts. Read as much as possible about the culture and customs of the country you are going to visit. Investigate the human rights situation too. Many repressive regimes actually take comfort from the presence of tourists – as long as they stay on the beach. Make contact with people from the country you are visiting who live in your locality.

A number of organisations have put together thoughts for tourists visiting the third world. Again these focus on maximising the economic and cultural benefit of such tours. The Christian Council of Asia writes: 'Travel in a spirit of humility and with a genuine desire to learn . . . Be sensitive about taking photos; cultivate the habit of listening and observing . . . Instead of looking for a beach paradise, discover the richness of another culture . . . Remember you are only one among many visitors; do not expect special privileges. When shopping, remember your bargain is only possible because of low wages . . . Spend time each day reflecting on your own experiences in order to deepen your understanding.'

The Center for Responsible Tourism in the USA adds: 'Stay in accommodation run by locals . . . eat the national foods; local food is usually fresher, less expensive and more varied than imported western cuisine . . . Take local transportation; buses, train and taxis not only cost less, but offer contact with the people of the country.'

As you travel around, think what you will say to friends

about the holiday, and about the country and its people.
What is it that colours your view? Are you seeing the 'real
thing' or the result of the influence of tourism on the local
culture?

Although it is desirable to look beyond the large operators
to the small specialists, most of us cannot yet do so, as the
choice is limited. It is also beyond the scope of this book to
evaluate the many small operators. But when you are leafing
through the brochures for third world locations, look carefully at the images used; what are they saying about the
country . . . and about the tour operator or travel agent?
Choose a company that is prepared to talk about the issues
raised here.

✔ Of the larger companies, travel agent **Hogg
   Robinson** and tour operator **Kuoni** emerge best
   from the survey, though not without reservation.

✔ **North South Travel** is a small independent travel
   agent offering low priced flights and accommodation. Closely involved in the 'alternative
   tourism' network, it donates its profits to charitable
   projects concerned with the third world.

✔ There are several small specialist tour operators that
   address some of the issues in this chapter. There are
   too many to give addresses, or to attempt a rating
   here, but further information can be obtained from
   CART (the Centre for the Advancement of
   Responsive Travel), whose handbook gives
   information about many of the independent
   operators.

✔ Most importantly, join **Tourism Concern**. This is a
   network of people concerned (and taking action)
   about the impact of tourism on host communities.
   You can obtain from them advice, the CART
   handbook, up-to-date information and the means to
   become a sensitive tourist.

✔ Frank Barrett's very good book, *A Guide to Real Holidays Abroad*, published by the *Independent* newspaper, lists a large number of 'alternative' tour operators.

✔ Start asking questions of your travel agent or tour operator. Tourism Concern have useful material to help with this job. The best tour operators and travel agents will be able to respond to the questions.

On your return

Give your tour operator or travel agent feedback; they are there to ensure that your holiday fulfils your expectations, and they can only respond if you do. You will have invested a lot, and your holiday should come up to scratch. Perhaps you could be the first person to complain about too much luxury!

Send feedback also to Tourism Concern; that way, information about the record of the tour operators and travel agents will be made available to other tourists.

Processed Foods

The diversity and complexity of the processed foods market makes it difficult to develop a simple set of issues. Food products contain a great variety of ingredients; the major ones for the purposes of this book are sugar, cocoa, fruit and vegetables, meat and fish, and the issues they present are explored in their individual product chapters. In this chapter we look at the overall response of the major food manufacturers.

Some large manufacturers are 'vertically integrated' – involved in all stages of food production from growing of crops to the production of consumer goods. These companies are in a good position to ensure beneficial changes. Others are less powerful, but still share with consumers the responsibility of ensuring that purchases are of maximum benefit to the third world. They should be monitoring the effects of the trade they are a part of and developing policies responding to the issues that arise.

However, as we have seen in other chapters, it is clear that for most manufacturers this is unfamiliar territory; by and large it is only those companies with direct involvement in third world operations that have made even faltering steps to address the issues.

Associated British Foods is one of the UK's largest food manufacturers, involved in milling and bread production as Allied Bakeries, in biscuit production (*Ryvita* and *Burtons*), canning, and is also market leader in the speciality tea and herbal tea market, through *Twinings* and *Jacksons of Picadilly*. In December 1990, ABF acquired **British Sugar**, having fought over it for several years with Tate & Lyle.

ABF did not respond to the questionnaire, nor give any information. There is no evidence of any policies addressing the need for improvements in wages and working conditions in the third world, the use of pesticides on crops, human rights violations, nor the sustainable sourcing of meat or fish used in the products sold in its stores. In fact, the only mention of its tea business in its annual report concerned the 'weather and economic factors' and the resulting increase in producer prices putting margins under pressure.

Allied-Lyons is mainly known for its tea and coffee, through such well known brand names as the *Tetley* range of teas and *Lyons* fresh ground coffee. Allied-Lyons declined to fill in the questionnaire (though it did provide a statement), so it is difficult to assess its level of involvement in the third world. The company states: 'So far as we are aware, our operations have not had adverse social or environmental effects – no-one has been forced out of occupation of traditional lands, we have not destroyed forest habitat – we have sought to operate on a socially responsible basis.' The company did not, however, provide any examples or documentation.

Allied-Lyons states that the products it imports are commodities that are in surplus – tea, coffee, sugar, cocoa and edible oils. It is not the first-hand importer or processor, and 'As far as we know, our trade broadly assists third world countries rather than deprives them of supplies.' In most cases that is likely to be true; the commodities mentioned are export crops that provide valuable foreign exchange earnings.

The company considers that simply purchasing commodities is beneficial, and has not made any response to the issues raised relating to the trade in these products, on the grounds that international institutions should take care of this. The company states that its plants participate in the community through fundraising for local educational institutions, sponsoring sports events and helping local charities. Initiatives range from support for a flying doctor service in Zimbabwe and assistance for victims of Hurricane

Gilbert in Jamaica, to a donation of cordials to the Zimbabwean Army's Sports Day. The parent group also makes charitable contributions to the third world, for example £34,000 was donated from the Allied-Lyons Charitable Trust to the Water Decade, towards wells in Africa. Employees of Allied-Lyons around the world are raising £300,000 for the Save the Children Fund.

Allied-Lyons has gone to great lengths to provide details of its charitable contributions and community involvement, clearly regarding itself as a good corporate citizen, but does not provide information about any initiative to ensure that its everyday business runs in accordance with the same values.

Though a major biscuit manufacturer, **BSN Groupe**'s processed food involvement is through the *HP* range of bottled and canned foods. The company has been built up by Antoine Riboud, who has a reputation for progressive employment practices in Europe, including the facilitation of pan-European collective bargaining. However, BSN did not respond to the questionnaire, and there is no indication of any policy addressing the social and environmental issues arising from its involvement and trade with the third world.

CPC International Inc. is a worldwide processor of packaged consumer foods, which account for 81% of its total sales, and has major corn refining operations, producing mainly artificial sweeteners. In the UK some of its best known brands include *Marmite* and *Bovril* spreads, *Mazola* corn oil, *Knorr* soups and sauces, *Napolina* Italian foods and *Hellmann's* mayonnaise. In response to the New Consumer questionnaire, CPC said that each of its 43 third world subsidiaries manufactures almost exclusively for the market of the host country and that exports and imports are negligible.

Regarding unions, CPC says 'suffice it to say . . . one can find countless unions, workers' councils, and many other forms of employee representation and participatory management.' The company believes that there have been no major labour problems in recent years. CPC has a very brief environmental policy statement, referring to little more than that they 'protect the environment'. Its policy on community relations refers to support for community activities rather than to monitoring the social effects of its sourcing of raw materials. No further policies or initiatives regarding the other issues arising have been notified to New Consumer.

H J Heinz Company Ltd manufactures more than 57 varieties (over 4,000 in fact) of processed foods, including sauces, soups, baked beans, oils and fats, tinned fish, pet foods and slimming foods. Heinz is an American company and is a market leader in the UK with 46% of the tinned soups market and 59% of the tomato sauce market to name but two. Heinz has a very clear idea of its role in developing countries, and its involvement is well documented. It has established joint ventures with national enterprises in Zimbabwe, Thailand and China, to manufacture and market processed foods in the respective domestic markets and for export to surrounding countries.

The reason for establishing plants in those developing countries was that ' . . . our first unsettling discovery was that 85% of the world's population had not been exposed to the Heinz brand.' In order to expand, Heinz needed to look beyond the stagnating Western market. Among the criteria Heinz has devised to assess the prospects for entering into a joint venture in a developing country are: that a company is staffed by nationals and not reliant on expatriates; it does not rely heavily on imported raw materials; and has a ready domestic market and so is not dependent on exports. With regard to employing nationals, Heinz says: 'We have a predisposition to believe that, all things being equal, the local is better than the importee. And that's not just a benediction to local sensitivity; it has major cost implications. Americans overseas are expensive.'

Heinz obviously looks at the host country as well, evaluating tax and pricing laws, political stability, population size and growth rate, and natural resources, among other factors. Heinz decided not to invest in Zambia for instance as the Zambian government and the IMF clashed over mechanisms for control of the economy. Heinz manages a Lowest Cost Operator programme, to produce at reasonable prices, recognising that disposable income is lower in developing countries. Regarding use of labour, Heinz says: 'we sometimes need to apply different rules, using production techniques that might be more labour intensive than we would allow in our US or UK plants.'

In Zimbabwe, Heinz has a joint venture with the country's largest food and soap company and was able to persuade the government to change the law that restricted foreign corporate ownership to 49%. Heinz insisted that it should have managing control of 51%, a need 'based not on corporate chauvinism but on a very practical understanding of the workings of the marketplace'.

In Malaysia, where foreign investment is limited to 30%, Heinz was 'not willing to place ourselves or our investments at the mercy of such restrictions.' In China, Heinz seemed overwhelmed at the potential market for its baby food, given that 22 million babies are born there each year! The company opened a baby food factory in Guangzhou in 1986 and sees its presence as contributing to a nationwide effort to improve public health.

Heinz is a large and powerful company, able to make real changes in the third world. While there is evidence of quite imaginative policies and a good deal of research into the impact of its operations in the third world, this does not seem to be matched (yet) by equivalent work on its sourcing policies. While Heinz declined to fill in the questionnaire, it did provide a good deal of supporting material. However, we have found no information suggesting initiatives intended to maximise the development potential of its sourcing of foodstuffs in the third world, other than its dolphin-friendly *Starkist* tuna brand.

We have not found any examples of pressure applied to governments to improve legislation on working conditions, for example, to match changes to foreign ownership legislation. In the light of this, one can only say that Heinz compare favourably with other food manufacturers, but have a long way to go.

Through a series of takeovers, **Hillsdown Holdings plc** is now one of the largest food manufacturing companies in the

UK. Its wide-ranging subsidiaries are involved in food processing and distribution, furniture, housebuilding, property and building materials, insurance and other businesses. Hillsdown owns Premier Brands which manufactures tea (*Typhoo*, *Glengettie* and *Ridgways*), chocolate drinks and biscuits under the *Cadbury* label. Marmalades and jams (*Hartley's*, *Chivers* and *Rose's*), pet foods (*Butch* and *Cat's Choice*), cooked meats (*Culrose*, *Beechwood* and *Wirral*), sweets (*Needlers* and *Bluebird*) and ice cream desserts (*Fiesta* and *Hortons*) are among the wide range of products made by Hillsdown subsidiaries. Hillsdown is also responsible for *Marvel* dried milk and *Smash* instant potato, *Buxted* poultry, *Daylay* eggs, *Allinson*, *Smedley's*, *Morrell*, *Lockwoods* and *Wilson's of Scotland*. It also owns *The London Herb & Spice Company*.

As well as being a major supplier of own label products to the major retail outlets, Hillsdown is involved in the wholesale trade. It is a major wholesaler of fresh fruit, flowers and vegetables, it prepares and distributes meat (sourcing meat from Argentina), and even has a fellmongery business using the hides and skins that are the by-products from the abattoirs. Hillsdown declined to fill in the questionnaire, and there is no indication of policies or initiatives addressing the social and environmental impact of its trade with the third world.

Nestlé SA, a Swiss company with a turnover in excess of £19 billion, a figure greater than the GNP of the vast majority of third world countries, is the world's leading food manufacturer. It has 39 subsidiaries in the third world, employing 52,000 people, and accounting for 20% of its turnover. Nestlé launched the world's very first instant coffee in 1938 and is still the world leader in its manufacture. Nestlé is also the world's leading manufacturer of infant formula and baby foods, and a major manufacturer of confectionery, ice cream and frozen foods and pet foods. Some of its best known brand names in the UK are *Nescafé*, *Libby's*, *Rowntree Mackintosh*, *Crosse & Blackwell*, *Findus* and *Chambourcy*.

Nestlé has been subject to boycott calls since the 1970s

over its policies in marketing infant formula in the third world. The International Organisation of Consumer Unions has been monitoring the compliance of 20 infant food companies with the World Health Organisation resolutions on the marketing of breast milk substitutes and infant foods, in 42 countries. It rates Nestlé third worst, behind the Japanese Meiji and **Boots'** *Farleys*.

Nestlé's many third world operations have largely been set up to serve the domestic markets, though there is a limited amount of export of finished and semi-finished goods to industrialised and other third world countries. Around 1% of the total personnel in the third world are expatriates; there is a policy to have a combination of locals and internationals, and the trend is towards attaining a completely local staff. Since 1987, five production facilities were opened and two joint ventures were established, one production facility was closed and one was transferred. Nestlé states that it avoids relocation wherever possible, and that it 'favours good labour and union relations'.

Regarding health and safety, Nestlé indicates that there is no difference between industrialised countries and developing countries and that the company follows local regulations or company standards if stricter. It does not state whether information is monitored and kept. Labour turnover and proportions of temporary workers are monitored and discussed between HQ and local management.

The 1989 annual report, in the section on sales of prepared foods, states: 'In the developing countries we have concentrated, in all product categories, on creating varieties that are accessible to the lower-income segments of the population. The use of local raw materials and simple packaging are two factors enabling us to keep the prices of these products low, while using our experience to retain their nutritive value.'

Raw materials sourced directly from the third world are, not surprisingly, coffee, cocoa, sugar, tea, soya and cereals. The company's purchases of coffee and cocoa account for 11% and 10% of total world production respectively. Nestlé does not as a policy own farms or plantations.

The company states that it is a reliable purchaser,

promptly paying a fair price, though what is meant by a fair price is unclear. It does not believe it should pay more than the market price. The company rarely has direct contact with growers and does not seem to recognise any responsibility for initiatives to improve prices, wages or working conditions. It does, however, claim that it encourages the growers to use fewer pesticides by enforcing strict quality control standards.

Nestlé has no policy to favour the use of cane sugar; around 40% of the sugar used in food manufacturing is from cane. The company uses HFCS, but it is not clear in which products. Beef from Argentina and Brazil is used, and subsidiaries purchase local beef according to price and availability. There is no indication that Nestlé has any initiatives to ensure that such meat is not reared on forest land, or land from which people have been forcibly removed.

The company purchases a small amount of canned tuna from Thailand, but has no policy ensuring sustainable sourcing of the fish.

Philip Morris is the largest international cigarette manufacturer (its *Marlboro* brand leads the world), and is now one of the world's largest food companies, having bought up companies such as General Foods (*Maxwell House, Kenco, Hag* and *Bird's*), *Kraft* (now combined into *Kraft General Foods* in the UK), *Jacob Suchard*, the chocolate manufacturer, and *Miller*, the world's second biggest brewer. The company has a wide ranging programme of corporate giving which is mainly focused on the USA, but it has also donated money to help Caribbean victims of Hurricane Hugo. The company did not respond to our questionnaire, and there is no indication of policies or initiatives addressing the social impact of the sourcing of its third world products.

Ranks Hovis McDougall plc is one of the UK's big food companies, manufacturing a wide range of products under labels such as *One-Cal, Capri-Sun* and *Just Juice* soft drinks, *Keiller, Robertson's* and own brand preserves, as well as *Mr Kipling, Cadbury* and own brand cakes and a range of breads. More recently, *Sharwood's* brand ready meals have been launched. Though the company now has no third world operations, many of its products use materials sourced from there – in particular fruit juice, sugar and cocoa. While the company has clearly responded to many social issues in its UK operation, it seems that it has not yet begun to look at the social and environmental impact of its raw materials sourcing in the third world. We have no evidence of any initiatives intended to address this.

Though **Sara Lee** may sound like a cottage industry it is in fact the world's biggest manufacturer of frozen desserts. The company also owns *Douwe Egbert* and *Van Nelle*, the two Dutch coffee giants, and, strangely, *Aspro-Nicholas* pharmaceuticals and *Kiwi* polishes (available in 140 countries throughout the world). The company allocates space in its annual report for its responsibility to the public, covering community and environmental concerns, though no specific information is given. Further details are available, but were not forwarded in response to our questionnaire. There is no indication of policies or initiatives addressing the social and environmental impacts of Sara Lee's sourcing of products in the third world.

Unilever is made up of two parent companies, one Dutch and one British, operating as nearly as is practicable as one entity. Involved in the manufacture of a wide range of processed foods, beverages, detergents and personal products, Unilever is one of Europe's largest consumer goods companies and has a long history of substantial involvement in agribusiness, manufacturing and marketing in the third world.

Some of the UK market's best known and most diverse range of brand names come from the Unilever stable: *Birds Eye* frozen foods, *Mattessons* processed meats, *Walls* ice creams, *Flora* margarine, *Radion* washing powder, *Timotei* shampoo, *Brooke Bond* teas and *John West* canned fish to name but a few. By the end of 1989, Unilever employed 300,000 people worldwide; around 130,000 in the third world. It had 42 principal subsidiaries in 34 third world countries, as well as 12 associates.

Given this extensive and long term involvement, it is

surprising that Unilever has no formal written policy relevant to the sourcing of products and services from the third world. It states, though, that its 'ability to provide quality goods at reasonable prices depends on our ability to trade freely in the world markets. Our standards of integrity, fair dealing and concern for product safety, health and safety at work and for the environment apply to the third world in the same way as to the developed world.'

Unilever sees its involvement in the third world as beneficial, in part because any venture there is considered as long term rather than short term or speculative; it is not aware of any closure of any foods factories in the last three years. In replying to the questionnaire, it states that it is concerned with working conditions worldwide, and benefits to the third world resulting from its involvement include provision of training; enhanced use of local resources already available, including labour; the stimulation of ancillary industries like marketing, packaging and transport; the provision of finance, technology and research capability; standards of product safety and concern for working conditions. Unilever produces literature on how it sees its role in the third world and particularly its plantation businesses.

Unilever stresses that while advice is given to subsidiaries, they are autonomous; for instance they are largely responsible for raising their own investment capital, they negotiate their own wage rates and working hours, and are responsible for their own information gathering and monitoring of many of the issues covered in this book. Unilever policy is that wages and conditions should be at least what is normal within any business sector and country. While 'normal' can vary from the reasonable to the desperate, it is held that Unilever wages compare favourably with others.

Unilever does have a policy for health and safety at work that applies to all subsidiaries, and such standards are monitored centrally (for example, all employees involved in applying pesticides are trained in safe handling and application). But there is no central policy to monitor and improve other aspects of working conditions, such as wages, which makes any assessment of policies on working conditions difficult, either for the consumer or the company. There is apparently closer monitoring on plantations and in South African subsidiaries. Unilever recognises the right of employees to be members of trade unions, and states that most of its workforce are. The vast majority of its personnel in senior positions are nationals, but proportions were not specified. It has a policy of developing local management structures, but has a small number of expatriate managers in each country to give managers international experience, and achieve transfer of skills to local employees.

Most of the manufacturing facilities in developing countries have been set up to serve local markets. They use, where possible, locally available raw materials, and very little is imported and exported. Raw materials exported directly include oils and oilseeds, tea and coffee. The company does import processed foods from the third world; *John West* canned foods, for example, are canned by subcontractors in several third world countries. It does not have any specific policy of increasing the third world's share of value added. Of the sugar the company uses, about 80% is currently from cane.

Unilever has a cattle breeding operation in Zimbabwe, that it states is located in an area unsuitable for intensive communal farming due to water shortage. Unilever says it actively seeks to conserve the wildlife on the ranch, and carries out regular game counts to check on this. The company does not have its own meat production facilities, but seeks and obtains assurances from producers that processed meats it uses (which include corned beef raised on traditional ranching lands in Brazil) are not from sources that raise or graze stock on land cleared of forest for this purpose.

Unilever is involved in prawn farming in the third world and sources tuna from there. Its policies are detailed in the Fish chapter.

In summary, Unilever has many policies relating to the impact of its own operations in the third world; the length of its experience and the detailed research work undertaken ensure this. However, the company has far less well developed policies to monitor the wider social impact of its sourcing of products from third parties.

United Biscuits is the leading biscuit producer in the UK, but the group also includes *KP* snacks and *Ross Young's* frozen foods. The company has operations in the third world, though these are involved in supplying the local market, rather than sourcing for the UK market, and UB works primarily with local companies rather than establishing wholly owned subsidiaries; its recently opened operations in China, Brazil, the Philippines and Trinidad are all joint ventures.

The local management is responsible for the selection of new staff, though UB staff are sometimes involved in interviews for senior managers. UB takes no part in decisions regarding the status of unions at its operations, though health and safety standards are influenced by the policy to ensure UK hygiene standards.

UB uses fish caught in the third world, relying on the monitoring of the industry's association to ensure that catches are properly reported, but no initiatives addressing the social and environmental impact of the operation were reported. The company also uses third world beef in its products, but this is apparently sourced in Botswana. It is unaware of any environmental problems arising from this. UB also stated that where possible, it purchased raw materials only where there was an excess of supply.

The company is involved in a project to breed an export quality peanut for growing in China, and a 'genetic catalogue' of cocoa, though has not yet formulated any policy on the application of biotechnology.

UB is unusual in having a clear and public statement of ethics and operating principles. It includes statements such as, 'Beliefs and values must always come before policies, practices and goals.' The company values lasting relationships with suppliers, recognising that it has great power over them, which must not be used 'unscrupulously'. This document was produced in 1987, however, and makes no reference to environmental or social issues relating to the third world.

UB responded in some detail to our questionnaire, providing operational information to an unusual degree. However, in view of the company's ethos, one would expect UB to be amongst the first to develop policies addressing the issues that arise from the sourcing of agricultural produce and fish from the third world; there is no indication that this has happened.

CONSUMER CHOICES

Clearly, when addressing such a wide range of issues, it is difficult to develop an objective evaluation of company policy. Here we are looking at a company's overall response to a package of issues and attempting to identify a 'corporate culture'. Not surprisingly, no company has moved far down the road of responsible sourcing of food products in the third world, but several, with a more international outlook, have clearly taken on board some issues as part of enlightened management practices.

United Biscuits, **Heinz** and **Unilever** stand out in this regard, and **Allied-Lyons** rates a mention in view of its community and charitable activities.

A small but increasing range of processed foods is becoming available from organisations such as **Traidcraft** and **Equal Exchange**. Many of these are processed in the country of origin and all are sourced from organisations working with poor communities in the third world. The range includes nut butters, nuts (brazil nuts from the rainforest), honeys and muesli, as well as tea, coffee and other food products mentioned in previous chapters.

The Major Retailers

As well as thinking about the global impact of individual products, it is worth looking separately at two major groups of retailers that have considerable influence on the UK market – the supermarkets and the mixed retailers (variety and department stores). Covering a wide range of products, these shops are powerful enough to affect the policies of manufacturers. Supermarkets account for nearly 60% of the food we buy, and more in certain products, such as coffee or frozen food. Their own brand lines often lead the market – for example in fruit juice and ready cooked meals.

The big supermarkets covered here are **Asda**, the **Co-operative movement, Gateway, Iceland, Kwik Save, Marks & Spencer, Safeway** (Argyll), **Sainsbury, Tesco** and **Waitrose** (John Lewis).

Mixed retailers are responsible for sales of some £17 billion each year, and again are particularly dominant in certain markets, for instance textiles and soft furnishing, and clothes, where they take 41% and 31% respectively. The companies covered are **Argos, Boots, Debenhams** (Burton), the **Co-op Movement, Great Universal Stores (GUS), House of Fraser, John Lewis, Littlewoods, Woolworths** (Kingfisher), **Marks & Spencer** and **BhS** (Storehouse).

In the context of this book, the primary responsibility of retailers is that of setting standards for the suppliers and monitoring their compliance, to ensure that the impact of their trade on the third world is beneficial. They are able to influence the trade directly through the production and sourcing of their own brand products, and indirectly through their choice of other brands stocked. They are big enough to make manufacturers think twice.

Few retailers are in direct contact with the source of supply in the third world, and so it could be argued that they have little impact on working conditions, environment and the terms of trade. But in as much as there is free trade in their products, they can and do already set quality standards and price constraints. They can also develop initiatives to assess and respond to the social and environmental implications of their business.

Supermarkets should develop purchasing policies addressing the need for food manufacturers and traders to ensure that progress is made on: higher and more stable prices for tea, coffee and cocoa; working and living conditions of workers on plantations; smallholder contracts; the use of dangerous chemicals; the development of processing industries in third world countries; human rights among agricultural workers; the use of real cocoa rather than substitutes and of tropical oils and especially coconut oil; the social and environmental impact of the sourcing of meat, fish and prawns.

Mixed retailers similarly should be addressing: the sustainable sourcing of tropical wood; the need to add value to products in the country of origin; the employment conditions at their suppliers' and subcontractors' factories.

But how far have the big retailers come in taking on these issues? In general, companies with direct involvement in the third world, mainly manufacturers, are far more aware of the issues than those who merely go shopping there. This is unfortunate, given the great power that retail chains have in the market place.

While some retailers have begun to address the more obvious environmental effects of their sourcing, few have given any indication of even the beginnings of progress on the crucial social impacts. The usual response from retailers when questioned on social responsibility is 'We buy only from reputable suppliers'. In practice of course, though consumers can express their preferences, the responsibility for defining what 'reputable' means, and for monitoring compliance with that standard, rests with the retailers alone.

Having said that, there are some interesting things to report; in some cases, retailers have taken action in respect of particular products, usually sold under own brand labels. Where relevant, these are included in the product chapters. Here we'll concentrate on the overall policies of the main supermarket and mixed retail chains.

THE SUPERMARKETS

Argyll Group is one of the UK's leading food retailers, owning the supermarket chain Safeway, which accounts for over 70% of its revenue. The Presto supermarket chain that is also part of the group is being merged with Safeway, though some stores continue to trade under the Presto name.

Asda Group had 199 stores in 1990, which included the acquisition of 60 Gateway stores. Asda also owns Allied Maples, the furniture chain, with 160 stores. It has no subsidiaries in third world countries.

The Co-operative movement was founded primarily for the social benefit of its members, its origins stemming from the initiatives of the famous 'Rochdale pioneers'. The original system of bulk food purchasing and profit sharing was addressing the poor quality of food available to the ordinary people at that time. Now comprising 80 separate societies, of which the Co-operative Wholesale Society and Co-operative Retail Services are the largest, the Co-operative movement is Britain's largest retailer, selling food, clothing, furniture, electrical goods, DIY, alcohol and tobacco. The CWS, as well as being Britain's largest farmer, is involved in production and purchasing on behalf of the total Co-op in the UK.

While the CRS is unique in having written policy statements on social objectives, which attempt to formalise the practice of social responsibility, it has no written policy on trading with the third world. The Co-op states, however, that it takes an interest in ethical trading practices and welcomes the rise in consumer awareness of such issues. The Co-op sees its role in raising consumer awareness of social issues as crucial, setting it apart from other retailers. Through its Co-operative College Trust, development projects involving cooperatives in Bangladesh, Botswana, Nigeria and Thailand are supported. These initiatives are not, by and large, matched by awareness of the movement's role in development through trade.

The CWS is a major importer of canned foods: 'For commercial as well as ethical reasons, there is an increasing trend towards the import of finished products.' Examples given are pineapple from Botswana, tuna from the Solomon Islands and sardines from Morocco. This is a worthwhile initiative; it would be good to see it applied to other products. The Co-op also states that it does not source Co-op brand canned meat products from Latin America, though it does not seem to make any such stipulation of other manufacturers from whom it buys. A similar initiative to influence the sourcing of shrimps and prawns from the third world would be useful, in view of the social and environmental impact of these operations. The Co-op brand sugar is 100% cane sugar.

Through supplier audits, the Co-op seeks information on environmental and ethical policies. This is an essential requirement for any company taking social and environmental issues seriously, but it is not clear from the response to the questionnaire whether any action is taken should these policies not come up to scratch.

Gateway Foodmarkets is owned by Isosceles plc, set up in 1989 to buy Gateway Corporation plc, at the time the food retailer with the most outlets in the UK after the Co-op. Even after 61 of the larger stores were sold to Asda, and 86 Medicare stores were sold to Kingfisher plc, it had 700 stores, including a new chain called Somerfield Fine Fresh Foods.

Iceland Frozen Foods is a multiple retailer of frozen foods, groceries, chilled foods and domestic appliances. In 1989, Iceland acquired its main competitor, Bejam, and now operates over 500 stores. 65% of Iceland frozen lines are own label, implying a good deal of control over the product specification. Iceland states that it does not buy products from third world countries directly, but estimates that around 3% of its products are purchased from the third world via 'reputable' suppliers.

The John Lewis Partnership is known for its unique structure; it is owned by its employees and all share capital is retained in the group. Profits are used to subsidise social and health amenities. After paying preference dividends and interest, providing for amenities, pensions and reserves, the remainder of the profit is distributed to members or 'partners' as staff are referred to, in proportion to their pay. Staff elect members to a 140 strong central council. The central board, which is equivalent to a board in a publicly quoted company, is the working forum where the chairman and the central council meet to determine policy and conduct of the partnership's affairs.

The company controls 22 department stores, under several names – Bainbridge, Peter Jones, Pratts, John Lewis among others – 90 Waitrose supermarkets, owns furniture and fabric manufacturing operations and runs farming estates.

Kwik Save is a UK-based food retailer with 650 outlets under the Kwik Save name, and 312 off licences under the Best of Cellars name. The trading philosophy is to operate smart 'no-nonsense' foodstores with national brands at low prices. It does not sell own label produce. The company has a subsidiary, Coleman Meat Company Ltd, which operates a franchise system within the Kwik Save stores, selling fresh produce; meat, fruit and vegetables. Another subsidiary operates late night stores under the Lateshopper name.

Marks & Spencer, with its 679 stores, is one of the best known names in high street retailing. While clothing accounts for just under half M&S turnover, foods in 1990 accounted for 38%. M&S is known for its policy of procuring as much as possible from British manufacturers, and is also known for the extremely high standards of quality control it demands from its suppliers. Marks & Spencer does, however, source some clothing items from the third world. Of the foods and furniture it retails, some will by their very nature contain products sourced in the third world. One example is french green beans that are grown for M&S on a farm in Zimbabwe. This farm grew only tobacco until it began growing mange-tout peas and subsequently other vegetables on contract for M&S in the early 1980s.

J Sainsbury is one of the largest food retailers in Europe, now with sales of over £7 billion a year, though it retains something of its family origins, since members of the Sainsbury family are still major shareholders and serve on the board. The company has a good reputation for quality standards and has been one of the supermarkets most aware of green issues in recent years.

Besides its initiatives in, for example, reducing dependence on CFCs, the company is increasing its range of organic foods and monitors pesticide levels in its other fruit and vegetable products. It is proud of the degree to which its staff select and work with suppliers to ensure that they meet the required standards of quality and safety.

However, it is clear that the perspective is very much one of customer care rather than any awareness of the position of the producers of the merchandise. While the annual report is replete with mentions of the needs of staff, the consumer and the environment, there is no mention of suppliers (apart from some appreciation of their role in increasing food quality). The monitoring of the standards met by suppliers can in principle be applied to the area of working conditions. Sainsbury's was the first supermarket to respond to concern about the killing of dolphins by tuna fishing.

Tesco is the second largest supermarket chain in the UK, with nearly 400 stores. It has been one of the main contenders for the 'green' label for some time, both through its product range and its operation. Its slogan, 'Tesco cares', is applied in company literature to suppliers as well as customers and staff. However, it is surprisingly silent about the social and environmental impact of its sourcing policies in the third world; the company did not respond to our questionnaire.

The company carries a major range of own brand goods, and is thus responsible for the production process, as well as for the appropriate sourcing of other products; 'We have a real impact on our society and the world around us.' The company does have a tough monitoring policy for pesticides in foodstuffs, but no reference is made to the impact of these chemicals on the people who do the growing.

Responses

The **Co-op**, alone among supermarkets, responded in some detail to the questionnaire. **Iceland** returned the questionnaire, but felt it was irrelevant to its current operation, though it did clarify certain points raised in the profile. **Argyll** declined, in spite of its proud record of being voted two years running the 'greenest' supermarket by *The Green Consumer's Supermarket Shopping Guide*. That a company should put so much into its 'green' effort makes it all the more surprising that it does not see any parallel responsibility for the third world's involvement in the global crisis. The same could be said of **Sainsbury** and **Tesco,** who similarly did not respond. No response either, from **Gateway** and **Asda**, though Asda stated in a previous New Consumer questionnaire that it had no policy on sourcing from the third world.

John Lewis and Marks & Spencer declined to complete the questionnaire; John Lewis because of a policy of completing questionnaires only where there is a statutory requirement to do so, and M&S because 'We do not have the resources available to complete it.'

The majority of supermarkets did not indicate any policies addressing the social and environmental issues arising from their trade with the third world, such as the need for improvements in wages and working conditions in the third world, the use of pesticides on crops, human rights violations, or the sustainable and just sourcing of meat or fish.

Iceland states that 'We have a commitment to our obligation in the third world countries but have not yet formalised it into a policy document.' The company states that it is in the process of compiling a 'comprehensive document for dealings with our agents'. The company purchases canned tuna from John West and Gerber Foods. It has indicated that it talked with John West regarding the sourcing of 'dolphin-friendly' tuna, and sent a statement it received from John West, and copies of correspondence it has had with the Whale and Dolphin Conservation Society. This positive action by Iceland is an encouraging sign and it will be interesting to see how this policy works once it is up and running. Because a large proportion of Iceland sales is own label, the company should in theory be able to successfully put pressure on its suppliers to make the required policy changes.

Kwik Save declined to fill in the questionnaire, and instead wrote explaining that it does not purchase from or manufacture directly in the third world. 'The companies we deal with are the well known larger concerns who we trust are conducting themselves in a socially responsible manner with regard to dealings in the "third world".' The company states, 'We would however be interested to learn of any evidence that your organisation has that suggests anything to the contrary. If this were the case we would then possibly review our trading relationship with such a concern.' Given Kwik Save's market position, it is likely that such influence as it does bring to bear tends to emphasise the need to reduce costs, rather than to reflect social and environmental concerns, though the company challenge this interpretation, stating, 'Our company does have and has had over many years both social and environmental concerns. I am a little surprised that an organisation such as yourselves is so unaware of what actually goes on.' No indication is given of specific policies addressing social or environmental issues arising from trade with the third world.

It is clear that **M&S** makes the resources available to oversee a high level of involvement with suppliers, many of which are highly dependent on the company. M&S is in a strong position to influence the way business develops. However, there is no indication that this involvement extends to setting employment or environmental standards for sourcing from the third world.

Regarding produce from **South Africa**, most supermarkets follow Argyll's line: 'Safeway believes it is solely up to our customers to decide what to buy, rather than retailers making that decision for them. We are seeking and stocking alternative lines to South African produce, in keeping with the majority of our competitors; the only difference is that our choice of alternative lines is usually larger than most.' All claim to label such products clearly. However, **Tesco** stores in Brixton and Bristol apparently refrain from stocking any South African products. The **Co-op** is unique among major retailers in that since 1985 it has banned the sale of products from South Africa. It was also the first retailer to sign the Whale and Dolphin Conservation Society's agreement for the protection of dolphins.

In summary, the policies developed by the **Co-op**, while at an early stage of development, are laudable and make the Co-op something of a 'best buy' among the major multiples. However, these policies seem to apply only to the sourcing of own brand products, and relate more to the 'extra-curricular' aspects of the movement's work than to its trading operation.

THE MIXED RETAILERS

Argos, Britain's leading catalogue showroom retailer, sells a wide range of branded electrical goods, hardware, sports goods, toys, jewellery, audio and visual equipment, DIY, household textiles and furniture. The company was owned by BAT plc, the financial services and tobacco company, until it was demerged in April 1990. At the time of the demerger, Argos had 254 showrooms, Superstores and Best Sellers stores.

Argos estimates that, in value terms, about half its products are sourced overseas, but does not say what proportion is from the third world. Of the company's range, it is likely that electronics goods, textiles and furniture are the most significant in this regard.

Boots, one of the best known high street retailers with over 1,000 stores, is seen primarily as a chemist, but it is involved in a much larger range of activities. It is a major pharmaceuticals manufacturer, producing own brand products for the Boots stores as well as over the counter and prescription drugs, including the popular Nurofen. Boots manufactures Farley baby products and Ostermilk. Boots is also involved in the DIY market through its merged operation with W H Smith, under the Payless/Do-It-All names and owns other retail chains including Halfords, FADS, and Children's World. Boots is also the UK's second largest chain of opticians, and the second largest health food retailer.

The Burton Group, a leading clothing retailer, had 1,965 retail outlets in September 1990, under such well known high street names as Burton, Top Shop, Top Man, Principles, Dorothy Perkins, Evans, Champion Sport, Harvey Nichols and Debenhams. It has no subsidiaries in third world countries.

House of Fraser operates the well known department stores House of Fraser, Binns, Rackhams, Barkers, Dingles, Army & Navy and, of course, the flagship store Harrods.

Great Universal Stores (GUS) is the market leader in the home shopping market in the UK. It produces mail order catalogues under 20 different names including Marshall Ward, Family Album, Great Universal, Choice, John England, Fashion Extra, John Myers, John Noble, Trafford and Kit. It also produces clothing under the Burberry label, and is involved in finance, property and information services.

The company does not have subsidiaries in third world countries but has two in South Africa, where it has 340 retail outlets selling furniture. In the company's statement in accordance with the European Community Code of Conduct for Companies with Interests in South Africa, it states that 'Retail unions are not represented in most areas where we trade as our shops are very widely spread and very often in deep country areas.'

Kingfisher, formerly known as Woolworth Holdings plc, is a major retailer, and owns the Woolworth chain, B&Q DIY stores, Comet electrical goods retailer, and the Superdrug drugstore chain.

The Littlewoods Organisation is a major retailer, with 117 outlets, runs several home shopping operations – Janet

Frazer, Littlewoods, Brian Mills, Peter Craig, John Moores Home Shopping and Burlington. Littlewoods announced that the home shopping division was up for sale in January 1991. It also owns the Littlewoods football pools. The company is privately owned by 32 members of the family of Sir John Moores, the founder and President.

Storehouse is a major retailing group, best known through its BhS mixed retailer chain, the Habitat furnishing chain, the Mothercare mother and baby retailer and the Richards and Blazer fashion shops. The group has altogether over 600 shops in the UK.

Responses

The policies of the **Co-op**, **Marks & Spencer** and **John Lewis** have already been mentioned, as they have supermarket operations.

Argos, **Boots**, **Burton**, **Kingfisher** and **Storehouse** did not respond to the questionnaire, and there is no indication in company literature of policies developed to address the social issues that arise from the sourcing of their products in the third world. **Kingfisher** did, however, send details of its environment policy, mainly relating to its B&Q subsidiary and covered in the DIY chapter. Interestingly, its Superdrug chain stocks rubber gloves from Malaysia; a good example of added value! Kingfisher has also recently sponsored the publication of a book on corporate social responsibility which includes a small section on the third world; while the company admits that it has only just begun to explore these issues, it is a welcome initiative.

While little is known of **Boots'** third world involvement generally, the company was rated second worst offender behind the Japanese company Meiji, when monitored on its breast milk substitutes and infant foods marketing in third world countries (see page 266–7).

Storehouse is suffering badly from the downturn in the consumer market, and cited the consequent lack of resources to devote to the task of completing the questionnaire. It is reported that the Storehouse subsidiary Habitat had a policy to replace mahogany with dark stained poplar, but it is not known to what extent this has affected the range in the shops. The company stated that little tropical hardwood was used, but that most came from 'government-approved renewable resources' in Indonesia. The annual report, focusing on the need to improve financial performance, does not mention sourcing of clothing or furniture.

The **House of Fraser** did not fill in the questionnaire either, though in response to the recent campaign on working conditions in the clothing industry initiated by Traidcraft, House of Fraser stated, 'This company has taken a number of initiatives which I am confident have played some part in protecting the rights of workers in the third world.' It states that the buyers of oriental carpets sold to the company visit production sites wherever possible to ensure that child labour is not used.

GUS did not respond to the questionnaire but was among a number of clothing companies mentioned in a 'World in Action' programme in 1984 that looked at the involvement of British companies in the exploitative garment manufacturing industry in Bangkok. GUS denied direct involvement as it purchased through agents and indicated that it had changed its agents, and had stopped purchasing from Thailand until it was 'satisfied with the position'. It is unclear what steps if any the company has taken to ensure that working conditions are satisfactory in the factories where its garments are made.

While **Littlewoods** declined to complete the questionnaire, the company is innovative in its policy on sourcing, and was the first to establish a code of practice including reference to social issues for those doing business with Littlewoods. The code states that the merchandise (or its components) produced for retail sale by Littlewoods must be produced in conformity with a) the UN Charter, Chapter IX, Article 55, governing economic and social cooperation with specific reference to workers' rights and working conditions, and b) the regional and local laws covering workers' rights, minimum wage and working conditions in the country of manufacture. Article 55 itself states that the UN 'shall promote: a) higher standards of living, full employment, and conditions of economic and social progress and development; b) solutions of international economic, social, health, and related problems; and international cultural and educational co-operation; and c) universal respect for, and observance of, human rights and fundamental freedoms for all without distinction as to race, sex, language, or religion.'

It is known that **Littlewoods** has terminated contractual arrangements with suppliers of garments on ethical grounds, but the company would not elaborate on this. Nor does the company say how it intends to monitor its suppliers' adherence to this policy. This is likely to be difficult in the absence of specific criteria, given the charter's very general wording. It will be interesting to see how well this enlightened policy works in practice, once it has been in place for a while.

CONSUMER CHOICES

Retailers generally do not display a particularly impressive appreciation of the issues of concern, but there are two initiatives worthy of recognition.

Overall, the **Co-op** is the supermarket to try first, on the basis of its social policies generally, and with respect to development and the third world in particular. The Co-op is also a mixed retailer, though in this area **Littlewoods'** Code of Practice also brings it into the best buy category; questions still arise, but it is a good start.

However, there is room for improvement. Write to the **Co-op** and suggest they look at developing further policies to address the many issues covered in this book, and to retailers expressing your concerns.

Write also to **Littlewoods**; the code of practice is a good start – a recognition of responsibility – but it is not yet known how successful it will be. Ask how the code is monitored, and what success it is having.

Development Agencies

In addition to making informed choices about what you buy, a very positive way to invest money in the development of third world communities is to support development agencies. There are many organisations in the UK, large and small, contributing to development in the third world in one way or another. For many of us, the decision as to which organisation to support is based on partial knowledge. We may not have come across many agencies that we wish to support; we may be unclear what the differences are between them. In this section we have selected development agencies that rely on public donations for a significant proportion of their work. We have limited ourselves to those having a reasonably wide geographical coverage, both in terms of overseas operations and UK fundraising, both for practical reasons (there are too many specialist agencies to cover here) as well as to ensure relevance to a wide range of readers. We have also chosen to concentrate on agencies whose work is biased towards long term development as opposed to disaster relief, important though the latter is.

Each organisation was sent a questionnaire covering its aims, development philosophy, structure, accountability and mode of operation. It was not an easy questionnaire to answer and we are grateful to their staff for devoting the necessary time.

Of the issues raised in the questionnaire, the most difficult one is that of accountability. Agencies, like commercial companies, are in principle accountable to their donors (for wise use of the money), to their partners or recipients and their communities (for their policy and practice), and of course to the charity commissioners. In practice, most are accountable to a board of some kind, usually self-appointed, which holds the organisation to its principles on behalf of the other groups. National bodies are accountable financially at least to the regulatory authorities in the country where they are based, though there have been some concerns that international organisations can escape this scrutiny.

Few organisations seem to have any structure allowing the donor or the recipient a formal voice in the creation of policy. To be fair, it is clear that many do listen at operational levels, and that it is not easy to include genuine representatives from 'developing' communities when the people who matter are such a hugely diverse group. But accountability has recently become more of an issue; we expect commercial companies with overseas operations to have management and direction from the local population. As with any organisation in a free market, development agencies may be more responsive to the demands of 'customers' (donors) than those people overseas who depend on them.

One controversial area in which individual donors may express a preference is the means by which money is raised. Some organisations profess to direct donors' money to specific projects. This raises the issue of who determines the priorities. If donors favour one project over another, does the agency respond by making up the difference or does one project, already approved, go hungry? No organisation would arbitrarily abandon a project; in practice, the money may only notionally be committed to a specific project.

Child sponsorship has been argued about long and hard; it is an effective way to raise money, as it encourages donors to feel involved in a personal way, but critics argue that it distorts priorities away from the needs of the community as a whole and more effort goes into meeting the needs of the donor than with other methods.

Commercial sponsorship is another key area; in today's economic climate, companies are increasingly expected to take a role in funding charities. But are there limits to this?

Do agencies select their potential sponsors? Do they allow commercial sponsors to influence their priorities? Any large donor is likely to have some influence, if for no other reason than that the agency cannot afford to lose the money. This is as true of government funding as commercial sponsorship, of course.

This section is not intended to encourage you to consider changing your policy on development support; if you are a regular supporter of an agency you will already know more about it than we can write in such a short space. But if, having considered the limitations of your power as a consumer, you are considering redirecting money through these channels, this will give you a flavour of the market.

AFRICA NOW

PO Box 165, London SW10 9LX.
Established: 1982   Income: £411,000 pa

AFRICA NOW aims to help communities in Africa achieve self-sufficiency by providing grants, low interest loans and training for small scale economic, technological and agricultural projects. It currently has twenty-eight projects in East, South and West African countries. With the vast majority of income coming from public donations, fundraising costs are high, so the organisation is currently attempting to increase the level of funding from other sources such as trusts and corporations.

Project selection begins with requests for project support, following which prospective recipients fill in a Needs Assessment Questionnaire. AFRICA NOW works jointly with both NGOs and government agencies who are selected according to their particular skills. Evaluation of projects consists of quarterly internal monitoring, self-evaluation by beneficiaries against the original objectives, and an external evaluation by a consultant about two thirds of the way through the funding of a project, allowing time for recommendations to be incorporated before handing the project over. Policy decisions are taken by the Council of Management which consists of individuals selected for particular expertise. The Council is appointed by the honorary director. Overseas partners are involved in planning, implementing and evaluating projects.

AHRTAG
1 London Bridge Street, London SE1 9SG.
Established: 1977   Income: £919,000 pa

AHRTAG (Appropriate Health Resources and Technologies Action Group) supports community health care and appropriate technology projects overseas. Its Resource Centre holds information on all aspects of primary health care and community-based rehabilitation. A key part of its work is assisting overseas groups to produce newsletters and disseminate information on all health matters.

Partners are selected if their approach to health care is comprehensive and if they have a proven background in the area. The emphasis is on local training and long-term infrastructure development. Evaluation is made jointly with the overseas partners using base-line indicators agreed beforehand. The Executive Committee is selected from the Council, whose members are either elected at the AGM or co-opted at other times throughout the year.

AHRTAG will not accept funds from drugs or baby milk manufacturers or from any company whose activities have a detrimental effect on health. Funders include several of the larger development organisations and UN agencies.

ApT Design and Development
29 Northwick Business Centre, Blockley,
Moreton-in-Marsh, Gloucestershire GL56 9RF.
Established: 1984   Income: £95,000 pa

ApT is a small engineering firm that provides both technological and managerial training to small-scale industries in developing countries, mainly teaching people to manufacture their own equipment. It receives most of its income from fees for work carried out on behalf of other agencies. Half of its expenditure in 1988 paid for the engineers to provide training overseas. ApT does provide some training in the UK for its overseas partners. One of the staff has performed an external evaluation of a $2 million UN programme aiding small enterprises in Bangladesh and has been asked to write a proposal for another similar programme.

Most overseas partners first contact ApT and a relationship is built up from there. ApT staff travel widely, running small workshops which thus far have all been internally evaluated, although external evaluations are now budgeted into projects. Workshops are evaluated by looking at the use of taught skills one year later. ApT is financially still a very small organisation and accordingly policy decisions are made by an executive committee consisting of two of the engineers.

CAFOD

2 Romero Close, Stockwell Road, London SW9 9TY.
Established: 1962   Income: £20,013,000 pa

CAFOD, the Catholic Fund for Overseas Development, is the Catholic Church's official agency for overseas development. It supports over 500 mainly small projects in 75 countries in the areas of food production, water development, preventive health care, agriculture and education, and also responds to emergency situations. Nearly £2 million of its income in 1989 was raised by parish groups, and includes family fast days and Friday self-denial.

Wherever possible, CAFOD works using the Catholic Church at national, regional and local level as an intermediary, and therefore does not need to employ local staff. Alternatively it will work with trusted local partner agencies. CAFOD sometimes seeks an independent pre-funding evaluation of project proposals. Ongoing projects are evaluated through narrative and financial reports supplied by the project proponent, which are read and evaluated by CAFOD Project Officers, whilst staff members undertake periodic visits to monitor and evaluate projects. In cases of difficulty an external evaluation or audit may be arranged. The management committee is accountable to the trustees who are themselves appointed by the Catholic Bishops' Conference to whom they report annually. CAFOD has a project advisory committee in each of the three continents where they are active. Individuals can subscribe to various newsletters and participate in advocacy initiatives whereby they are able to lobby for changes in policy.

CARE Britain

36 Southampton Street, London WC2E 7HE.
Established: 1985   Income: £10,690,000 pa

CARE Britain is one of the 11 national member organisations of CARE International through which it has access to an extensive range of projects throughout the world. Although the organisation as a whole started in the US over 40 years ago, CARE Britain has more recently become independent. CARE offers technical assistance, training, food and management to projects in the areas of health, food production and income generation.

CARE International has overseas offices in 40 different countries employing mostly local staff who, in conjunction with host governments and non-governmental organisations, prepare project proposals for the members of CARE International. From these projects CARE Britain selects the projects that it wishes to support. Projects are evaluated both during and after the period of support by multi-disciplinary teams, mostly from outside CARE, against project achievement indicators defined at the outset of the project. Executives are accountable to a voluntary board of non-executive directors, which includes the Deputy Chairman of one of the high street banks. Each national CARE contributes members to the board of CARE International.

CARE Britain seems to be unique in having a specific association of companies involved in sponsorship of its work. Over 60 companies are members of CARE Britain Corporate Council, sponsoring individual projects and contributing between 1% and 2% of total funds. Donations from the corporate sector have been steadily increasing.

Christian Aid

PO Box 100, Interchurch House, 35 Lower Marsh Street, London SE1 7RT.
Established: 1944   Income: £31,239,000 pa

Christian Aid is an official agency of the British and Irish Churches, working on agricultural projects, technical and health training, self-help community development and human rights counselling. It also has an education programme at home. One fifth of expenditure in 1990 was used for emergency relief.

Christian Aid has no staff based overseas, instead always working through other bodies including local churches and secular organisations. Partners are either recommended or apply and are then visited. Projects must serve the local community and not just the members of the partner organisation. In evaluating projects, the criteria used include technical and financial efficiency and the social impact on the whole community, in particular vulnerable groups such as women. The evaluation is performed by persons decided by consultation with the partners if an evaluator is not already available. The Director of Christian Aid is accountable to the Board which is itself accountable to, appointed by and comprises representatives of, the sponsoring churches. Country Policy Papers are drawn up in conjunction with overseas partners who are sometimes represented at meetings by nationals resident in the UK. Christian Aid is in the process of developing a policy on corporate funding sources.

Christian Outreach

1 New Street, Leamington Spa, Warwickshire CV31 1HP.
Established: 1967   Income: £865,000 pa

Christian Outreach was formed as a response to destitute children in the Vietnamese war and works with children and refugees in medical, construction, business and community development projects. Major sources of funding include the ODA, the UNHCR and Tear Fund (see later profile) with whom they work closely.

Christian Outreach has expatriate workers in the field in refugee situations who select projects in consultation with the UK office and committee. In addition, over 1,000 local and refugee staff are employed overseas. In other circumstances, Christian based local partners overseas may be found. Each project is monitored by project staff, quarterly reports and regular visits by UK based staff and might include monitoring health statistics and the birth rate. The executive committee is appointed by the trustees. There is normally a management team of refugee staff responsible for much of the policy within a particular programme. Most donors give to general funds but where donors specify a particular project, the donation is put into the existing budget for that project.

Christian Outreach will not accept funding from companies involved in arms or tobacco or in cases where they feel the donation has ulterior motives.

FARM Africa
22 Gilbert Street, London W1Y 1RJ.
Established: 1985   Income: £370,000 pa

FARM (Food and Agricultural Research Management) works in particular with small farmers (mostly women) and herdsmen. It pioneers new techniques and strategies in crop production and animal husbandry and spreads knowledge of better farming practices to agriculturalists. There is an emphasis on environmentally sustainable agricultural systems.

FARM Africa recently merged with the Send a Tonne Development Fund (SATDF) and has close contacts with the National Farmers' Union. FARM responds to project requests from overseas organisations, some familiar with previous FARM projects. Proposals are forwarded to national and international agencies and private organisations for funding, which may be provided as 50, 75 or 100% of project costs. Donors include governments, trusts and companies who are involved in the evaluation process. Evaluation is against initial project objectives and 'base line data' such as the amount of milk being produced or the mortality rate of adult stock. Fundraising in the UK has to date concentrated largely on the farming community, and has included 'Sheep Aid' and 'Milk Aid'. The Council of FARM Africa is elected from its members (invited by the council) at the AGM.

Harvest Help

318 St Paul's Road, London N1 2LF.
Established: 1985   Income: £200,000 pa

The Harvest Help appeal supports work with poor rural communities, helping them to produce more food. It also works on health, marketing, veterinary and education projects.

Projects are selected after staff visits, and must be capable of self-development by local communities at every stage, with possible guidance by local agencies. Evaluation is performed externally by experts such as sociologists, comparing physical, social and economic measures against those in the original plans. The Executive Committee meets monthly and is accountable to the Full Committee. This body is itself accountable to the Trustees of Voluntary and Christian Service who also make the appointments. The committee includes technical specialists and donor supporters. Prior to commencement, funding sources are approached for specific projects, and covenanted gifts from individuals are similarly used.

Health Unlimited

3 Stamford Street, London SE1 9NT.
Established: 1983   Income: £423,000 pa

Health Unlimited sends teams to run primary health care training programmes in communities isolated during, or as a result of, conflict. The long term aim is to establish self-supporting health care systems.

Health Unlimited responds to requests from communities received via contacts from other agencies. Projects are usually in areas where other agencies are not working in the health field. Although working in areas of conflict, the local situation has to be stable enough to support a training programme at the village and district level, and the partner be willing to use local resources to support the programme. Teams are usually composed of expatriate professionals on one or two year contracts.

Funding sources include British Government and European Community grants and the larger development agencies. Projects are evaluated by staff on an annual basis and external evaluators are appointed for a selection of projects, usually towards the end of the funding period. Health Unlimited was set up by a group of health professionals who formed the original Management Committee and ran the organisation on a voluntary basis. New members are co-opted up to a maximum of twelve. There is a 'Friends of Health Unlimited' scheme which gives supporters a chance to meet project officers, although at present there is no formal representation of the Friends on the Committee. The results of discussions with local communities overseas are communicated back to the London offices for consideration.

HelpAge International
St James's Walk, London EC1R 0BE.
Established: 1983   Income: £549,000 pa

HelpAge International works overseas in the areas of grants to local organisations, health promotion, ophthalmic work, relief of urban destitution, income generation schemes, refugee work, age care development and training and the provision of emergency relief. Help the Aged is a member organisation of HelpAge International. HelpAge International funds projects through its member organisations. All member organisations contribute 2.5% of their annual income and must have a proven record of commitment to developing age care services and a local fundraising base.

Project selection and evaluation are carried out by the member organisations who submit proposals both for themselves and for other organisations in that country.

Evaluation is performed by local specialists and through feedback from beneficiaries, for example trainees' own assessment of workshops. All member organisations have the right to appoint a representative as a member of the Council. The Council is accountable to the Executive, the members of which are elected from the Council. In 1990 the Council Chairman came from HelpAge India and two of the three Vice-chairmen were representatives of member organisations in Kenya and Colombia. In cases of corporate sponsorship, the Secretariat will ask a member organisation if it objects to receiving funding from that source.

Intermediate Technology

Myson House, Railway Terrace, Rugby CV21 3HT.
Established: 1965   Income: £4,837,000 pa

IT was founded by Dr E F Schumacher, the author of *Small is Beautiful*, and provides technical information and advice, training, equipment and financial support for small scale technology projects with poor communities in the developing world.

IT projects generally begin in response to requests from overseas groups and always involve the use of local materials and labour. IT's partners for projects include government ministries, multilateral agencies and other non-governmental agencies. Ongoing evaluations are carried out by social scientists working with the project, although external specialists make more substantial assessments. Evaluation processes are currently under review. Policy decisions are taken by the Director and Chief Executive who are accountable to a voluntary Committee elected from the organisation's members. In the five countries where IT has overseas offices, recipients are able to feed into policy decisions. Donors include several companies and some of the larger development agencies.

International Christian Relief

Interaid Ltd, PO Box 80, 16 St Johns Hill, Sevenoaks, Kent
TN13 3NP.
Established: 1978   Income: £1,191,000 pa

Interaid Limited is an affiliated fundraising body of Interaid
International. ICR provides assistance with medical, agricultural and educational projects in developing countries and
also responds to emergencies. Most of its income in 1989
came from individual donations, including its child sponsorship programme which accounts for the biggest portion of
expenditure. At least 14 UK companies made donations to
Interaid in 1989, the most substantial of which came from one
of the high street banks.

Project selection emphasises consultation with the elders
of prospective recipient communities from which field
workers make formal proposals. Funds are transferred from
a central European Fund where money received is pooled
and administered by the European financial director of
Interaid International. Donors are invited to designate how
their donations should be used. There is also a fund called
'Where most needed' to which donors can subscribe, leaving
the choice of investment to management. Projects are
budgeted and evaluated by country directors but monitored
by the organisation's international accountants. The board of
Interaid Ltd consists of five UK and two international
directors, and is self appointing. The whole range of policy
decisions are taken at regular clearance meetings which
involve fundraising directors and senior field management.

International Planned Parenthood Federation

Regent's College, Inner Circle, Regent's Park, London
NW1 4NS.
Established: 1952   Income: $73,523,000 pa

IPPF is a federation of Family Planning Associations (FPAs)
in 137 countries worldwide. It aims to promote family
planning and responsible parenthood. The FPAs provide
family planning advice, information and services through

clinics and mobile units and give training and support to wider community programmes being developed by local groups.

Individual FPAs are set up and run by local people and work in partnership with government health programmes. Member FPAs submit annual work programmes for which they seek funding from IPPF and other agencies. Evaluation criteria include the number and type of contraceptives distributed, and attitude surveys of recipient communities. IPPF's policies are formulated and agreed by representatives of its member FPAs. They elect representatives to Regional Councils which in turn elect representatives to the Central Council, which determines IPPF policies and directs the Federation's work. Every three years a Members' Assembly reviews the role of IPPF and considers the way its objectives can best be accomplished.

IPPF does not accept cash or in-kind donations from manufacturers of contraceptives or fertility drugs.

Methodist Church Overseas Division

25 Marylebone Road, London NW1 5JR.
Established: 1973   Income: £4,514,000 pa

The MCOD was formalised after a reorganisation of the Methodist Church and works in partnership with churches and local groups overseas in areas including education, health, agriculture, by supplying personnel and by making grants.

Projects are selected by overseas partners, primarily churches with historical links with the British Church. Evaluation is the responsibility of local partners but MCOD staff sometimes make visits. The Committee of MCOD is accountable to the Methodist Conference and includes two representatives from each Methodist district and seven from the Methodist Church in Ireland. Two of the senior executives are members of overseas churches and West African churches are consulted to discuss joint budget proposals. Members of the Methodist Church are automatically members of the MCOD. Most of the support for the MCOD comes from churches. Specific projects – the Second Mile Projects – are supported by groups of churches in units of £500.

The Ockenden Venture

Guildford Road, Woking, Surrey GU22 7UU.
Established: 1952   Income: £2,370,000 (15 month period)

The Ockenden Venture works with refugees and displaced persons, providing homes, education and medical facilities, and runs skills training, literacy and cottage industry projects. Grants from the ODA, EC and UNHCR make up the bulk of the funding. Similar amounts, around £1 million each, were spent in 1989 on UK and overseas projects.

Overseas projects are researched by the Overseas Director and when selected put forward as a proposal for funding. Projects are selected with a view to handing the project over to local people after initial training. The Overseas Director constantly evaluates projects and reports back to the committee members. Monthly reports on projects may be required, and any of the directors may visit projects at any time. Policy making is handled by a self-appointing General Committee which includes refugees currently resident in the UK. Questions concerning formal mechanisms for including the views of staff in policy decisions are currently being addressed.

One World Action

59 Hatton Garden, London EC1N 8LS.
Established: end of 1989   Income: approx £400,000 pa (unaudited)

One World Action was founded in 1989 in memory of Bernt Carlson, the UN Ambassador to Namibia killed in the Lockerbie air disaster while on his way to the signing of the Namibian peace settlement. One World Action sees itself as a partnership between women and men in the third world and supporters in Europe aiming to end poverty, discrimination and inequality. It has a special focus on Southern Africa.

Its partners are women's groups, trades unions, co-ops

and NGOs, selected on the basis of their commitment to equitable distribution of resources, challenging gender bias, and participative and democratic methods. Project evaluation is based on reports and visits, with grants given in instalments conditional on progress. Executives are responsible to a group of trustees who appoint a management committee. Having no overseas staff, the agency seeks the opinions of partners about priorities, including development education in the UK.

Oxfam

274 Banbury Road, Oxford OX2 7DX.
Established: 1942   Income: £62,078,000 pa

Founded to relieve famine and sickness in Nazi-occupied Greece and Belgium, Oxfam's main activity is funding of projects of other groups and organisations in the areas of social development, health, education, production, agriculture, and emergency relief. Oxfam's concern to enhance public awareness of the causes of poverty (based on the experiences of its overseas partners) has given the organisation a higher than average and sometimes controversial profile.

Projects are selected through Oxfam's field offices, where the mostly local staff visit groups to discuss proposed projects. The final decision to fund a project is made overseas except in the case of very large grants. Criteria for selection include the prospective partners' level of organisation and motivation, the likelihood of achieving objectives, technical appropriateness and economic viability. Field officers decide which projects to evaluate. Senior officers are accountable to the Council of Management, or Trustees. The current Council's 49 voluntary members include 21 women. Periodic regional meetings are held around the world to discuss work strategies.

Oxfam reviews every source of corporate funding to ensure that it does not contravene the principles of its overseas work. The organisation has about 900 shops throughout the UK and Oxfam Trading, an alternative trading organisation, sells produce made by small groups in the third world and returns the profits to these groups. Oxfam operates a textiles and aluminium recycling scheme called Wastesaver, processing unsold items from the shops.

Quaker Peace and Service

Friends House, Euston Road, London NW1 2BJ.
Established: 1978   Income: £1,434,000 pa

QPS is the international department of the Religious Society of Friends in Britain and Ireland. Areas of work include rural medical projects, counselling and workshops and provision of teachers.

Projects are often carried out by local voluntary agencies with funding from QPS. The organisation also works closely with overseas partners that share Quaker beliefs in peace, justice and equality. Evaluation is performed by Area Committees who may commission academic studies or professional consultants to perform an independent evaluation. Except when the project's goals are very material, evaluation concentrates on consideration of the attitude of the recipient community. The senior officers of QPS are accountable to the membership of the Religious Society of Friends, through its executive body representing the Friends all over the UK and Ireland. This body delegates policy decisions to a committee of 26, which it appoints.

QPS is reluctant to accept more than 20% of funding from the UK government and has an active policy not to accept money from organisations involved in activities such as the arms trade. QPS has a policy of ethical investment and is informed by the Ethical Investment Research and Information Service which it helped to establish. The amount spent on projects in the UK is two thirds of the amount spent on overseas development.

Save the Children

Mary Datchelor House, 17 Grove Lane, London SE5 8RD.
Established: 1919   Income: £52,196,000 pa

Long term health, nutrition, education, community development and welfare programmes form the principal part of Save the Children's work overseas. Throughout Save the Children's history, the Rights of the Child have been at the heart of the organisation's work and have now become the United Nations Convention on the Rights of the Child, which was adopted in 1989.

Projects, run by 2,500 overseas indigenous staff, must fall within the scope of the Convention, must involve working with children in one of the above areas, be based on community participation and involve working with the local health or welfare authorities where possible. Monitoring of projects is a continual process and is performed by field staff, although independent evaluation is also carried out. The directors are accountable to the Council, which consists of up to 20 members, 11 being elected, the rest co-opted or members by virtue of their office.

The majority of expenditure is on overseas projects, but one fifth goes on UK based projects. Save the Children will not accept links with products or companies whose activities directly contradict or work against the best interests of children. The organisation has a network of 150 shops throughout the UK, as well as 800 local branches.

Scottish Catholic International Aid Fund
5 Oswald Street, Glasgow G1 4QR.
Established: 1965   Income: £2,073,000 pa

SCIAF is the official agency of the Catholic Church in Scotland and the equivalent organisation of CAFOD in England and Wales. It supports long term development projects mainly in the areas of primary health care and agriculture and also responds to emergencies.

SCIAF provided one of the most detailed sets of guidelines for project selection which emphasises self-sufficiency after an initial period of assistance. Specifically mentioned is the long term desire to eliminate the roots and causes of poverty, although as in all cases there is no clear distinction between preventive work and patching up wounds. The guidelines also include factors that would exclude a project from funding, notably any that require large capital investments. Two years ago, for the first time, overseas partners were encouraged to apply for funding for a period of several years in order to assist with their long term project planning. SCIAF has reduced its number of 'priority' countries to 23 in order that project officers can have a greater knowledge of the areas in which they are working. Projects are initially evaluated by Project staff and then by the Projects Committee. Regular field trips are made to liaise with overseas partners. The Management Committee is appointed by the Catholic Bishops' Conference of Scotland and, like the Projects Committee, consists of both diocesan representatives and individuals with expertise in the field of development work.

Shared Interest

52 Elswick Road, Newcastle upon Tyne NE4 6JH.
Established: 1990   Income: £90,000 pa

Shared Interest provides a channel through which people in the UK can invest in job creation and income generation projects in developing countries. The organisation differs from a bank in that there is a possibility of making a loss on investments should projects fail. Individuals' investments however are not allocated to specific projects. Capital invested by individuals currently stands at £550,000, paying interest at 5.25%. Shared Interest is one of 240 members of the Ecumenical Development Cooperative Society (EDCS). The invested money is lent to small enterprises on favourable credit terms and when repaid, the money can be reinvested elsewhere. The EDCS has itself invested in over 125 projects in 15 years.

Projects are currently selected by the EDCS. Primarily they should be sustainable business enterprises which can service and repay capital investment, but whose business and profits are aimed to serve the interests of the poor, usually through charitable, cooperative or community ownership. Evaluation is also done by indigenous EDCS

Project Development Officers. Measures include normal financial projections, the ability to generate foreign exchange surplus (where applicable) and the income and employment created for the community.

Shared Interest is mainly self financing from the investment returns. The Board of Directors is appointed at the AGM and is accountable to the Council, which is elected from investors. Members of the Board generally have financial skills, and the Council members are mainly lay. EDCS still make the project decisions at present and the majority of its board come from a variety of developing countries.

South American Missionary Society
Allen Gardiner House, Pembury Road, Tunbridge Wells, Kent TN2 3QU.
Established: 1844   Income: £872,000 pa

SAMS is a long standing Anglican agency linked to the Church of England and involved in a combined missionary and developmental role. It is working with the Anglican Church in developing countries in South America and the Iberian Peninsula on medical, agricultural and educational programmes.

Staff make frequent visits overseas and have occasional meetings in South America to discuss policy issues with the dioceses which it serves. The General Council is accountable to the Board of Trustees and nominees for positions on the Council are appointed with a view to achieving a reasonable gender balance and geographical spread from British Anglican dioceses. Whilst SAMS places equal emphasis on material and spiritual aid, the actual work carried out reflects the greater funding available for the former. About one third of expenditure is on development education in the UK.

Tear Fund
100 Church Road, Teddington, Middlesex TW11 8QE.
Established: 1969   Income: £14,871,000 pa

Tear Fund works with evangelical alliances around the

world, mainly in the areas of water provision, health care, agriculture and vocational training, as well as organising relief aid.

Tear Fund works with partners who share its religious beliefs. Projects are evaluated by local specialised consultants or by Tear Fund staff. Projects must be appropriate in terms of both the needs of the community and the size of the church undertaking the project. The Logical Framework developed by the ODA is used here as a guide by Tear Fund. Tear Fund is a limited company and the Board are accountable to the Council of Reference and Members. Council members are appointed by the Board and represent a broad spectrum of evangelical denominations and churches.

Other than the ODA and the EC, funding sources are Christian based organisations, churches and individuals. Tear Fund sells third world produce through a mail order catalogue as Tearcraft. Tear Fund also operates child sponsorship schemes which currently cover over 20,000 children sponsored at £13 per month and providing over £3million of income.

Tools for Self Reliance
Netley Marsh, Southampton SO4 2GY.
Established: 1978   Income: £137,000 pa

TFSR sends recycled second hand tools to cooperative communities in developing countries where it also promotes tool making.

TFSR works through indigenous partner groups who propose recipient communities. Volunteers in the UK collect, clean and renovate old tools and then send them overseas. Partner organisations then distribute the tools themselves and provide reports on progress made with the tools. Field studies by UK staff are kept to a minimum and overseas representatives sometimes make visits to the UK. TFSR sees itself not as running its own projects but supporting the projects of overseas partners. The organisation is notable for its questioning of the motives behind much Western development aid and is very self-critical. TFSR is currently involved with one Zimbabwean group in a dialogue about 'the motivations and ethics which lie behind aid and the mutual responsibility of partnership', following complaints from the group that agencies dominate, rather than work with, beneficiaries. Members, including several representatives from overseas, elect directors to the board for a period of three years. Staff can be members but not directors. There is strong emphasis on everyone within the organisation taking part at all levels, from manual work to policy making.

In the past an offer of funding was turned down because of South African links. TFSR now has a formal policy not to solicit donations from the 'big four' banks and has never sought funds from the British Government aid programme. Tool production overseas represented about one third, and tool refurbishment in the UK plus shipping abroad one quarter, of expenditure in the last financial year.

Traidcraft Exchange
Kingsway, Gateshead, Tyne & Wear NE11 0NE.
Established: 1979   Income: £270,000 pa

The Traidcraft Exchange encourages and develops 'fair trade' with producer groups in the third world establishing better trading links, both financially and in terms of security, than would otherwise have been possible. The Exchange is linked to Traidcraft plc, which contributes to its funding. Some of the other larger agencies also contribute. The Exchange is involved with overseas projects in an advisory role, by helping small community businesses to break into the European market and by educating consumers in the UK.

Standard business criteria are applied when selecting and evaluating producer groups as well as the social and employment benefits of establishing trading links. Following an initial request from a potential producer group, a visit and background survey follow. Executive officers are accountable to a self-appointing Board of Trustees which is itself accountable to a Trust Deed.

Individuals can purchase produce through the mail order

catalogue or retail outlets of Traidcraft plc, which is also involved in establishing trading links with producer groups and shares the same board of Trustees. The two groups collaborate on some projects, although the Exchange is involved in a wider area of work than the company. The Exchange has been instrumental in setting up Shared Interest (see earlier profile).

Water Aid

1 Queen Anne's Gate, London SW1H 9BT.
Established: 1981   Income: £2,747,000 pa

Water Aid is a specialist water and sanitation development agency working on safe water supplies and adequate sanitation projects using low-cost and simple technologies. Nearly one half of funds raised comes from water industry employees or appeals sent with water bills.

Water Aid works with partner organisations overseas, including the water departments of foreign governments. The local people must demonstrate that they are willing to organise and manage their own projects and show that they are committed to completing the work. Projects are evaluated by Resident Engineers, by visits from the Overseas Projects Officer and by independent assessors. The Council members are elected at the AGM by the members who consist of representatives of the 10 main water plcs, 28 water companies, various union bodies, Lions Clubs and individuals.

World Vision of Britain

Dychurch House, 8 Abingdon Street, Northampton, Northamptonshire NN1 2AJ.
Established: 1981   Income: £9,207,000 pa

World Vision is a Christian motivated agency working on projects in the areas of income generation, agriculture, health, education, relief and rehabilitation. World Vision was established in 1950, World Vision of Britain being a more recent affiliate.

Where conditions permit it is the policy of World Vision to employ local national staff to administer its work in the field. The Field Offices of World Vision exist in nearly 60 countries and provide the immediate liaison with partner communities, who in most cases approach World Vision for assistance. Partners consist mainly of Churches from a variety of denominations. The field officers and the local communities then jointly formulate proposals which are offered to member organisations in the developed world for funding. Projects are selected with a view to their sustainability, community participation and the 'level of need'. Evaluations are performed by both World Vision International and by the British member organisation. Evaluation criteria include the level of use of new facilities provided by a project.

World Vision of Britain has a non-stipendiary Board of Directors. Membership is rotated, with new members being invited on the Board by existing members. The Board includes representatives of business and the major Churches. Each national office of World Vision operates through World Vision International, jointly determining policy.

About one third of funding comes from child sponsorship schemes and one fifth from a 24 hour 'famine' on its national fundraising day. Funds raised in child sponsorship are mainly used for community-wide support rather than going directly to the child. 42% of total funding comes from the government and the European Community. Equal amounts are spent on development projects and relief aid.

Y Care International

640 Forest Road, London E17 3DZ.
Established: 1984   Income: £1,300,000 pa

Y Care International is the development agency of the YMCAs of Great Britain and Ireland. Y Care is a department of the English National Council of YMCAs, but the National Councils of Wales, Ireland and Scotland have Y Care committees which nominate a person to sit on the Y Care International Committee.

Projects involve working mainly with young people worldwide and include vocational training, health and education programmes, a reafforestation scheme and also emergency relief. Worldwide YMCAs have over 30 million members in over 100 countries. Projects are selected and managed by overseas YMCAs and evaluated in conjunction with staff from Y Care International. Policy is made by the Y Care International Committee which is accountable to and also appointed by the National Council of YMCAs of England Board.

Going Further

It would be neat to let things rest at this point; to assume that consumer power is here to stay, and that we can solve the world's problems by choosing more carefully where we shop and what we buy. But there are, of course, limitations to individual action of this sort and other ways in which to address the impact of rich countries on the third world. The importance of campaigning groups, unions and neighbourhood committees that have been working for many years to improve the impact of trade on the people of the third world should not be underestimated.

One issue of particular importance, and which governments and international institutions have not yet effectively addressed, is the power of transnational companies to operate across international boundaries. This is the proper concern of consumers as voters, and, as New Consumer's role is to focus on consumer choices in the context of social values, we would encourage you to explore these issues with the help of the agencies listed at the end of this chapter.

Where next?

We hope we might be able to produce a second edition of this book; many companies have barely begun to take the issues seriously, and we should expect change. In particular, retailers characteristically do not see that they have any responsibility save to provide goods for their customers. Manufacturers frequently do not think too hard about the social and environmental aspects of the raw materials they use. Most have yet to realise that some of the 'goods' consumers want are closely bound up with the way products are manufactured and traded. The green consumer movement began a process; it is by no means finished. We have reported many statements of company policy; the challenge facing consumers and consumer groups is to assess the extent to which these are reflected in practice. An essential, though enormous, task.

A major concern to which we have only occasionally alluded is companies' records in the manufacture and distribution of goods for sale in the third world. It is a huge area in which many more companies are involved, including drugs manufacturers and car companies. This we hope to follow up in the future.

In some cases, government policy is of major significance, and you should voice your concerns to the appropriate people. But this book is not about lobbying; advice can be had from the World Development Movement and other specialised agencies. Addresses are given at the end of the chapter.

Alternative trade

For many years now, a number of trading organisations set up specifically to address the need for fairer trade with the third world have existed. Products are made by community groups, cooperatives, or even commercial companies that provide better employment conditions or wages, or perhaps better participation in decision making. They also seek to build better relationships with their suppliers, based on loyalty and avoiding the abuse of power.

These trading groups are small – even the biggest have turnovers of less than £10 million – and locally-based, which helps them to be sensitive to the needs of their partners. Although this does mean that the products are not widely available to Western consumers, certain items – especially foods, beverages, crafts and clothing – are available in local shops or by mail order; details are given in the buyers' guides in relevant product chapters. Addresses of the larger alternative traders are given at the end of **Going Further;** you can find local sources of supply from them.

From the margins to the mainstream – The Fair Trade Mark

During 1992, consumers will see the introduction of the 'fair trade mark', when a small range of products carrying a special seal of approval will be promoted through mainstream outlets. The 'fair trade mark' will guarantee that the brand carrying the mark has been sourced and supplied from the third world in a way that provides the producer with a better deal than is the norm.

Companies will be able to apply for use of the mark providing they fulfil a set of product criteria. Initially the mark will be limited to food products, though in the future any third world sourced product could be considered as potentially eligible.

The mark will be administered and promoted by a number of development agencies, campaign groups and alternative trading organisations, who were inspired by a similar and very successful scheme in the Netherlands, and who will soon be setting up an independent foundation. The main task of the foundation will be to administer the use and promotion of the mark. In some ways similar to the Soil Association's organic seal, the foundation will be responsible for monitoring the use of the mark and developing criteria for additional products.

Some major companies as well as smaller ones have already shown interest and enthusiasm for the scheme, and at the time of writing negotiations on contracts are progressing. Look out for the Fair Trade Mark, particularly on coffee, tea and honey, over the coming months.

Write to your local supermarket and say that you have heard of the fair trade mark scheme and that you would like to know when brands carrying the seal will be available.

Once they are available, write to the manufacturer concerned (or retailer if it is an own brand) and congratulate them on taking part in the scheme. For updated informatio and further details contact the Fair Trade Mark at the address below.

Beyond the Global Consumer

The process of change can be continued, with the help of this book, by consumers acting together. One of the weaknesses of the consumer movement at present is that it really hasn't got beyond helping the great 'silent majority' to make effective their economic vote. We still consume alone. But if consumers are to make progress towards a new way of doing things it is vital that they come together. Only then will consumerism truly be a movement.

Consumer issues can be the natural concern of many important groups and not just the obvious citizen action groups that some of us belong to, such as the WI, Oxfam or Parents for Safe Food. Key consumers meet together and talk in anything from parent and toddler groups to keep fit classes. They don't meet to change the world, but these groups can be the seed bed of ideas on their way into everyday society.

The Global Consumer, while clearly written as a resource for the individual, will only be effective when you pass on the message to friends and neighbours. Find out how to take things further by sending for the leaflet, 'Beyond the global consumer'. You can become a supporter of New Consumer (see page 352). You could be in at the start of a movement!

In short, we see this book as opening the door to the world of corporate accountability, not tying up the issue once and for all; there is a long way to go.

Further reading

Because of the large amount of ground covered in this book, the analysis is necessarily brief. There are some very good books that go into more detail, and we hope readers will want to explore further. Many of the agencies listed below have a publications catalogue; Christian Aid and Oxfam ▪mong development agencies are worth contacting, as well as Traidcraft (see page 321) and Latin America Bureau and CIIR (page 318).

For further background on international trading trends and statistics it is worth looking at material produced by the United Nations Conference on Trade and Development (UNCTAD) – the *UNCTAD Commodity Yearbook* and the *Handbook of Trade and Development Statistics,* both published annually and available in most central libraries.

For economic analysis the World Bank's *World Development Report,* also published annually, is useful, particularly its tables. *The State of the World's Children,* compiled by UNICEF, and the *Human Development Report* produced by UNDP provide excellent comparative information on social and economic factors including health education and income distribution. All three are published by Oxford University Press.

Poverty and the Planet (Ben Jackson, Penguin) and *Our Common Future* (World Commission on Environment and Development, OUP) both look at the links between poverty and the environment. *The End of the Third World* (Paul Harris, Penguin) surveys the lessons to be learned from the NICs of SE Asia and Latin America and their manufacturing industries (electronics, footwear, clothing and textiles). *The Trade Trap* (Belinda Coote, Oxfam) looks at how the global commodity markets affect the third world. *The Third World Guide 91/92,* produced and published annually in the third world (and available from New Internationalist, 55 Rectory Road, Oxford OX4 1BW), gives useful country profiles. The annual *Amnesty International Report* provides a country by country summary of human rights.

On specific products, *The Hunger Crop* (Belinda Coote, Oxfam) looks at the sugar industry; *Green Gold* (Latin America Bureau) is an analysis of the banana industry of the Eastern Caribbean; *Common Interests: Women Organising in Global Electronics* (Women Working Worldwide) is one of the few books on the subject; *Rainforest Politics* (Philip Hurst, Zed) and *No Timber Without Trees* (Duncan Poore, Earthscan) look at the tropical timber industry.

Of the major newspapers, the *Financial Times* can be a

source of useful material on the industries and commodities featured in this book, and is good on international news and features. Finally, company annual reports, though very variable in the amount of information they give, can provide good insight into a company's culture and what it says about itself.

Useful organisations

Amnesty International (British Section) 5 Roberts Place, Bowling Green Lane, London EC1R 0EJ. Carries out and publishes respected surveys of human rights abuses in all countries, and campaigns for release of prisoners of conscience.

Anti Apartheid Movement 13 Mandela Street, London NW1 0DW. The leading agency campaigning for democratic change in South Africa.

Anti Slavery Society 180 Brixton Road, London SW9 6AT. Campaigns for, among other things, the abolition of child labour. A new campaign focuses on a non-child labour labelling scheme.

Centre for the Advancement of Responsive Travel (CART) 70 Dry Hill Park Road, Tonbridge, Kent. Aims to promote fairer forms of tourism, including reforms of the mass tourism industry. Publishes an informative handbook available to members of Tourism Concern (qv).

Catholic Institute for International Relations (CIIR) 2 Coleman Fields, London N1 7AF. Publishes good material on development and human rights.

Fair Trade Mark c/o New Consumer, 52 Elswick Road, Newcastle upon Tyne NE4 6JH. See Fair Trade Mark above.

Friends of the Earth 26 Underwood Street, London N1 7QJ. One of the leading environmental campaign groups, FoE has, through contacts with third world environmental groups, taken a lead in responding to the social issues surrounding environmental concern.

Greenpeace Greenpeace House, Canonbury Villas, London N1 2PN. Perhaps the most high profile environmental campaigning organisation, concentrating on pollution and endangered species.

Latin America Bureau 1 Amwell Street, London EC1R 1UL. Publishes books and booklets on social, political, economic and human rights issues in Latin America.

National Association of Development Education Centres (NADEC) 6 Endsleigh Street, London WC1H 0DX. National coordinating office of the network of local Development Education Centres. Can tell you where your local DEC, development resources, and some local third world trade shops are.

One World Week PO Box 100, London SE1 7RT. Coordinates a national week of events to raise awareness of development issues. Assists local groups to make the most of the opportunity this offers.

Tourism Concern Froebel College, Roehampton Lane, London SW15 5PU. A network for all concerned about the impact of tourism on host communities; linked with similar networks throughout the world.

Third World Information Network (TWIN) 345 Goswell Road, London EC1V 7TJ. Primarily acting as a facilitating link between producers in the third world and the UK market, TWIN can also supply a list of 'alternative' retailers throughout the UK.

Whale and Dolphin Conservation Society 19a James Street West, Bath, Avon BA1 2BT. For information on current progress on dolphin-friendly tuna.

Women Working Worldwide Box 92, 190 Upper Street, London N1 1RQ. Information and publications on women in global industries.

World Development Movement (WDM) 25 Beehive Place, London SW9 7QR. Campaigning and lobbying on behalf of the world's poor. WDM has many local groups and individual members, and a unique role in confronting the government with the impact of its policies on the third world.

Worldwide Fund for Nature Panda House, Weyside Park, Godalming, Surrey GU7 1XR. Focuses on conservation of natural resources, but also aware of the 'people issues' that are an essential part of this.

Useful companies

Ecological Trading Company (ETC) 1 Lesbury Road, Newcastle upon Tyne NE6 5LB. Imports timber from sustainable sources in the third world, as well as establishing the principles of verification.

ETC timber for craft and DIY use is available from Milland Fine Timber Ltd, Milland Pottery, Milland, Nr Liphook, Hants GU30 7JP.

Equal Exchange 29 Nicholson Street, Edinburgh EH8 9BX. An 'alternative trader' specialising in foods from the third world. Their products can be found in many wholefood shops.

North South Travel Moulsham Mill Centre, Parkway, Chelmsford, Essex CM2 7PX. A travel agent closely linked to the Tourism Concern network, and whose profits are given to charitable projects concerned with the third world. The company can arrange low cost flights and accommodation for independent travel, but does not handle package tours.

Oxfam Trading Murdoch Road, Bicester OX6 7RF. Sales of crafts, gifts, clothing and foodstuffs from community-based groups in third world countries; mail order catalogues and Oxfam shops.

Traidcraft Kingsway, Gateshead NE11 0NE. The largest independent 'alternative trader' in the UK; sells jewellery, clothing, crafts, paper, foods through mail order catalogues, a network of voluntary 'reps' and small shops. Contact them to find name of local supplier.

The Companies

Throughout this book we have suggested writing to the companies surveyed, either to encourage them to adopt some new policy or to reinforce their commitment to one they have already developed. The addresses of the companies we have researched are listed below, together with the turnover of the whole group (parent plus subsidiaries), where known, to give some idea of the resources they have available.

Wherever possible, we have given a UK address for foreign companies. Write to the Director responsible for Public Affairs. Mentioning this book will add weight to the request, as a focused consumer response will begin to be noticed.

Several companies are involved in a huge range of manufacturing businesses, often under different names. Few of us can be aware of the full scope of a company's activities, yet this is important for an understanding of a company's influence. **American Brands**, for example, makes *Gallaher* cigarettes, but also owns *Dollond and Aitchison* opticians, *Forbuoys* newsagents, *Whyte & Mackay* and *Vladivar* spirits and *Prestige* kitchen ware. **Hillsdown Holdings**, while not a household name, is involved in furniture, food, flowers, building and property. **Unilever** is widely known to be a huge company, and its range of activities is also huge: from food and fragrances to household cleaners and speciality chemicals. But the archetypal conglomerate is **Mitsubishi**. Mitsubishi Corporation is part of a grouping of companies involved in anything from mining to insurance, cars to logging, electronics to food.

For a complete listing of consumer brands and an assessment of the wider social performance of most of the companies featured in this book, order a copy of *Shopping for a Better World* (published by Kogan Page, price £4.99) from your bookshop or direct from New Consumer.

Adidas AG D-8522 Herzogenaurach, Adi-Dassler Str, Postfach 11 20, Germany (£1,730m in 1989)

Airtours PLC Wavell House, Holcome Road, Helmshore, Rossendale, Lancashire BB4 4NB (£155m in 1989)

Allied-Lyons PLC Allied House, 24 Portland Place, London W1 (£4,731m in 1990)

American Brands Inc. (Gallaher Ltd) Members Hill, Brookland Road, Weybridge, Surrey KT13 0QU (£7,789m in 1990)

Amstrad PLC Michael Joyce Company, 19 Garrick Street, London WC2E 9BB (£577m in 1990)

Argos plc 489–499 Avebury Boulevard, Saxon Gates, Central Milton Keynes, Buckinghamshire MK9 2NW (£818m in 1989)

Argyll Group PLC Safeway House, Millington Road, Hayes, Middlesex UB3 4AY (£4,143m in 1990)

Asda Group plc Asda House, Southbank, Great Wilson Street, Leeds, West Yorkshire LS11 5AD (£2,709m in 1990)

Associated British Foods plc Weston Centre, Bowater House, 68 Knightsbridge, London SW1X 7LR (£2,775m in 1990)

Barclays Bank PLC Public Affairs, Johnston Smirke Building, 4 Royal Mint Court, London EC3N 4HJ (£5,547m in 1989)

Edward Billington & Son Ltd Cunard Building, 3rd Floor, Liverpool L3 1EL (£110m in 1989)

The Body Shop International PLC Hawthorne Road, Wick, Littlehampton, West Sussex BN17 7LR (£85m in 1989)

Booker plc Portland House, Stag Place, London SW1E 5AY (£2,926m in 1990)

The Boots Company PLC Head Office, Nottingham, Nottinghamshire NG2 3AA (£3,381m in 1990)

British Airways Plc 200 Buckingham Palace Road, London SW1W 9TA (£4,838m in 1990)

BSN SA (Jacob's Bakery Ltd) 121 Kings Road, Reading, Berkshire RG1 3EF (£4,916m in 1989)

The Burton Group plc 8–11 Great Castle Street, London W1 7AD (£1,801 in 1990)

C & J Clark Ltd 40 High Street, Street, Somerset BA16 0YA (£636m in 1989)

C & A North Row, London W1A 2AX

C.P.C. International Inc. Claygate House, Littleworth Road, Esher, Surrey KT10 9PM (£2,885m in 1989)

Cadbury Schweppes p.l.c. Group Headquarters, 1–4 Connaught Place, London W2 2EX (£3,146m in 1990)

Casio Computer Co. Ltd Unit 6, 1000 North Circular Road, London NW2 7JD (£1,088m in 1990)

Chiquita Brands International Inc. 250 East Fifth Street, Cincinnati, Ohio 45202 USA

Co-operative Wholesale Society Ltd PO Box 53, New Century House, Manchester M60 4ES (£2,678m in 1990)

Co-operative Retail Services Ltd 29 Dantzic Street, Manchester M4 4BA (£1,230m in 1990)

Coats Viyella Plc 155 St Vincent Street, Glasgow G2 5PA (£1,904m in 1989)

The Coca-Cola Company Pemberton House, Wrights Lane, London W8 5SN (£5,094m in 1989)

Colgate-Palmolive Co. Guildford Business Park, Middleton Road, Guildford, Surrey GU2 5LZ (£3,217m in 1988)

Courtaulds Textiles plc 13–14 Margaret Street, London W1P 3DA (£983m in 1990)

Del Monte Foods International Ltd Del Monte House, London Road, Staines, Middlesex TW18 4JD

Del Monte Tropical Fruit Company PO Box 149222, Coral Gables, Florida 33114-9222, USA (£496m in 1990)

Dixons Group plc 29 Farm Street, London W1X 7RD (£1,771m in 1990)

Fyffes plc 12 York Gate, Regent's Park, London NW1 4QJ (£377m in 1989)

The Gateway Corporation PLC PO BOX 197, Bristol B14 0TJ (£2,370m in 1990; Isosceles PLC)

Geest PLC Whitehouse Chambers, Spalding, Lincolnshire PE11 2AL (£498m in 1989)

Gerber Foods (International) Ltd Northway House, 1379 High Road, Whetstone, London N20 9LP (£165m in 1990)

Great Universal Stores PLC Universal House, Devonshire Street, Manchester M60 1XA (£2,692m in 1990)

Hanson PLC 1 Grosvenor Place, London SW1X 7JH (£7,153m in 1990)

H J Heinz Co. Hayes Park, Hayes, Middlesex UB4 8AL (£3,458m in 1990)

Hi-Tec Sports Ltd Hi-Tec House, Aviation Way, Rochford, Southend on Sea, Essex SS2 6UN (£84m in 1990)

Hillsdown Holdings plc Hillsdown House, 32 Hampstead High Street, London NW3 1QD (£4,215m in 1990)

Hitachi Ltd. Hirwaun Industrial Estate, Aberdare, Mid Glamorgan CF44 9UP (£26,519n in 1990)

Hogg Robinson plc Church Gate, Church Street West, Woking, Surrey GU21 1DJ (£87m in 1990)

House of Fraser Holdings plc 14 South Street, London W1Y ⁸PJ (£1,133m in 1989)

Iceland Frozen Foods Holdings plc London Regional Office, 7 Parr Road, Honeypot Lane, Stanmore, Middlesex HA7 1LE (£725m in 1990)

John Lewis Partnership plc 171 Victoria Street, London SW1E 5NN (£2,046m in 1990)

Kingfisher plc North West House, 119 Marylebone Road, London NW1 5PX (£2,910m in 1990)

Reisebüro Kuoni AG Kuoni House, Deepdene Avenue, Dorking, Surrey RH5 4AZ (£149m in 1990)

Kwik Save Group P.L.C. Warren Drive, Prestatyn, Clywd LL19 7HU (£1,520m in 1990)

Ladbroke Group PLC 10 Cavendish Place, London W1M 9DJ (£3,659m in 1989)

The Littlewoods Organisation PLC 11th Floor J M Centre, Old Hall Street, Liverpool L70 1AB (£2,248m in 1988)

Lloyds Bank PLC Public Affairs, 71 Lombard Street, London EC3 3BS (£3,824m in 1990)

Lonrho Plc Cheapside House, 138 Cheapside, London EC2V 6BL (£5,476m in 1990)

Magnet Home Improvements Ltd Royd Ings Avenue, Keighley, West Yorkshire BD21 4BY (£265m in 1990)

Marks & Spencer PLC Michael House, 37–67 Baker Street, London W1A 1DN (£5,608m in 1990)

Mars Inc. 3D Dundee Road, Slough, Berkshire SL1 4LG

Matsushita Electric Industrial Co. Ltd Panasonic House, Willoughby Road, Bracknell, Berkshire RG12 4FP (£22,503m in 1990)

A T Mays Moffatt House, 9 Yard Street, Saltcoats, Ayrshire, Scotland (£2,880m in 1990; Carlson Companies Inc.)

MFI Furniture Group Ltd Southern House, 333 The Hyde, Edgware Road, London NW9 6TD (£595m in 1990)

Midland Bank PLC Corporate Communications, Poultry, London EC2P 2BX (£3,138m in 1990)

Mitsubishi Corporation (Princes Foods Ltd) Royal Liver Building, Liverpool L3 1JH

NFC plc The Merton Centre, 45 St Peters Street, Bedford MK20 2UB (£1,493m in 1989)

National Westminster Bank PLC Corporate Affairs, 1st Floor, 1–2 Broadgate, London EC2M 3BS (£5,627m in 1990)

Nestlé S.A. St George's House, Croydon, Surrey CR9 1NR (£19,369m in 1989)

Next PLC Desford Road, Enderby, Leicester, Leicesterhsire LE9 5AT (£949m in 1990)

Nike Inc. Coniston House, Washington 4, Tyne and Wear NE38 7RN (£1,263m in 1990)

Paterson Zochonis plc Bridgewater House, 60 Whitworth Street, Manchester M1 6LU (£205m in 1989)

Pepsico Inc. Eurasme House, 2 Woodgrange Avenue, Kenton, Harrow, Middlesex AJ3 0XD (£8,660m in 1989)

Philip Morris Co. Inc. St George's House, Bayshill Road, Cheltenham, Gloucestershire GL50 3AE (£25,431m in 1989)

Philips NV Philips House, 188 Tottenham Court Road, London W1P 9LE (£17,341m in 1989)

The Procter & Gamble Co. PO Box 1EL, City Road, Newcastle-Upon-Tyne NE99 1EL(£12,158m in 1990)

Puma AG D-8522 Herzogenaurach, Wurzenburger Str., 13 Postfach 1420, Germany (£183m in 1989)

Quaker Oats Company PO Box 24, Bridge Road, Southall, Middlesex UB2 4AG (£3,252m in 1989)

Ranks Hovis McDougall PLC King Edward House, Box 527, 27–30 King Edward Court, Windsor, Berkshire SL4 1TJ (£1,771m in 1990)

Reebok International Ltd Reebok House, Silverwell Street, Bolton, Lancashire BL1 1PP (£1,790m in 1989)

Rothmans International p.l.c. Denham Place, Denham, Uxbridge UB9 5BL (£1,549m in 1989)

Royal Bank of Scotland PLC 36 St Andrew Square, Edinburgh EH2 2YB (£1,164m in 1990)

J Sainsbury plc Stamford House, Stamford Street, London SE1 9LL (£7,257m in 1990)

Samsung Co. Ltd Cowpen Lane Industrial Estate, Royce Avenue, Billingham, Teesside TS23 4BX (£17,524m in 1988)

Sara Lee Corp. Carnaby Industrial Estate, Lancaster Road, Bridlington, North Humberside YO15 3QY (£6,561m in 1990)

Sears plc 40 Duke Street, London W1A 2HP (£2,092m in 1990)

Sharp Corp. Sharp House, Thorp Road, Manchester M10 9BE (£4,643m in 1990)

W H Smith Group PLC Strand House, 7 Holbein Place, London SW1W 8NR (£2,130m in 1990)

Sony Corp. Sony House, South Street, Staines, Middlesex TW18 4PP (£10,796m in 1990)

Standard Chartered PLC 38 Bishopsgate, London EC2N 4DE (£1,005m in 1990)

Storehouse PLC The Heal's Building, 196 Tottenham Court Road, London W1P 9LD (£1,130m in 1990)

Tate & Lyle PLC Sugar Quay, Lower Thames Street, London EC3R 6DQ (£3,432m in 1990)

Tesco PLC Tesco House, PO Box 18, Delamare Road, Cheshunt, Waltham Cross, Hertfordshire EN8 9SL (£6,346m in 1991)

Thomas Cook Group Ltd 45 Berkeley Street, Picadilly, London W1A 1EB (£368m in 1989)

The Thomson Corporation (Thomson Tour Operations) Greater London House, Hampstead Road, London NW1 7SD (£5,112m in 1989)

Thomson SA (Ferguson Ltd) Cambridge House, 270 Great Cambridge Road, Enfield, Middlesex EN1 1ND (£7,594m in 1989)

Toshiba Corp. Europe Office, Audrey House, Ely Place, London EC1N 6SN (£15,939m in 1990)

Unilever PLC Unilever House, Blackfriars, London EC4P 4BQ (£22,258m in 1990)

United Biscuits Holdings plc Grant House, PO Box 40, Syon Lane, Isleworth, Middlesex TW7 5NN (£2,130m in 1990)

Index

Join New Consumer today!

You are helping to make Britain's top companies more socially responsible every time you use this book. You are sending a clear message by buying from those companies responding to social and environmental issues rather than from those who pursue short term gain regardless of the costs.

Help us to continue this work and keep yourself informed by joining New Consumer. Members receive a quarterly, fact-filled magazine and updates to this shopping guide. There's also a free advisory service for ethical savings and investment.

If you are not sure you want to join at this stage, but would like to know what more you can do having read *The Global Consumer*, send for a free copy of our leaflet, 'Beyond the global consumer', from the same address.

Membership £15 (or £18.50 including a free copy of *Shopping for a Better World*, retail price £4.99)
Special Membership £55, including a free copy of *Changing Corporate Values* (retail price £48)

Total cost £..............

Name ....

Address ....

.... Postcode ....

Visa/Access No. .... Expiry ....

Card Holder's name .... Signature ....

or enclose a cheque payable to New Consumer Ltd.

Please return with payment to *New Consumer, Freepost, 52 Elswick Road, Newcastle upon Tyne NE4 5BR*.

Charity Number: 1003268